The Books of
KAHLIL GIBRAN

The Madman (1918)
Twenty Drawings (1919)
The Forerunner (1920)
The Prophet (1923)
Sand and Foam (1926)
Jesus the Son of Man (1928)
The Earth Gods (1931)
The Wanderer (1932)
The Garden of the Prophet (1933)
Prose Poems (1934)
Nymphs of the Valley (1948)
Spirits Rebellious (1948)
A Tear and a Smile (1950)

This Man from Lebanon: A Study of Kahlil Gibran
by Barbara Young (1945)
The Kahlil Gibran Diary (annually)

THESE ARE BORZOI BOOKS
PUBLISHED BY ALFRED A. KNOPF IN NEW YORK

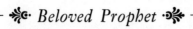

Beloved Prophet

Kahlil Gibran and Mary Haskell
drawn by Gibran

Beloved Prophet

The love letters of
KAHLIL GIBRAN
AND MARY HASKELL
and her private journal

Edited and Arranged by
Virginia Hilu

Alfred A. Knopf New York 1974

THIS IS A BORZOI BOOK
PUBLISHED BY ALFRED A. KNOPF, INC.

Copyright © 1972 by Alfred A. Knopf, Inc.
All rights reserved under
International and Pan-American
Copyright Conventions.
Published in the United States by
Alfred A. Knopf, Inc., New York,
and simultaneously in Canada by
Random House of Canada Limited, Toronto.
Distributed by Random House, Inc., New York.

ISBN: 0–394–43298–3

Library of Congress
Catalog Card Number: 70–79342

Manufactured in the
United States of America

Published March 23, 1972
Reprinted Twice
Fourth Printing, November 1974

———————————— ❧· *Editor's Note* ·❧ ————————————

THE LETTERS AND JOURNALS on which this book is based are
part of the Minis [*Mī-nus*] family papers, the Mary Elizabeth
Haskell–Kahlil Gibran series, in the Southern Historical Collection at the University of North Carolina Library, Chapel
Hill. There are 325 letters from Gibran to Mary in the years
1908–31 and nearly 290 of hers to him. Her 47 "five-lines-a-
day" diaries are records of Mary's personal activities as well
as brief accounts of her meetings with Gibran. Twenty-
seven notebooks are devoted exclusively and at length to
their meetings, and include quotations of his views on literature, art, philosophy, religion, and other topics; descriptions
of what he was working on, his clothes, health, diet.

If the letters and journals were reproduced in their entirety,
this book would be several thousands of pages long. Perhaps
at some later time the complete record may be reproduced,
but for now I have cut and edited freely and heavily, attempt-
ing to weed out that which would be of interest chiefly to
the specialist and to put together the story, in their own words,
of the relationship between the two. Part of the spell cast by
these letters and journals derives from the glimpses they afford
of Gibran's struggle to come to terms with himself and his
world, but what is far more startling and unexpected is the
compelling personal chronicle they reveal.

Cuts have not been indicated. Eighteen-page letters, for instance, in a few cases have been telescoped to one or two pages. In some places, entire sequences are recorded. In others, they are not. Names appear, now and then, of persons who may have been friends or relatives, and are identified where possible or desirable. There are, as will be noted, few letters between them during the six years preceding Gibran's death.

For scholarly research, one must refer to the entire body of correspondence at the Southern Historical Collection at the University of North Carolina.

Virginia Hilu
April 1971

─────────────── ❧ *Illustrations* ☙ ───────────────

All illustrations are from the work of Gibran.

Beloved Prophet

MARY ELIZABETH HASKELL'S ROLE in the life of Gibran has for years been a matter of conjecture and speculation. Her name is mentioned only occasionally, if at all, in the few books about Gibran. It is unlikely that anyone living at the time knew of their secret meetings in New York at his studio or at Mary's school in Cambridge, the secluded strolls in Boston, the excitement, joy, tumult, despair of the early years, or the strength of the bonds between them. Until the disclosures of this collection of letters, there was little that could definitely be said about her and Gibran.

The existence of the letters came to light after Gibran's death. His biographer, Barbara Young,* found them in Gibran's studio while she was working with Mary Haskell to set Gibran's affairs in order. She must have been shocked when the large box containing the letters was pulled out and opened. For a number of years before his death, she had served as a scribe for Gibran, yet had known nothing of his relationship with Mary Haskell.

Barbara Young recognized what Mary's letters represented. What had occurred between the poet, now dead, and this woman alongside her in Gibran's studio, who was knowl-

_____

* *This Man from Lebanon* (New York, 1945).

edgeable about so much of Gibran and his life, and whose letters spanning a quarter of a century now came spilling from a carefully hidden box? Although she implored Mary to burn the letters, pleading that misunderstandings would arise, Mary, who at first agreed, refused. These were the letters of her life with Gibran. She had saved all of his letters to her. How could she have known that he had treasured her letters as she his? Who can know the surge of emotion, the grief and the happiness that must have washed over her when she saw all those letters and recognized her handwriting? Mary believed that the letters, hers and his, belonged to a future that would cherish Gibran as she had. She took them with her to her home in Savannah, Georgia, where she lived out her remaining years.

WHEN HE DIED IN 1931 in New York City, Kahlil Gibran was forty-eight years old. He had achieved some fame in America and in the Middle East as a Lebanese poet and artist, and as the author of a number of slim, black books. After his death, these little books, *The Madman*, *The Forerunner*, *The Prophet*, *Sand and Foam*, and *Jesus the Son of Man*, attracted ever-growing audiences throughout the world.

One could not have known, however, or even have anticipated that in America alone, forty years after his death, his books would be selling close to half a million copies a year, that on college campuses he would be quoted as often as Jesus and Ayn Rand, that his words would be incorporated into baptismal ceremonies, weddings, and funerals. He had captured the hearts of millions. In 1970, almost fifty years after it was published, *The Prophet*, of which nearly four million copies had already been sold in America alone, continued to sell at the rate of approximately seven thousand a week.

When he died, Gibran had also achieved some fame as an artist and had painted a great number of canvases. Many hung in fine homes, and five were destined later to hang in New York City's Metropolitan Museum of Art.

In the Middle East, Gibran's books had caused a great stir. His death in America was major news in Lebanon.

In 1931, Kahlil Gibran, a bachelor, was living in a one-room studio apartment at 51 West 10th Street in New York. There he had resided for almost twenty years. It was a large room, and Gibran had furnished it sparely—a sofa, drapes, a small table, an occasional chair, a stove. He referred to his studio as "The Hermitage."

Gibran's health was never robust. In letters to friends and relatives he often mentioned physical ills—the grippe or the flu, heart palpitations, stomach ailments, bad teeth, and, for a long while before he died, some vague but serious illness. We still do not know the identity of this elusive affliction. In the last years of his life, however, it stalked him. His suffering dismayed his friends. He wasted away. Never a great eater, he now ate even less; always thin, he was thinner than ever. He would not go to the hospital.

Gibran consulted a number of doctors. One insisted that at least temporarily he abandon his poetry and painting and relax at the home of his only remaining sister, Marianna, in Boston. She was an anchor and a refuge. In 1925, hoping that this change of scenery and style of living might work, Gibran sublet "The Hermitage" and left New York for Boston.

Marianna, who worked as a seamstress, enjoyed caring for her brother and wanted desperately for him to regain his health. She prepared the Lebanese foods he loved, entertained his numerous Arabic friends who came calling, pleaded with him to take short summer strolls. Marianna and Kahlil, brother and sister, loved each other dearly. Their parents were both dead, as were Peter and Sultana, their brother and sister.

In 1928, Gibran was ill again with what he termed "summer rheumatism." In March 1929, he was ill once more but with what? And, in 1930, he seems to have had intimations of never recovering the good health for which he yearned.

A number of Gibran's acquaintances were artists with whom he had shared models, visited museums, hunted for lofts; others were people he had painted or who had come to attend his poetry readings and had stayed to try to know better the shy man whose words struck responsive chords in the hearts of so many. Poets, writers, childhood neighbors from the "old country"—in fact, Syrians on all levels—were among his friends.

And there was Mary Haskell—much more than a friend and about whose closeness to Gibran no one knew but Marianna. Mary had been a part of Gibran for nearly thirty years.

When Gibran died, his will left everything to Bsherri, the village where he had been born, whose essence had been locked in his heart since he had left it as a child, whose air, earth, sounds, and colors he longed for but to which he returned only after death; to Marianna, his only living relative, who had worked tirelessly as a young woman, supporting both Gibran and herself on meager earnings as a seamstress so that he could devote himself to his painting and writing; and to Mary Elizabeth Haskell.

Marianna had always known of Mary. Mutual affection and respect characterized their relationship. They cared for each other, although the worlds from which they came and in which they traveled were far apart. Both women had simple tastes, a purity of heart, and a common goal: to help Gibran, to enable him to develop to his fullest in whatever area he chose. They were united in their belief in his greatness.

Mary Haskell appeared at Gibran's funeral in Boston and was introduced as a friend by Marianna to the many who were there. Whereas all the others were weeping, Mary was observed to be quietly happy. She had been aware of Gibran's inner struggles over the years and of his efforts to draw closer to his unnamed Spirit—the sacred spirit who is a vital part of everything he has written. Mary was convinced that the occasion of Gibran's death, though sad for his friends, was no occasion for tears. He was at last with the Spirit toward whom he had been striving all his life.

KAHLIL GIBRAN WAS BORN in the village of Bsherri, Lebanon, on January 6, 1883. His parents were Maronites—Christians of an Eastern rite obedient to the Roman Pope, but differing from the Latin church in having a Syriac liturgy and married clergy.

His father, who appears to have been a farmer, was a strong, vigorous man with little education. He was, according to several sources, often drunk, and quarrelsome and abusive to his wife and children.

Kamilah Rahmi, Gibran's mother, was the daughter of the village priest and the widow of Abdal-Salam Rahmi, by whom she had a son, Peter. She had no education. But, unlike her husband, as the family grew to include Kahlil and two sisters, Sultana and Marianna, so did her ambition for a better life for them. In 1895, the family comprised the father and mother, eighteen-year-old Peter, twelve-year-old Kahlil, and the two younger daughters.

Gibran's father spent most of his tiny income on drinking; food was never plentiful, nor was there relief from anxiety. In distressing poverty and in an atmosphere constantly charged with tension and bitterness between a drunken father and a despairing mother the children spent their early years.

Gibran craved solitude and loved to sit alone near the cave of the monastery of Mar Sarkis drawing in pencil and in charcoal. Some biographers claim that he was influenced when he was seven or eight years old by Da Vinci and Michelangelo, but it is difficult to balance this with what we now know about Gibran's painful childhood. His father, who seems to have preferred exhibitions of great physical prowess, often beat him if he found him sketching. Determined that her children should have a better life, Gibran's mother began to think of emigration.

In 1894, when he was eleven years old, Gibran came to America with his mother and her three other children. (Some claim they arrived in June 1895.) Gibran's father did not accompany them. The family may have made its escape while the father was serving a prison term, although we will see from Mary's journals that Gibran claimed other reasons. Conditions must have been desperate for Gibran's mother, who spoke no English (and who could neither read nor write her own language), to abandon her native land, her friends, and the life she had always known to cross the ocean to a strange land. From New York, the Gibrans continued on to Boston, where they settled near what was then Boston's Chinatown. There was a small Lebanese community in and around Hudson Street; the Gibrans lived nearby on Edinboro Street.

Here they all went to work except for young Kahlil, who attended school. Three years later, at fifteen, he returned to Lebanon and entered the Al-Hikmat school in Beirut, a school run by the Maronite clergy. He seems to have concentrated on Arabic, French, and writing. Not enrolled full-time, Gibran tended to choose courses in which he was especially interested rather than those which were required.

Gibran spent his summers in Bsherri. His father was now drinking so heavily that he was impossible to live with. He stayed therefore at the home of one of his aunts.

In the autumn of 1899, Gibran returned to Boston. He neither went back to school nor looked for work. He chose instead to concentrate on his painting and writing. For the next two years, his mother and his two sisters worked as seamstresses in Boston, and his half-brother, Peter, was employed in a shop. Kahlil sketched and painted.

On April 4, 1902, Sultana died of tuberculosis. In March 1903, Peter died of tuberculosis. Kahlil's mother, whom he revered, died of cancer in June of that year. (Some years later, Mary Haskell, who had by then become extremely close to Marianna, talked with her about these three deaths and their effect on Gibran. Their conversation is recorded later in this book.)

Gibran continued with his writing and painting. Marianna continued to work as a seamstress, supporting them both on her salary of sixty dollars a month. By 1904, he had a number of canvases, and Fred Holland Day, a well-known photographer in Boston, offered him the use of his studio for an exhibition. Day wrote to his friend Mary Haskell that he had met a young artist—Gibran was just twenty-one—and that he wanted Mary to come and see what this young man was doing. At this time Mary was running a boarding school for girls, the Haskell-Dean school, which she and her sister had started in 1897.

On May 10, 1904, in Day's studio, Mary Elizabeth Haskell, thirty-one years old, the daughter of a bank president and distinguished veteran of the Confederate Army, and Kahlil Gibran met.

She was born on December 11, 1873, in Columbia, South Carolina, and had five sisters and four brothers. Her father was Alexander Cheves Haskell. His honors were many, but just after the Civil War the family was quite poor. Life was not easy for any of them, and Mary had to learn early how to manage on little. The money-stretching habits she learned as a child stayed with her all her life, so that when she did come into money, it became increasingly difficult for her to bank it or to spend it on herself. Money had to be used— it had to be put to some good purpose. If Mary needed a new dress, she dyed an old one. If, through Mary, some artist could be freed to paint or some young person enabled to go to school, Mary was fulfilled. When she was a student at Wellesley, if relatives came to visit her she would beg not to be taken to lunch but instead to be given the money that would have been spent, so that she might buy books.

After graduation from Wellesley in 1897, Mary went to Boston to join her sister, Louisa. In 1902 or 1903, Louisa left the school to marry Reginald Daly. Mary then took over as headmistress.

At the exhibit in Day's studio, Gibran explained to Mary what he had been trying to do in his sketches. Something about the young artist captivated her, and the next day Mary spoke of him to Émilie Michel, the young woman who taught French at the school. According to all reports, Micheline, as she was affectionately called, was charming and vivacious.

After the exhibit closed, Gibran hung his paintings at the Haskell-Dean school, where Mary introduced him to Micheline. Micheline was twenty—attractive, enthusiastic, gentle—and Gibran painted her a number of times. Later, when he was in Paris, Micheline came to see him. After these visits, both he and Micheline would write separately to Mary—Micheline reporting on Gibran's health and state of mind, Gibran saying how wonderful it was to have a visit from Micheline and then going on to worry about her health.

The exhibit at the boarding school brought Mary and Gibran closer, although both were shy and distant in their own ways. He got into the habit of visiting on Wednesday and Friday evenings, although he never came without an invitation from Mary. Sometime during 1904, she got the idea of sending Gibran to Paris to study painting.

After discussing the plan with Marianna, Mary approached Gibran and offered to pay his transportation to Paris and to send him seventy-five dollars a month. He accepted, and arrived in Paris on June 13, 1908. As prearranged by Mary, he was met by Micheline, who helped him find quarters.

Another friend of Mary's who visited Gibran in Paris was Charlotte Teller. She was a suffragette and a playwright, who wrote unsuccessfully under a masculine pseudonym. For a while, Mary was supporting Charlotte also. Charlotte wrote Mary hundreds of lengthy letters in which she discussed drama, art, philosophy, history.

Charlotte wrote Mary of Gibran's progress in Paris. When she visited him, Charlotte linked Mary's name with various prominent men in Cambridge and Boston, and "confided" in him about the kind of man she hoped Mary would eventually marry. These "confidences" were not encouraged by Gibran. Charlotte saw Gibran in Paris irregularly in 1908 and occasionally in the spring of 1909. During this time, he worked hard at his painting. In June 1910, Ameen Rihani, one of his friends from Lebanon, arrived in Paris and the two took off to visit the museums and art galleries of London.

Gibran returned to New York on October 31, 1910, and to Boston the following day. Leaving his belongings with his sister, Marianna, he hurried over to see Mary.

ON FEBRUARY 12, 1908, Kahlil Gibran had written to Ameen Guraieb: "And now since you have heard my story you will know that my stay in Boston is neither due to my love for this city, nor to my dislike for New York. My being here is due to the presence of a she-angel who is ushering me toward a splendid future and paving for me the path to intellectual and financial success." *

* *Kahlil Gibran: A Self Portrait*, by Anthony Ferris (New York, 1947), p. 23.

---·❦ *KG* ❦·---

October 2, 1908
14 Avenue du Maine
Paris

My dear Mary—

I had a long rest in the country with Syrian friends, a rich man with a great heart and a woman with both a beautiful soul and face. They both love poetry and poets. The town in which they live, is like a large garden divided into little gardens by narrow paths. From a distance the houses with red roofs look like a handful of corals scattered on a piece of green velvet.

I am painting, or I am learning how to paint. It will take me a long time to paint as I want to, but it is beautiful to feel the growth of one's own vision of things. There are times when I leave work with the feelings of a child who is put to bed early. Do you not remember, dear Mary, my telling you that I understand people and things through my sense of hearing, and that *sound* comes first to my soul? Now, dear Mary, I am beginning to understand things and people through my eyes. My memory seems to keep the shapes and colours of personalities and of objects.

And now while I am in perfect health, both physically and mentally, I wish to say that the few pictures and drawings, which you have now, are all yours if I should die suddenly here in Paris. All the pictures and studies found after my death in my studio here in Paris are yours. You are free to do whatever you wish with them.

The above statement, dear Mary, is not well worded but it expresses my wishes and feelings. I hope I will live long and be able to do some things worthy of giving to you who is giving so much to me. I hope that the day will come when I shall be able to say, "I became an artist through Mary Haskell."

It is almost midnight. The woman with a sweet voice, in the opposite studio, is no longer singing her sad Russian songs. The silence is profound. Good night, dear Mary. A thousand good nights from

Kahlil

November 8, 1908
Paris

When I am unhappy, dear Mary, I read your letters. When the mist overwhelms the "I" in me, I take two or three letters out of the little box and reread them. They remind me of my true self. They make me overlook all that is not high and beautiful in life. Each and every one of us, dear Mary, must have a resting place somewhere. The resting place of my soul is a beautiful grove where my knowledge of you lives.

And now I am wrestling with colour: The strife is terrible, one of us must triumph! I can almost hear you saying, "And what about drawing, Kahlil?" and Kahlil, with a thirst in his voice says, "Let me, O let me bathe my soul in colours; let me swallow the sunset and drink the rainbow."

The professors in the academy say, "Do not make the model more beautiful than she is," and my soul whispers, "O if you could only paint the model as beautiful as she really is." Now what shall I do, dear Mary? Shall I please the professors or my soul? The dear old men know a great deal, but the soul is much nearer.

It is rather late, and I shall go to bed now, with many thoughts in my heart. Good night, dear Mary. God bless you always.

Kahlil

⸱⸱❧ KG ❧⸱⸱

1908
Christmas Day
Paris

May God bless you, dear dear Mary. May the Unknown who gave birth to the spirit of Christ give birth to a great joy in your heart. May you see this same holy day many times in happiness and in peace.

I think of you today, beloved friend, as I think of no other living person. And as I think of you Life becomes better and higher and much more beautiful. I kiss your hand, dear Mary, and in kissing your hand I bless myself.

Kahlil

❧ *1909* ❧

—————— ❧{ *KG* }❧ ——————

June 23, 1909
Dear Mary—   Paris

I have lost my father, beloved Mary. He died in the old
house where he was born sixty-five years ago. His last two
letters make me weep bitterly each time I read them. His
friends wrote saying that he blessed me before the end came.
I know now, dear Mary, that he rests in the bosom of God;
and yet I cannot help but feel the pains of sorrow and regret.
I cannot help but feel the heavy hand of Death on my forehead. I cannot help but see the dim, sad shadows of the bygone
days when he and my mother and my brother and my young
sister lived and smiled before the face of the sun. Where are
they now? Are they somewhere in an unknown region? Are
they together? Do they remember the past as we do? Are they
near this world of ours or are they far faraway? I know, dear
Mary, that they live. They live a life more real, more beautiful
than ours. They are nearer to God than we are.

The veil of seven folds is no longer hanging between their
eyes and Truth. They no longer play hide and seek with the

Spirit. I feel all this beloved Mary and yet I cannot help but feel the pains of sorrow and regret.

And you—you dear sweet consolation, you are now in Hawaii—in the islands so much loved by the sun. You are on the other side of this planet. Your days are nights in Paris. You belong to another order of time. And yet you are so near me. You walk with me when I am alone; you sit across the table in the evening and you talk to me when I am working. There are times when I feel as though you are not here on earth.

I am taking notes of the different works of modern artists like Rodin and Carrière and Henry Martin and Simon and Ménard. Each has something to say and says it in a different way. The work of Carrière is the nearest to my heart. His figures, sitting or standing behind the mist, say more to me than anything else except the work of Leonardo da Vinci. Carrière understood faces and hands more than any other painter. He knew the depths, the height, and the width of the human figure. And Carrière's life is not less beautiful than his work. He suffered much, but he understood the mystery of pain: he knew that tears make all things shine.

Remember me to the valleys and mountains of Hawaii.

I kiss your hand, dear Mary, I close my eyes now and I see you, beloved friend.

Kahlil

1910

---- *KG* ----

New York
Monday, October 31, 1910

And here I am in New York, dear Mary. My heart is full of longing and I am almost happy.

I shall be in Boston tomorrow evening. Write me a little word to 15 Oliver Place. I must see you before seeing other faces.

O, you are so near now.

Kahlil

Our introduction to Mary is her journal entry of November 1, 1910. It is brief, merely a quick note in a diary, far different from the entries she would later make. Gibran was lonely, as Mary points out, and also very much attached to her.

Boston
Tuesday, November 1, 1910

K. to supper. First time after his return from Paris. Very lonely. No close friends here now, I fancy. Dreary two rooms. Looking for one.

Boston
December 7, 1910

Kahlil came back to Boston from Paris this October . . . two years and four months after he went there to learn to paint. Since his arrival, I have seen him two or three evenings every week.

In the following journal entry Mary records Gibran's memories about his childhood. They are interesting and important in light of the fact that his recollections of his childhood and of his father do not coincide with the facts as we now have them.

We know, for example, that the family was destitute, that the father drank heavily, that the mother's fight for survival was desperate and tenacious. Gibran may indeed have remembered when a summons was served on his father, for one story has it that his mother was able to flee with the children when Gibran's father was serving a term in prison. Gibran obviously chose to tell Mary a fanciful tale about pet lions, orchards, old family wealth and grounds, rather than the sad truth.

[J O U R N A L]

Boston
December 7, 1910

Tonight he talked of his family. His maternal grandfather was the bishop of the Maronite church—one of the Eastern branches—Estefanos Rahmi by name—famous for scholarship (Greek, Latin, French, Italian, and Arabic), his personal charm and power, and for his wonderful voice in speaking or singing. He had seven children, four sons and three daughters. Kamilah, Kahlil's mother, was the youngest and his favorite. He called her "my heart that goes before me" and Kahlil he loved better than all his own children and grandchildren too. His properties were immense—whole towns, vineyards, fields. He was an only child and his father's brother too had died childless, leaving him that additional property. But at Rahmi's death one year before the Gibrans left Syria, his family went to pieces and squandered the fortune. Two of the sons lived hard into early graves—one is a good doctor. They have all lived and died (except Kamilah) in Bsherri, about thirty-five miles from Tripoli, or two hours by train north of Beirut.

The grandfather on the Gibran side was a man of leisure—wealthy, aristocratic, athletic, brilliant—who kept lions as pets.

Gibran is not proud of him because he is out of sympathy with his aristocratic attitude. His son, Kahlil Gibran's father, was a peculiar man. At twenty-eight he married Kahlil's mother, then a widow of twenty-two with one child, Peter. Her first marriage had been very happy and Kahlil believes the second was a love-match, for she was lovely, and Gibran magnetic and a man of tastes. He was however a tax collector for the government, and he had an enemy. He was accused, when Kahlil was eight, of embezzlement of taxes. Three years the trial lasted. Kahlil remembers the morning when the summons was served on his father—how the crowd rode into the courtyard of the big old house and how his mother stood bravely smiling. At the end of three years, Gibran was found guilty, all his property, houses, orchards, fields, the old family dwelling, the statues, books, curios, furniture, etc. of which he had a great number and many of which had been long in the family, was confiscated so that the family became guests of the government in their own house. Gibran was taken to the capital and given partial liberty—freedom within a radius of one mile from the courthouse—and Mrs. Gibran began to move heaven and earth to get him cleared. She went from city to city, exerting personal and family influence, and at last to Paris. The government restored a good portion of the property, but the suit had cost so dear that the recovered lands and house had to be mortgaged and the family had only the little that was Mrs. Gibran's. With that she and the children came to Boston, after moving about in France. Peter opened a Syrian shop and did well. But he not only made a great deal—he also spent freely. The oldest daughter, Sultana, contracted consumption and died; Peter died of it; and Mrs. Gibran; all within nine months. Peter left heavy debts. With the help of Syrian friends, Kahlil wound up his business and cleared his debts. This was in 1902.

In the spring of 1903 I met Kahlil. Lionel Marks said to me one day: "Mary, there's an exhibit of pictures at Mr. Day's studio that you ought to see. You'd like them."

Next week he asked me if I'd gone. It was my first year as principal of this school. I said no, too busy. Next week he asked again. No. A few days later he said, "Tomorrow is the last day of that exhibit at Mr. Day's. You *must* go."

I went and was deeply interested. While I lingered before a red-pencil drawing, a little dark young man came up and said in a gentle voice, "Are you interested in that picture?"

When I said I was indeed, he offered to explain them all to me and did. Miss Keyes (art teacher in private school) next day suggested that I try to get the exhibit at school because it would be good for the girls to see the work of a man of promise before he won recognition. Mr. Gibran readily let us have them. They hung here several weeks and he was often in during the afternoon to explain them.

After the pictures went, I never quite lost sight of him. Once or twice a winter I'd invite him to supper. He never refused—nor did he ever come without an invitation. In the five winters that I've seen more or less of him he has never come unexpectedly—nor once asked leave to come.

[JOURNAL]

Boston
Friday, December 9, 1910

To Museum to Frick Collection: three beautiful Rembrandts, several fine Van Dycks. Saw them in a new way because of Kahlil's teaching.....Kahlil to supper and we talked pictures all evening.

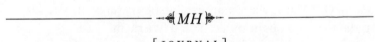

[JOURNAL]

Boston
Saturday, December 10, 1910

To Museum for Frick pictures. Kahlil there. Looked at Rembrandt, Millet, Corot, Rodin, Turners together till 12. Kahlil spent the evening. Told me he loved me and would marry me if he could, but I said my age made it out of the question.

"Mary," he said, "whenever I try to get nearer to you in speech, to be personal at all—you fly up into remote regions and are inaccessible." "But I take you with me," said I. And I said I wanted to keep our friendship enduring, and feared to spoil a good friendship for a poor love-affair. This was after Kahlil had explained what he meant.

The next afternoon Kahlil was here a while and I told him yes.

[JOURNAL]

Boston
Wednesday, December 21, 1910

Kahlil in evening. President Eliot* will let him draw his head. Did R. Cabot† today. Was much pleased with it. R. sat and worked while Kahlil drew and Kahlil said it was simple, direct, subtle work. My disillusionment series of camp snapshots of myself failed. I had collected all the old snaps of myself that I had—some are ghastly—to show Kahlil and give him a distaste for me. He was utterly unmoved.

* Charles William Eliot, of Harvard University.
† Richard Clarke Cabot, chief of the medical staff at Massachusetts General Hospital, Boston.

1911

—⟨ KG ⟩—

Boston

January 1911

Yes, beloved Mary, I would like to go to the Symphony Saturday evening and hear Elman,* for I feel a strange hunger for music in these days. And it will be so good to sit in your shadow for a few minutes afterward.

Mary, beloved Mary, when you are alone, in the silence of the night, send me a breath, a little breath from your heart, and I will work better.

Good night.

Kahlil

—⟨ MH ⟩—

[J O U R N A L]

Boston

January 10, 1911

Since he has always found me hard to draw because "I'm always thinking of you, or of myself when I draw you," I've decided on a strictly impersonal-minded attempt tonight. I almost slept in a little chair while he did a good profile in less

---

* The violinist Mischa Elman (1891–1967).

than half an hour. He was pleased—liked the quality of the drawing. The values are fine and delicate.

Boston
January 28, 1911

Kahlil to Symphony and I to door of hall with him. Fierce wind—he tired when came back—long silent, just resting. Told him my idea of test by Paris and why I am bound for two or more years. He feels absolutely sure—no need of test.

[JOURNAL]

Boston
February 19, 1911

Home by the Esplanade—in cutting wind—bearing Kahlil's Swinburne on Blake. I told Charlotte in the studio that Kahlil and I want to be married when we can and she said she had hoped since she saw him in Paris that it might be.

Again Mary records what Gibran tells her about his coming of age and his early years in Lebanon. On the whole, the recollections included here are far from the truth.

25

Boston
Friday, March 24, 1911

[*Mary:*] "What is the earliest thing you remember?"

"Being fished out of a little pool—the fountain in the court-yard. I was playing with a large ball—the ball fell in, and I after it. They told me afterward I was two and a half."

When the family came here, the father sent money—more at first than later—but Peter did well. Peter through mother, the mother through Peter, sent Kahlil to college, and his father gave him pocket money and other expenses while he was there. Mother always had "comfortably" enough while she lived. She and Peter died only four or five weeks apart—Sultana having died before. Very soon after that, Mary went to work. Father died leaving many debts.

Father loved Peter, his stepson, very much. "Much more than me. I never minded that." He [Gibran's father] loved [the] mother; she respected and admired him, and loved him too. But there was a subtle silent gap in understanding between the two. He had an imperious temper, and was not a loving person. "I admired him for his power—his honesty and integrity. It was his daring to be himself, his outspokenness and refusal to yield, that got him into trouble eventually. If hundreds were about him, he could command them with a word. He could overpower any number by any expression of himself. And he was an agreeable man to my mother. He cared for her as much as he could care for anybody—and he had unfailing tact when he cared to use it.

"My father hurt me often. I remember once especially. I had just written a poem. I was in college—about sixteen or seventeen, and it had been published. I was proud and conceited, and thought everybody would be interested and would speak to me about it when I went home. Well, my father gave a dinner-party—one of the guests was Salima, a literary man

26

I was anxious to see. I longed to appear well in his eyes. During the dinner one of the ladies told me she had read my poem and liked it. Then several praised it. The lady said, as a woman of fifty would say to a boy to encourage him, 'And shall you write more, Kahlil?' 'Yes, in fact I wrote one last night,' glad to say it in the happiness of her commendation. 'Oh! how interesting. I'd like to hear it. Won't you read it to us after dinner?' Then the others said, 'Yes, Kahlil. Read us your poem.' I looked at my father, and he made a face—of contempt.

"After dinner we went into the hall, where coffee was served. Presently one of the men asked me to read my poems, and the lady said, 'Especially the one you wrote last night.' 'You are so kind,' I said, 'to remember I wrote one last night.' My father said, 'I don't believe, Kahlil, that our friends will find such things interesting.' Then they insisted—and I said to myself that I would *be* myself and I got out the poem and read it. It was my first reading ever to a selected audience. I cannot describe what it was to me. But they all were with me —they were loving me. And my father said—'I hope we shall never have any more of this sickmindedness.' That hurt my innermost being.

"My father wanted me to be a lawyer. My mother was just opposite to him—very sympathetic, and a critic too. She always encouraged me."

Kahlil read Hearn* with much difficulty. His English is faulty in pronunciation, and in grammatical number, third person singular and the singular of plural nouns. But his voice and intonations in reading are delightful—and as he goes slowly, I find it a musical and pensive pleasure to hear him. He likes to do it, partly for the practice, partly because he is happiest when active. Utterance soothes him. His reading the passage the Cabots sent me from Tolstoi revealed to me—it

---

* Lafcadio Hearn (1850–1904), British writer; his chief writings were an attempt to interpret Japan to English-speaking peoples.

was easy for him—the justness and nicety of his inflections and how sensitively he reflects each nuance of an idea—and how thoughtful and exceedingly sweet his voice in prose is.

[J O U R N A L]

Boston
Friday, April 14, 1911

Joy reigned at night, too, when the Greenes came to supper. She! she wore a Grecian gown of white—with one red rose—and he was echo to her chiming enthusiasm. They really loved K.'s work—*Rose Sleeves* was a "fairy tale" to them—*Consolation* a spiritual message—*Charlotte* a sybil—*Angele* the vestiture of a dream—and when I told them Kahlil had never dipped brush in oil before the fall of 1908, she said, "Then you're only two and a half years old!" And when I said he could work only three hours a day in his studio and that all they saw here except the Paris studies had been done since the last week in January, I felt their amazement in their momentary silence. Then they spoke at once of a room in their house that was good for morning work. And when he said he wrote during the morning, they asked about that, and cried that Mrs. Joe Smith knows Arabic and he must know Mrs. Joe Smith. So they took his address and phone number, and next Friday at luncheon or supper this Mrs. Joe Smith he shall meet!

The three went off together a little after nine—finding each other a joyful discovery—and the Greenes saying they wanted him to paint their Francesca.

It seemed to me that it was the moment of the opening of the door between Kahlil and the world that shall love him and into whose heart he shall surely feel he is pouring his work. I *think* his future is not far away now!

And so I made up my mind to follow what seems to me the

final finger of God—I put definitely to myself the possibility of being his wife. And though every waking hour since has been drenched with inner tears, I know I am right, and that the tears mean joy, not pain, for the future. My age is simply the barrier raised between us and the blunder of our marrying. Not my age constitutes the objection—but the fact that for Kahlil there waits a different love from that he bears me—an apocalypse of love—and that shall be his marriage. His greatest work will come out of that—his greatest happiness, his new, full life. And it is not many years distant. Toward the woman of that love, I am but a step. And though my susceptible eyes weep, I think of her with joy—and I don't want to have Kahlil, because I know she is growing somewhere for him, and that he is growing for her.

[JOURNAL]

Boston
Saturday, April 15, 1911

I wanted so much to think, that I practiced hard new hymns and walked all morning for a chance. When Kahlil came in after the symphony, and we had swapped news, I said, "I've something to say to you tonight, if I have strength." And when we were on the old sofa in the library, and I could command my voice, I said, "Everything in me protests against my saying it, except the one thing that makes me say it, but I know the one thing is right. You will acquiesce in what I say —but my heart longs to be overpersuaded. Still I know in the end I should not be persuaded."

"What is it, Mary? Is it something bad?"

"Bad for me—good for you. Don't mind if I cry. I've shed many tears since I saw you last night. But there is that in my heart beyond tears."

"You won't cry," he said, "you won't cry."

He held my hand hard, and I said, "I've stopped thinking that I shall ever be your wife—and I want to be." He went white and when in a minute I spoke of my last night sense of his future opening now—and I told him all—how every time I've thought or spoken of him or to him since early December as mine, or of myself ever married to him, I've felt obscurely that I was wrong—how slowly I had grown into the full passion for him which from the beginning I knew must come—so that until mid-March I had not entirely lost my lifelong sine qua non of great physical strength in a lover or husband—how with me as with him I had felt "the big structure," as he says, come right—but how insuperable remained to me my age, the fact that I am worn and wearing, that in spite of a certain youthfulness and my great vigor, I shall be soon on the downward path while he will still have a long climb upwards—that he is yet unripe, has still his best work and his best love before him, and that they will come together. But I am not the woman—how if he were tied to me when this new love came, all that is honorable and chivalrous in him would cry out in my behalf—and I should be chained upon him by gratitude—and whatever else his presence and silent loving listening brought to me to say. He wept and I got him a handkerchief. But he could not speak. Near the beginning in one of my many pauses he said brokenly, "Mary, you know I cannot say things, when I am this way," and hardly another word. The only comment he made was to love me. When it was over I opened my arms to him—but he soon had me in his, and the heart is not flesh that would not have been comforted.....When it grew late I put his right palm to my lips —and then indeed the tears came—but they drew me simply nearer to him. I kissed that wonderful hand as I have often longed to do, but as I have not before, because a mere touch on it moves him so. It answered like a heart.....Again at the door I cried a little—while he wiped my eyes, saying only, "Mary—Mary—Mary." And as he went he said as well as he could, "You've given me a new heart tonight."

Upon my tears after I went to bed it was suddenly as if a great peace and light broke—and he and I were in it—so that I cried, "Thank you, God, thank you!" again and again. I was so ineffably happy. That I have given him up I realize. But it has not parted us—it has brought us even much nearer together.

Boston
April 17, 1911

He forgot his notebooks on Saturday that he wants to show the Greenes on Tuesday night. So I took them and the red and orange scarf to the studio in the afternoon. K. was at work on the atmosphere study—putting in figures in the swirl and flame, with touches meaningless near and full of beauty at a little distance. I sat silent by him—too full and too tired at heart to speak or move for awhile except in response to him. But I draw life from the intensity of his presence.

I told him of the peace and light that came suddenly to me —both of us in it—and the sense of greater union than ever, on Saturday night. He said, "Yes, a new world of oneness— that I had never imagined before. I feel as if the last veil had fallen from between us."

"I think sometimes," said I, "that I hear from that being who guides you—that he tells me about you."

He answered, "I think sometimes *you are* that being."

"A great fear" is what he has felt at the idea of marriage— just what he tried to express to me one night while he was still maintaining that he wanted to marry. I said tonight I hoped he *would* marry: because it is a big, vital experience and the men of this age who have done best work have married. But it is plain he has not realized himself fully enough yet. When he does, and has "conquered life," he will probably marry.

In loving more, yet no longer expecting to marry, lies a difficulty which I thought well to face with him at once. "You are so clear," he said, "and so holy. Isn't it better to desire and to change and lift the desire to something higher—than not to desire? You be just as you have been—just as you are—and don't mind me. If you hear me wanting, don't listen."

[JOURNAL]

Boston
April 20, 1911

We began on Swinburne—with a big chair for our feet— "Oh! what a good time I do have here! I live here and only here—other times I'm not living," with a laugh.

"You make me feel warm and.....clear—inside.—I want for nothing—just clear and quiet and warm all through."

I can almost *see* him growing—he is changing and developing so fast—and the sense he has spoken of—of other things being great in life (besides work—of life itself, with work just a phase of life) is growing in him. His personal life is getting a new relation to the life of others, closer and more realizing, more sharing. I think that from gentleness and a certain tenderness, he is moving on through a deeper life of his own.

The big lines of his character are growing more pronounced, more dominant, steadier. A simplicity is coming to him thereby. And I feel sure a new knowledge of loving is coming to him. His own experience is an astonishment to him. Things he has only imagined he is now realizing. The whole basis of consciousness is broadening within him. About loving, he often says that he is living in a revelation. People are apt to say that with each love—I've always heard it—but in his case I see it and feel it in him—in greater degree than his spoken English expresses.

If the following account as related by Gibran is true, it is the record of the only time he turned away from his artistic and literary quests to take a job. This seems to have been the only "regular" work he ever had.

[JOURNAL]

Boston
Saturday, April 22, 1911

We got on the subject of gifts. "When my brother died, he left the store with 23,000 or 24,000 dollars in debt—and goods to about half that amount. My mother had had money from many poor Syrians, who would come to her and say, 'Here's fifty dollars I've saved, or here's five hundred. Please keep it for me.' They were afraid of the banks, and she was like a kind of church to them. She trusted my brother absolutely— no one knew his life was slowly going—and she turned the money over to him. He put it into the business. When he died there were no papers to show about these people's money— but Mother made a list of them all before she died. After she died there was nothing. The two or three hundred dollars from the things we had sold we used to give Mother the kind of funeral she should have had. Everyone knew I had no money, and some of these poor people were very much agitated about their money. There was a Syrian shepherd near us—an old man with white hair and beard. That night I slept hardly at all—but early in the morning I fell into just a wink. And at that hour came the old shepherd, opened the door softly, came up to my bed and said, 'Effendi, Effendi.' That was all. I hardly waked, it seemed to me that I dreamt he was there. But late in the morning when I had got up and my sister went

33

to the sofa where I slept to make it look like a sofa for the day, she found a roll of bills, one-dollar bills, dirty and worn —two dollars, ten fifty dollars—seven hundred and fifty dollars in all. So quietly had the old man come and gone that at first I had been impressed hardly enough to realize now where the money had come from. I went out at once to find the old man and return the money.

"He was sitting at the end of a long alley near his door, talking. When he saw me enter the other end of the alley, he just vanished. I ran after him, and when I came near, he turned and said, 'You haven't come to hurt me, have you?' He went on to tell me what our family had meant to him. I accepted the money and in six months was able to pay it back.

"I went into the store—and by taking our two largest creditors as partners we managed to clear all the debts. In a little over a year everything was clear except two or three hundred dollars. I went to them then and said, 'I must leave this business,' and I did. It was killing me—my life was just going in that shop."

------------------------ ❧*MH*❧ ------------------------

MISS HASKELL AND MISS DEAN'S SCHOOL
314 MARLBOROUGH STREET, BOSTON

Sunday morning, April 28, 1911

I sat down fifteen minutes ago—and have not brought to words the prayer for you that has been filling me—for strength to you from this strong sun, and lightness of heart from your faith. The long silences filled with you—are they vocal anywhere, anyhow, I wonder? Certainly they bring me something from you. They bring me more simply near. They are like bands of silver set about the days.

Mary

34

*Gibran moved to New York City in April 1911. Lonely and not
really happy in Boston, he may have felt that he was not making any progress in painting and writing. The first room he
found was at 164 Waverly Place. He soon became involved
with Syrian friends in Brooklyn and in Manhattan, and a childhood friend, Rihani.*

*In May, Mary joined him. Together they visited the museums
of New York. Mary records them as happy visits. On May 16,
Gibran moved to 28 West 9th Street.*

*He started to paint Charlotte and then introduced her to his
friend Rihani. They seemed to take to each other.*

*In late June, Mary left Boston for her annual summer trip
to her beloved American West, returning in the early part of
September.*

[Boston]
April 29, 1911

On Sunday I beautified things! Went through all your
treasures that we have here—for they *are* treasures—and
sneaked a few of them on to the walls! *Mary* I transferred to
where *Micheline* and the imaginative head hung—the dining-
room side of the library mantel—and she glows in the dark.
The Fountain of Pain I hung in *Mary's* place by the dining-
room door—and it floats there like a flower; *Spirits of Night*
is opposite, by the piano, deep and distant—and the old round
gilt-matted *Aching Heart* one with blue veil is by the pantry
door—most moving color.

'Way upstairs we've put in a glass sky-light—and in the full
glare I've two casts and the thing you did here one night—
large immortal face with wee man and woman in—flame in

35

her hand. It looks like loftiness and space, even from the hall below—so that our housetop seems suddenly to open heavenward. Do tell me lots of things—everything.

Love,
Mary

New York
Monday, May 1, 1911

I run through the streets of this gigantic city, and shadows run after me. I gaze with a thousand eyes and listen with a thousand ears all through the day; and when I come home late at night I find more things to gaze at and more voices to listen to. New York is not the place where one finds rest. But did I come here for rest? I am so glad to be able to run. I spent yesterday afternoon in the Museum—and I am astonished to find so many wonderful things in it. It is surely one of the great museums in the world in spite of its being *only* fifty years old. America is far greater than what people think; her Destiny is strong and healthy and eager. Just think, Mary, that fifty years ago there was not a masterpiece in any of the museums of America. And now they are seen even in private houses. Something besides wealth brings the beautiful and noble things from the old world. It is the Hunger of the *unwealthy* for public properties. I am so glad that you are reading *Zarathustra*. I want so much to read it with you in English. Nietzsche to me is a sober Dionysus—a superman who lives in forests and fields—a mighty being who loves music and dancing and all joy.

And must I use hair tonic, beloved Mary? Have I not enough on my head?! There are times when even my hair is in my way! But I will be anointed as soon as I reach Boston.

I shall use it every day and be like the priests of Chaldea who poured the sacred oil every morning on their heads.

O, Mary, why did you send more money? I have enough. You gave me more than enough before I came. May the Heavens bless your open hands. Good night, beloved Mary. I wish you were here now.

Kahlil

164 Waverly Place
New York
Tuesday, May 2, 1911

Seven times have I cursed the cruel Fate which made Syria a Turkish province! The influence of the Sultans follows the poor Syrians over the seven seas to the New World. The dark shadows of those human vultures are seen even here in New York. The Turkish ambassador, Riza Pasha, is in town. He is a feeble man with little brain; but he knows how to make one Syrian hate another. I am to dine this evening with his Excellency at the house of Mr. Mokarzel, the Editor of a daily Syrian paper. I do not know what will happen nor what I will say. I wish things were different with me, my sweet friend.

New York
Wednesday, May 3, 1911

It was a wonderful banquet at the Mokarzels last night. The guests were both Americans and Syrians. The ambassador was trying all the time to be *sweet* and *gentle*. We talked about

37

art, and he even invited me to visit him in Washington. That is the Turkish way of smoothing down the things that stand in the way! I made a little speech—Mr. Mokarzel forced me to, but it was all like fire under ashes. Poor Syria. Her children are nothing but poets. And though we sang as angels in her ear, she would not hear. Poor Syria!

Love from Kahlil

At this time, Gibran was trying to come up with some ways of earning money through his painting. He thought it would be a good idea to make portraits of some of the leading figures of the period and then try to sell them as a collection. He asked all of his friends who could be of help for introductions to various prominent persons. Mary wrote a number of letters on his behalf.

In the following letter, we see that he painted Arthur Farwell, the American composer and teacher, well known at that time for his symphonic music and string quartets.

New York
Friday evening, May 5, 1911
11:30

Beloved Mary. At nine o'clock this morning I was downtown planning things with a Syrian editor, and at half past two I reached Mr. Arthur Farwell's studio. The drawing I made of Mr. Farwell is among the very best. He said it expresses his whole inner being, and he *must* have a photograph taken from it. Afterward Mr. Farwell and I went to an exhibition of paintings by some of the New York artists. Mr. Farwell introduced me to Mr. Macbeth, the art dealer. At seven o'clock I came back to this place to get ready for a good dinner with Rihani and some of his friends. And now it is almost midnight and your Kahlil is quite tired out. I wish I could rest my head on your shoulder for ten minutes. I wish your hands were on my burning face.

New York
May 7, 1911
Sunday afternoon

Just came from the museum. O how much I want to see these beautiful things with you. We *must* see these things together someday. I feel so lonely when I stand alone before a great work of art. Even in Heaven one must have a beloved companion in order to enjoy it fully.

Good night, dear. I kiss your hands and your eyes.

Kahlil

New York
Wednesday, May 10, 1911

Every other person you see on the streets of New York is a Jew; and at noon, when people are out for luncheon, you see nothing but Jews. Today I saw two thousand of them walking on Fifth Avenue. The sight awakens one's imagination and inspires profound thoughts. It reminds the historian of the slavery of the Jews to the Babylonians and their miserable days in Spain. It makes a poet think deep thoughts of their past in Egypt and their future in this land. Perhaps a day will come when the dwellers of the East side will march toward Fifth Avenue even as the people of Paris marched to Versailles! The Jew is king in New York, and Fifth Avenue is his palace—and History is apt to repeat itself too often. But there is something eternal about the Jew—the world began when he was born, and the world is his to win and to lose and to win again! Yes, Mary, there is something everlasting in that strange race which we admire sometimes but never could like.

O these letters of yours, these rich letters. Each one is a feast for this hungry soul of mine.

I want to bring to you something beautiful, beloved Mary. I want you to gaze at a new picture as you did twice before. Do you remember? You gazed and my heart grew twice larger and my vision of life became less dim. Do you not remember? And now I am going to bed with *Zarathustra*, and we will read together, You and Kahlil.

New York
Friday morning, May 12, 1911

Mr. Arthur Farwell came with two ladies. One of the ladies said to Mr. Farwell, "Arthur, your mother must see this portrait of you—she will see in it her real son and the man who is going to do great things." These words gave me much joy, dearest Mary.

I spent an hour with my sick friend in Brooklyn. I read poetry to him, and I read poems in his pale sensitive face. As I was leaving him he took my hand tenderly and said, "Gibran, go to Syria—go to your Old Mother—she loves you much—go to Syria, Gibran."

I left him with unseen tears in my eyes. He is longing for Syria himself. He is afraid of death.

Kahlil

28 West 9th Street
New York
Tuesday, May 16, 1911

I took a room—a small room—in this old house where Rihani lives, and I feel so funny in it after being in a flat all by myself. But everything goes beautifully, and I do my work in Rihani's large room. When I am a stranger in a large city I like to sleep in different rooms, eat in different places, walk through unknown streets, and watch the unknown people who pass. I love to be the solitary traveler!

A large canvas is bought this afternoon and I will start work tomorrow. Will you not come and sit beside me while working? Come every afternoon, beloved Mary, and help me.

[New York]
Saturday, May 19, 1911

Here I am trying to preach "Self Reliance" to the Syrians who rely on the new regime in Turkey. I want these poor people to understand that a beautiful lie is as bad as an ugly one. The throne of the mighty sultan is built on wet sand. Why kneel before a tarnished idol when there is an immeasurable space to gaze at?

New York
Tuesday, May 30, 1911

—And guess what I did this afternoon? I made a drawing
of a man whom you admire very, *very* much—Mr. Charles
Russell.* It was a great joy to draw his remarkable face and
to talk with him about art in general and the eternal question
of the Near East. Mr. Russell's knowledge of drawings is that
of an Artist. He has an eye for fine lines and he knows where
to look for the poetry in things.

My dear Mary, why did you send more money? I do not
need it. You have given me too much too much! Bless your
open hands, and bless your many unseen hands. Good night,
dearly beloved Mary.

Kahlil

*Mary and Kahlil did not communicate often during the sum-
mers. Mary was always off to the West. She loved the mountains and the solitude. It was her time for rejuvenation. She
tried to encourage Gibran to travel but was seldom successful.*

*On holidays and in the summers he frequently joined his
sister in Boston and then traveled to quiet islands off the Maine
and Massachusetts coasts.*

* Charles Edward Russell was Socialist candidate for governor of
New York in 1910 and 1912, and for U.S. senator in 1914.

New York
June 28, 1911

I have not been out of this room for the last three days.
The Grip is my guest and I stay home to keep *Him* company.
A summer Grip is as mischievous as a winter one, and I know
them both so well that we usually get on beautifully. The
only thing about a Grip that I dislike is this bitter taste in my
mouth. It makes me feel as if I had swallowed a Turk half
way down!

Oh what a June this is! It is dark and cold and dreary. Even
the air is lifeless. I feel as if I am in a prison. This bitter taste
in my mouth adds to my longing for sweet air and bright
sunshine.

Now, Mary dear, I am going to rest. I shall close my eyes
and turn my face to the wall and think and think and think
of you—you the mountain climber—you the life hunter.

Good night, beloved.

Kahlil

Boston
September 14, 1911

And will you let me come and see you tomorrow evening,
beloved Mary? I have waited all these silent weeks for you
to come back so that I may see you before going to New
York.

My summer has been quite full—too full. I rewrote my
book *Broken Wings*, baptised it in fire and made a new
thing of it. How unhappy I would have been made if the publishers had taken it as it was. I did some work on my pictures,

made some decorations, and composed a few poems. I have a thousand things to tell you, and a thousand plans for this coming winter. Mary, I am just beginning to fall in love with Life! There are so many things to do, so many questions to solve, so many dreams to dream. But will you let me come and see you tomorrow, if you are not very tired? I will be here all day waiting to hear your voice over the telephone.

Kahlil

At this time boat lines operated between New York and Boston. From 1916 to 1937, there was a direct line, called the Metropolitan, which went by water from New York to Boston, on an overnight trip.

--------------------------------- ⚜{ *KG* }⚜ ---------------------------------

28 W. 9th St., New York
Tuesday, September 19, 1911

I had a mystic, sleepless night on the boat. No stateroom to be had and the berths had the odor of drunkenness so I spent the night on deck with stars, the bladelike moon, and then a remarkable sunrise. The memory of such a night remains forever. The music of the sea, strangely veiled with silence, and those bright, countless worlds sailing quietly through the immeasurable space made me think a million high thoughts.

Kahlil

28 W. 9th St., New York
Friday, September 22, 1911

I have taken a little, humble studio, dear Mary. It is on West 10th Street No. 51.* The little studio has an atmosphere and a small balcony! The light is good too—as good as that which I had in Paris—but it it *not* a sky light. The rent is only $20. Just think of it!

I know that you want me to have a better and larger studio but this little one will be good enough for me now. The good Great Spirit will lead me to the right place when the time comes.

I hope that in two weeks I will be working in this great, powerful city where the elements move as the imaginations of a god. I am visiting the places which we visited together three months ago. Things look so different when seen with two eyes only. But you will come again and we will see things with four eyes even as we saw them once before.

May God be with you, my dearly beloved.

Kahlil

A Miss Keyes taught art at Mary's school. In fact, it was she who had encouraged Mary to invite Gibran to hang his pictures at the school. Mary asked Miss Keyes—whom she considered an expert—to examine Gibran's paintings at the school and to comment on them. Undoubtedly Gibran's letter is a reply to Miss Keyes's remarks.

* The building at 51 West 10th Street was the first studio building ever built in America exclusively for the use of painters and sculptors.

New York
Dearly beloved Mary,   Sunday, October 20, 1911

All artists think that severe, unsympathetic critics are absolutely wrong. Miss Keyes is not wrong; she is simply conventional. She is a *slave* of the old, accepted forms of expression—and slavery is a misfortune. She and I belong to two worlds, we see art and life from two different points of view.

Technique is a power that could only reveal itself through *style*—and my style is only a month old. It was born with the *Beholder* and I am trying to bring it up as a mother would bring up her baby. I am trying to make it an instrument, a language, through which I will be able to express myself fully. Most people are apt to say that the technique is bad when they do not like the style of a work of art, and to like or to dislike a style is a matter of temperament.

I know too well what is wrong in my work and I am trying to make it right, but Miss Keyes does not know, and she thinks it is the technique. Even when my technique becomes perfect Miss Keyes will not like my work. She is too old in flesh and too young in spirit to accept new forms and new thoughts. And as to her idea of modern palette—well—it is childish and ridiculous.

She is not a painter. If modern palette cuts out burnt sienna, umbers and ochres, then Carrière, Whistler, Simon, Bonnard, Ménard, Blanche, Bache and Sargent are not *modern* artists, painting modern pictures, in modern France, modern Italy, modern England and modern America!! She also said that my lights are good but my shadows are bad. That, too, is an illogical statement; for how could anybody produce good lights without having good shadows. Good light, in a picture, is an optic illusion produced by good shadows. She probably wanted to say that those heads were out of construction, badly drawn, lacking in form.

46

But when Miss Keyes said that both the *Beholder* and *Dead Gods* suggest the beginning of another picture, she was paying me a great compliment. I hope that I shall always be able to paint pictures that will make people see other pictures (mentally) out beyond the left or right edge. I want every picture to be a beginning of another unseen picture.

These days are quite full. I am correcting the proofs of *Broken Wings* and I am trying to fix up the little studio so it will be warm and visitable and cheerful. At the same time, I am trying to make the Mohammedans of Syria understand that this war between Italy and Turkey is not a strife between Mohammedanism and Christianity. However, I shall write less and paint more during this coming winter. I *must* have a body of work before Spring comes.

It is getting dark in this place and I can hardly see what I write.

Kahlil

--- ❧ *KG* ❧ ---

New York
Tuesday, October 31, 1911

Mary, beloved Mary, I have been downtown, among my countrymen, all day long, working hard, and thinking harder. It is rather late and I am tired, but I could not go to bed without saying good night to you. You have been so near—so very near me today and yesterday. Your last letter is a flame, a winged globe, a wave from That Island of strange music.

These days, beloved Mary, are full of images and voices and shadows—there is fire in my heart—there is fire in my hands—and wherever I go I see mysterious things.

Do you not know what it is to burn and burn, and to know while burning, that you are freeing yourself from everything

you? Oh, there is no greater joy than the joy of
.

And now let me cry out with all the voices in me that I
love you.

Kahlil

There is an old Arabic song which begins "Only God and
I know what is in my heart"—and today, after rereading your
last three letters, I said out loud "Only God and Mary and I
know what is in my heart." I would open my heart and carry
it in my hand so that others may know also; for there is no
deeper desire than the desire of being revealed. We all want
the little light in us to be taken from under the bushel. The
first poet must have suffered much when the cave-dwellers
laughed at his mad words. He would have given his bow and
arrows and lion skin, everything he possessed, just to have his
fellow-men know the delight and the passion which the sunset
had created in his soul. And yet, is it not this mystic pain—
the pain of not being known—that gives birth to art and
artists? It is surely a noble thing to say "art for art's sake" but
is it not nobler to open the eyes of the blind so that they may
share the silent joy of your days and nights? True Art should
be made practical by revealing its beauty to people—I said
practical because anything that adds to our world of vision is
practical.

The studio is really very beautiful. I never felt more at
home in any other place.

And of course I have been working. I have already a little
picture—a little picture which is just a bit more than *Two
Crosses*. It is a little work in *the* Book.

As to us, seekers of the Absolute, whose loneliness has been made a garden, what is there left for us in Life but the joy of hunger and thirst? Have we not outgrown Realism through our love for the Real? Could we turn our eyes to see the gray faces of dead things? Who of us has two souls to send one to the mountain and the other to the valley?

Kahlil

--◆{ KG }◆--

New York
Sunday, November 26, 1911

O Mary, beloved Mary, it will be a real Thanksgiving day when you come. Charlotte told me some time ago that you were coming and I did not dare to ask you for fear that you will say "no." And Thursday will come like all the things we really desire. Thursday is no longer part of the future: it is the crown of this very "Now."

This is what I am doing in these days. I am putting my *House* in *order*. I am arranging my thoughts. I am getting rid of all the old spirits and shadows. To understand the world one must be far, far away from the world. To live is the greatest of all arts. To be an artist is to have glimpses of real Life. Real Life is God and God is everywhere. I am loving you all the time, Mary. I feel now what those Wednesdays and Fridays were to me. One must be at a little distance from great things in order to see them well.

O I have a million things to say to you. But Thursday is coming and the joy of Thursday is here even now.

Kahlil

Although Gibran's letters to Mary were always in English, his poetry in the early years was written in Arabic. When he was with Mary, Gibran would outline in English what he was doing and discuss different approaches and methods of expression with her. It was not until much later that he attempted to write poetry in English, and even then only after much encouragement from Mary. Later, we shall see how they collaborated when he began to write in English.

---------------------- ⊶⊰ *MH* ⊱⊶ ----------------------

[JOURNAL]

314 Marlboro St.
Boston
Wednesday, December 20, 1911

One of the most remarkable evenings I've spent with Kahlil. First, he helped me put round the Christmas candy bags on the girls' desks—tomorrow ends school—and when I gave him one for "Working so hard," he demanded a card too, and sent Miss Dean thanks.

Then we took up *Broken Wings*. He gave me an outline in English that lasted two hours. "Not one of the experiences in the book has been mine. Not one of the characters has been studied from a model, nor one of the events taken from real life. Authors often model upon their experience, but I have not. The characters and events are my creations—because I believe a book should have something new—an addition to life. I say this because the book dealing with a young man's awakening to life and with a love affair is sure to be called autobiographical."

It is in the first person—no name for the hero—but Sulma Karami is the woman, and Pharis Karami her father. "Sulma Karami I love very much. I've studied her carefully. She's a real person to me!

"I thought of this book first about three weeks after you spoke to me of Paris. I made the bare outline of it before I went, and in Paris I wrote it. This summer I rewrote it. And you were always with it—so you are in a way the mother of the little book!"

[JOURNAL]

314 Marlboro Street
Thursday and Friday, Dec. 21 and 22

Kahlil spent both evenings and Friday afternoon with me—working a little on Christmas bundles each time—and on Thursday recognizing his own, taking them from grandfather's table drawer—tiny Hawaiian salt bowls of wood, Japanese straw and strap slippers, Chinese brass spoon and small wooden slide top brown box, a Rossetti and a two-volume Swinburne like mine. Liked them all and was frankly sad that he'd nothing for me, since *Broken Wings* is delayed in press. "And I just didn't know anything else to give you."

1912

New York
Saturday, January 6, 1912

Tuesday was much more a birthday than today. The reality of those few hours is a door which leads to a new sense of joy and a new sense of pain and a new vision of Life. I have tried many times since that evening to write to you, but each time I found myself so completely overwhelmed by a strange silence—the silence of deep seas and undiscovered regions—the silence of unknown gods. And even now as I write, I feel that the most terrible element in Life is a dumb element. The hours that pass before a mighty storm and the days that come after a great joy or a great sorrow are alike, dumb and deep and full of outspread wings and motionless flames.

K.

New York
Sunday afternoon, January 7, 1912

Rihani and I had luncheon together. He and Charlotte came to the inevitable misunderstanding. They see each other now

Émilie Michel (Micheline)

Charlotte Teller

in a different light. Rihani said he will never see Charlotte again but I think he will! Charlotte said her house is always open to Rihani and I think she means it. The voice of an Unseen being said, "These two people are quite unusual and they should be friends," and I think they should.

Now I will say goodnight, as any other time. I kiss you and then I say goodnight and then I open the door and then I go out to the streets with a full heart and a hungry soul. But I always come again to kiss you and to say goodnight and to open the door and to go out to the street with hungry soul and full heart.

Kahlil

MISS HASKELL AND MISS DEAN'S SCHOOL
314 MARLBOROUGH STREET, BOSTON

Friday, January 5, 1912

Dear Hand, dear Eye, dear Thought, dear Fire, dear Love—

Thanks to the bon Dieu who gave you to your mother twenty-nine years ago—and one year ago drew you and me nearer together.

I've wept a little over these spirit-tenanted walls, and as yet have not touched them chiefly because my finger tips seem to shed tears at the thought of touching those places. It's been a priceless time, with them in the house, Kahlil.

You and the spring-floods of your new life with their power and strangeness and devastations and the passion of their lover to have the Earth drink them—Ach! it's so natural to think of you, sometimes so hard to write! All I am ever finally impelled to say, rather than *not* say, to you of yourself seems resolvable into, "Kahlil, you are in my heart—you are in my heart, Kahlil." When I look back over the years, it seems always to have been that—with changes only of depth and heat of your heart-place.

Lovingly,

M.

-··◄{ *KG* }►·-

[New York]

Sunday, January 21, 1912

The silent hour is not yet over and I am still in this little studio gazing at the shadows that pass between Hell and Heaven. I am living as I have never lived before. The days are filled with burning ideas and the nights are drowned in a sea of strange dreams. The hour that comes between the end of the day and the beginning of the night is veiled with a veil of seven folds.

There is much painful joy in life, and much sweet pain, too. Your Kahlil must sink into the depth of both joy and pain so that he may know how to paint a picture or write a line.

Kahlil

-··◄{ *KG* }►·-

[New York]

Friday, January 26, 1912

Beloved Mary. At last *Broken Wings* is out and I am sending you a marked copy (in Arabic!) which you cannot read now. Someday perhaps you will read it in a different tongue, and perhaps you will love it as an expression of the blessed year *1911*.

And did you ask me what am I doing, Mary? Well, I am working, working, working alone in silence.

I don't see much of anybody these days—I feel rather funny with *other* people—even those whom I care for. While one's heart is being transformed into a little world, one wants to be alone.

K.

···❧ *MH* ❧···

[JOURNAL]

[Boston]

January 28, 1912

Came from Kahlil a marked copy of *Broken Wings*, just out —with the dedication translated and the title of each chapter. The cover is green-gray paper, much like these 314 walls in effect, and good. Thus Kahlil translates the dedication, on the same page, above it:

"To her who gazes at the sun with fixed eyes; who touches the Fire with fingers that tremble not; who hears the songs of the Absolute while in the midst of the hollering blind— to M. E. H. I dedicate this book. Gibran"

In reply—I could only cry out of my speechlessness: To him who turns eyes sunward; who brings fire; who gives the Absolute a voice; whose immortality my name exults to hear —acknowledgment.

···❧ *KG* ❧···

[New York]

Thursday evening, February 1, 1912

I worked all through the afternoon—with burning hands.

The picture is getting along beautifully and I am almost happy.

My model was as good as gold—but, alas, she is not coming again. She gave up posing for a position as a secretary.

I have many things to say about Life after Death. I will not do so now. But I feel, and perhaps I shall always feel, that the "I" in me will not perish. It will not be drowned in the great Sea which we call God.

Mary, have you never been hungry, and without a thing in the house to eat? This is how your Kahlil is situated right now! I have not had anything to eat all day and I am so hungry! But I love it. Don't you love to be hungry and tired after a good day's work?

I talk to you, Mary, as I would talk with my own heart. You and my Destiny are inseparable . . . and what is there to hide from one's own Destiny?

Kahlil

———— ❧{MH}❧ ————

MISS HASKELL AND MISS DEAN'S SCHOOL
314 MARLBOROUGH STREET, BOSTON

February 1912

Dear Wrestler with Time and Mortality,

A Tuesday-written note from Charlotte in Washington says you "are in bed with a cold." Therefore my heart seeks you more than usual, if that can be with you whom I always find when I turn within. You no more slip from about my heart than Mary's bracelet from my arm. Perhaps I shall go to N.Y. a week from to-night.

If I do, shall I not bring the frames—or such of them as I can. *Autumn*'s anyhow, and the small or the large one maybe? And the *Three Women*? No hurry to answer this if you are still in bed—and it is in case you are that I write now instead of at the week end. But before I start, surely you will be about again—

[Boston]
Feb. 1912

Tell me what you'd like to have, and I'll bring what I can.
When I said, "Every pulse of your life is precious to me"—
my heart answered, "Foolish! to tell me I am precious to you!
You imply distance,—You meant, Precious the pulse-beats
together."—And so I did.

Ending a letter to you lays shadow on my heart.—I sneak
inside—and there you are, burning away like a bright fire!
So I warm up again till my fingers are limber enough to write
Ha ha! Let's laugh again—and God laugh mit!

Miss Haskell. M.E.H. Mary

MISS HASKELL AND MISS DEAN'S SCHOOL
314 MARLBOROUGH STREET, BOSTON

February 6, 1912

If there is one thing in the world I cannot feel hurried about
—it is You. Often I want to write to you, but I always do the
chores first, even write to the others first, with the common
consequence of not getting to you at all. And I have not even
the impulse to neglect job or joblets for you. I *add you*, I
never subtract from them.—Thought I find harder to regulate,
that *is* tempted to stray your way, and Mary's had to

"Go and call the cattle home"

from the Gibran pastures on several bright mornings.

Your dedication of *Broken Wings* to me is in my Dumb
world—with another gift from you—of which also I think I
have hardly even spoken to you—the other of these two dearest things that were ever given me—the little circle with my

59

initials on your *Autumn*. And even as I say it my letter comes to a standstill. I love them both so much—and so much more than love them. They are to me like the little pupil of the eye —that holds the heavens. I think they are in the ultimate drop of my heart's book. They have the reality of the incredibly strange. They are like another speech, yet I understand. They are books without words. I read them—yet I can't tell you what I read. But I should like to, because it is so dear to me, and you are so dear to me.

Goodbye. God lends me His heart to love you with. I asked for it when I found my own was too small, and it really holds you, and leaves you room to grow. I do long to see your beautiful new picture.

Mary

New York
Wednesday, February 7, 1912

My heart is full today, full of strange, calm serene shadows. I saw Jesus in my dream last night. The same warm face. The large dark eyes burning peacefully. The dusty feet. The rustic, gray-brown garment. The long curvey staff. And the same old spirit, the spirit of one who does nothing but gaze quietly, sweetly at Life.

O Mary, Mary. Why can't I see Him in my dreams every night? Why can't I gaze at Life half as calmly as He does? Why can't I find any one in this world so dearly simple and warm as He is?

Kahlil

New York
Thursday, February 8, 1912

There is something in these sonnets of Michelangelo that moves me as no other thing does. It is so hard to separate the man from his work. The greatest element in Michelangelo's soul was dumb and motionless. He went to his grave with a silent power in his heart—a power which he himself did not understand; and perhaps that is why he was always so unutterably sad.

K

[New York]
Friday, February 9, 1912

All the Arabic papers in this country are discussing *Broken Wings*. *Almoohajer* printed a whole page in which the book is compared to the work of those whose names would burn my lips if I should utter them. The book has not reached the Arabic world yet, and it will be a month or so before they start to give me cold and hot baths! I am proud only of the three English letters in my first page.*

I am working on a new picture. New in colour and feelings. It is twice as large as the *Beholder* and has more atmosphere than the rest of the pictures.

And now your Kahlil is going out to take his first meal. Come along, Mary, and sit with me.

Kahlil

* Mary's initials, MEH.

[Boston]
February 10, 1912

Saturday. Why! K.G.! how delicious! A from-you on the
hat-rack when I came in. I looked again, to make sure, for I
certainly hadn't tho't of any heavenly visitation earlier than
Monday. "Big mood inside," said the outside to me. "Something's doing—Papa's very active—his hand's in—or *Broken
Wings* is going well or embroiling him—skies are high and seas
deep!"—And sure enough, there it all was.

Greet the new picture from my heart—the fourth I have
not seen at all—since New Year's! And don't burn up, Old
Man, before we meet again, or, if you do, at least burn to my
windward, that the smoke may come to me.

Mary

314 Marlboro St., Boston
February 15, 1912

It never occurs to me to be anxious, but to-day the possibilities of illness have been hard thrust at me.

So I want to make sure

1. If you are still ill, that you know that yesterday you were
my treasure—"and where your treasure is there will your heart
be also"—that to-day you are my treasure—that to-morrow
you will be my treasure.

2. If you have any serious development, that I shall be told
of it,—and for that purpose I enclose a card. No one here will
read it—and I see all the mail first anyhow. I send it because
I fancy you use such little, and mayn't keep them handy.

For the rest, I know you are in a Hand to whose love of
you mine is but small—it is drawn from His. You have good

sense about illness,—and perhaps you've friends near enough to count on in time of need. They surely will count if they know of your illness—for it's not friendliness or affection that you lack among your acquaintance. God send you a Special Angel, from among them, or brand new!

Lovingly,
Mary

—⚜{ *MH* }⚜—

314 Marlboro Street, Boston
February 16, 1912

I wish I could come in to you as my mother used to come to me in the many illnesses I used to have—and as your mother must have come to you—like Life when I was empty of life —so freshly quiet and comforting, like sweet cool water, because I knew she loved me and bore me in her thought, and I had no fear. Always a peace was laid then upon my restlessness. I drank something beyond my craving from her presence, and for the moments she stayed my memory of suffering is as of a step by which I mounted to a clearer joy in feeling her, a more exquisite sense of her. Such balm I would bring you if I could, but I know that out of His countless hands and hearts God can send you more than I can even wish for you— and even with my eyes I can see how His will is towards you. So it is that praying for you becomes most simple.

Give yourself fresh air—Heaven's healing—and this food and drink that is good, dear one—and do not let considerations of cost enter it, I beseech you. You will not mind my saying this, and you will know you are in my heart.

Lovingly,
Mary

[New York]
Friday, February 16, 1912

It was nothing but my old friend the Grippe. He and I understand each other beautifully. We meet twice or three times every winter, we entertain each other as all old friends do, and then we part laughing!

Illness is more or less of a rest to me. It makes me feel like a baby who wants nothing but a soft bed to sleep on and a bright light to gaze at!

Kahlil

[New York]
Sunday, February 18, 1912

I am so glad that you are never anxious, dearest Mary. Far more painful than the grip is anxiety of those whom I love. I *will not* leave this strangely beautiful earth until I finish my work, and it is going to take me a long time to do that!

I worked rather well yesterday afternoon in spite of being weak. Today I feel much better. My hands and forehead are not burning half as much as last night. If I sleep well tonight, tomorrow will find me working, and singing too! And by the time you come to New York your Kahlil will be so strong that you will not recognize him!

Kahlil

[New York]
Tuesday, February 20, 1912

Forgive me, Mary, for not answering all the questions in my last letter.

Yes, of course I would like to have *Three Women* with me. The Spirit may move me any day to finish it. *Micheline's Head* is not very good—it has no place among the other heads which I would like to exhibit. The old drawings and pastels are little thoughts badly expressed. Let us keep them as shadows of the past, but we must not consider them while thinking of an exhibition.

I wish today was Thursday and I wish you were here now. I have many other wishes too, but I will keep them unuttered till you come.

May the hours run swiftly between now and Thursday, and on Thursday we will ask the hours to walk very slowly.

Kahlil

KG

[New York]
Tuesday (February 27, 1912)

I have not been able to think of anything else but this new spirit which you have breathed into my being. I don't know how or what to think of it. Perhaps I should not think but simply trust myself to that greater Mind which thinks for all of us.

May the Unseen help us both.

Kahlil

[New York]
Thursday, February 29, 1912

I have been working on this picture since Monday. The lower figure is finished and I like it much. Harting and Perry, two artists here in the building, think that it is the best figure I have painted, but I do not often trust the opinion of artists.

Mary, I am not feeling half as well as I should. That grippe is still hanging on and I am getting tired of dragging my body with my will. I am restless too. I envy those who are capable of relaxation. I simply can't relax. My mind is like a brook, always running, always seeking, always murmuring. I was born with an arrow in my heart, and it is painful to *pull it* and painful to *leave it*.

And I am always writing about myself to you. Tell me, Mary, are you not tired of "I am this" and "I am that" and "I am between this and that"? You see, Mary, I live so much within myself, like an oyster. I am an oyster trying to form a pearl of my own heart. But they say that a pearl is nothing but the disease of the oyster.

Kahlil

[Boston]
[Spring 1912]

What are you writing—and how does it go? And what are you thinking about—and how does *it* go? And what do you want to talk with me about?—and how do *You* go?

And why aren't your arms six hours long to reach to Boston?

And what old canvases have you been painting over?

And when will You come to me in a dream and make night sweeter than night?

Mary

[New York]
Sunday, March 10, 1912

Mary, dearest Mary, how could you, in the name of Allah, ask me if my seeing you gives me more pain than pleasure? What is there in heaven or on earth to inspire such a thought?

What is pain and what is pleasure? (Could you separate one from the other?) The power which moves you and me is composed of both pleasure and pain, and that which is really beautiful gives nothing but delicious pain or painful joy.

Mary, you give me so much of pleasure that it is painful, and you give me so much of pain too, and that is why I love you.

Kahlil

[J O U R N A L]

[Boston]
April 1912

We met on Friday—at 3:30 by the beautiful little marble band stand just being finished on the Common.

"This Common makes me ill," said Kahlil. "It could be so glorious! Look what the Italians would do with a place like this. And see! (the Civil War monument) Did you ever see anything uglier? Why don't they get Rodin to do something for them?"

The sun was warm. We found a bench facing it in the Gardens—and a little Jew boy ran about us after the pigeons, calling "Whoo! Whoo!" in great circles—while they fluttered calmly away. Sparrows hopped at our feet. We sat till after 6—and our most vital talk was on Kahlil's mind and habits in sex. He has had connection with few women in his life. He offered to tell how many but I said no. So few they have been, however, that it seems to him as if he had been actually guarded as by spirits—because started by a married woman so young, and with his temperament, he would naturally be expected to have run the gauntlet and lived hard. But the type of woman physically attractive to him is extremely rare, he says. He's met only three or four in his life—and what is not attractive is extremely repellent in physical intimacy. His actual sense of touch, extremely sensitive, keeps him remote from almost all women. All men seem to be a good deal approached by women with sexual offers. He is and always has been so approached from time to time—not in shadowy fashion—but as since I saw him in February by a woman he met who asked to come to his studio—and when he said he was engaged a good time ahead with models, bid him to tea at her house. He went and found, contrary to most teas, no one else there—her opening remark was that she had sent her husband away for the afternoon because she had fallen in love with him (Kahlil)—and asked as a second remark whether she should read him the poetry she had written him since! I write this almost with hesitation— because Gibran says such things with hesitation. He did it this time in fact only because I said I believed men thought themselves sexually approached sometimes when woman meant nothing sexual—and asked him point blank what he meant by such approach. We continued to talk on Saturday evening walking to the Symphony—and what I write is extracted from both talks. I had gathered from things he said to me that he had had a good many successive *liaisons*, and I confessed I had never been able to reconcile this with his stability and fastidious reserve, as I know him. So I gave him a list of his remarks from time to time and their inevitable significance to me. He was astounded—and didn't see at all that what he had said meant what to the English-speaking it must mean. Ignorance of certain English connotations explained some—his way of unconcreteness in matters that might give offense if in concrete words explained some—and his extreme brevity others; which he had left so that I thought he had entered into *liaisons* or at least had intercourse, when the affair was nothing but the offer from the woman. What I've known in the lives of other young men and of women, bears him out, if I needed corroboration —as to approaches made to him—and all I know of his physical reserve, his reserve in every way, the impersonalness underlying his gentle tact, the essential insignificance, despite his affection and human hunger, of personal relations in comparison with his work—and how the sex relation is not even predominant in his consideration of relations, but is only one among others almost as important—all this bespeaks the much-abstinence that I have always felt sexually in him. I said I had never been able to agree when people spoke of him as if he were a man of "affairs"—as they have—yet that his own statements had seemed to say the same thing—and when in N.Y. he said intercourse was no more than picking a flower, I could only say to myself that there were mysteries beyond my apprehension in the possible attitudes toward sex of clean minds. He himself brought up again that comparison to picking a flower —because he said it came to him what he had *seemed* to mean by it, and he was such a fool to say it. He meant that even picking a flower may be of great and mysterious significance and value—that great and small as we see them, are all great in reality. But that such phraseology was simply poetic and did not betoken lightness towards intercourse. He has not refrained because of Right and Wrong—but because he did not desire—did not wish what was before him. He believes in personal liberty—but in honor and cleanness and decency— and all those things are offended in—and the sense of privacy also—in most of the sexual approaches he had known. Once long ago he told me of the approaches of a rich leisure woman: the interest shown at first in a man's work; then an invitation to her house to talk; there a little talk, a little music—and another appointment; and shortly thereafter the direct offer.

I got a new sense too of permanency in our relation—because it was so explicit in him. When he asked me whether I realized surely that there is nothing in him he would not have me know, nothing he would not talk about or like to tell, I said I had thought he would not talk with me about his relation with women. A year ago, he said, he would not have, but he had learned to love me so much—had never conceived such freedom of confidence as possible, nor such sharing. Said as he has said before, that all his work he does with me. "And I never weary of being with you. There is no other human being, man or woman, that I can be more than two or three hours with without waiting to go off a while for a little rest" (he must have forgotten fellow-merrymakers, and just have meant tête-à-tête-ers), "but with you the time is never long enough."

He spoke of the impossibility of his marrying now and the probability that always the urge to express what is in him will absorb him too much for marriage. It would be unfair to two things—the two most concerned; to the woman and the work. And I think he believed me when I told him I was with him in thought and realized that he needs all of himself now for the work and isn't ready to marry. I gave him too my guess that after he is established he will marry a rare but younger woman. "Well, irrespective of that hypothetical ideal being," he said, "let me say that I want to work always with you, to grow always with you. I don't want to be left behind while you run on without me, and I don't want to run on and leave you behind. And my study is, how best to keep that third something, that relation, between us.—I make mistakes, many mistakes, in little things and in details. But about a big thing I've never yet been mistaken. And I feel that this thing between you and me is lasting. 70,000 years hence I shall be saying the same thing to you. Are you not conscious"—with a laugh—"of its being said 70,000 years ago? What to do to keep it unhurt, undimmed, living—that is my question."

I had been in a tumult over various questions of sex that had come up in my short three "calls" in New York—and he had known it—not alone from my mentioning it.

The smallness of the studio at 51 W. 10th St. is distressing because Kahlil can entertain but two at a time. "And it cuts into work because then I must have visitors often—and I can't have models and guests the same day. The guests usually want to come in the afternoon—and then I am working. I can't work from the model while I'm expecting people, nor pick up such work after they are gone. It makes something wrong in my head for it. I can write or plan in the morning—and now I've kept Monday, Wednesday and Friday afternoons for models—and Tuesday and Thursday I'm being visited."

I told him if I died I wanted him to take my little blue china jar, "though you've few blue things—just because I love it so."

K. "Do you know *why* I've so few blue things?"

M. "I supposed because you've room for not all the colors in your studio."

K. "No—it's because I love it so much. Blue is my color—my favorite. Not all blues—but there is a Persian blue, and Egyptian, that I love."

I said I had known he loved it, from his pictures—blue so predominates in them. Gold is his next favorite—"and that gray which is over colors."

Mary [his sister] had bought him a rug—for $7.00—an antique, full of yellow and brown, with some red. He'll use it for a table cover.

314 Marlboro Street
April 1912

Golden Links he finds going well. It is more virile than the Syrian Club in N.Y.—and counts more in Syria. The young men in it are not here to stay, as in N.Y.—but for college, and return to Syria. Kahlil finds they think more directly and forcefully and practically. The Italian bombardment of Beirut showed the Syrians, to whom Beirut is very dear, the second capital after Damascus, that Turkey is indifferent to them and therefore alienates Syria more for Turkey—and "anything is good that makes them hate Turkey."

I wrote the foregoing pages on Saturday, April 7, 1912, and Sunday p.m. he told me in the Library that what he was planning for and looking forward to was marriage! "As soon as I've conquered my work and a little of the world. I need a little time for that. But we are just waiting, Mary."

And on Friday he had said, as he had said months ago, that probably he would never marry!

Somehow in that interim he lived through a cardinal stage in himself. Somehow our relation became commensurate with his work. Somehow life together not only in spirit but also in house and home, became the essence of his thought and his plans.

I don't understand how it came about—unless it was just part of the expansion from nearness into oneness that our Friday and Saturday talks seemed to give—to give through my understanding his sex attitudes and his love for me—and through his understanding my love for him and my trust. Or rather, not trust, but knowledge.

I said, as I had said before, that I am too old to marry him—and gave my conception of the change that would come as he grew older toward liking women not his senior. He listened, in his ever-attentive way, and though he put up no argument versus my age—simply laughed when I said I'd studied the list, from Oedipus married to his mother, and through Browning to Elizabeth Barrett—and that I was not moved from my sense that in our case my age was insuperable—I felt through all our next meeting—Monday—that his mind had actually changed from friend-lover to friend-husband—and now—the Saturday night after his going—I have still the same feeling—as if now what he plans he plans for us together.

To deny that I long inexpressibly for marriage would be lying—but the drawbacks are so evident that I do not long to have it take place. And that it cannot take place indicates to me that perhaps the growth of readiness for that additional complexity in life is what Kahlil is to get from his full-grown love for me.

[JOURNAL]

[Boston]
April 1912

Even as I write—debating and analyzing—mud comes into the waters—I stop. I think in the natural, simple way—of life with Kahlil, as I believe he thinks of life with me—and the waters clear—and the beautiful wide calm that has filled me since I knew he loved me as I love him comes back. And zest for work comes! When I *debate* about Kahlil, it becomes hard to keep my mind on school; when I drop debate, and trust carefree-ly, thought about school is easy!

He takes joy so simply, so graciously, so unquestioningly and joyfully, that I feel nearer to him when I take it so too.

He said to me once, "When I am with you I often don't think; I just live—and I do things without realizing or even being fully conscious of what I do. But afterwards I remember everything and know just what I did." I have noticed it in him—with astonished delight—for he shows it by the thing that always touches me most deeply in him—complete unreserve and lack of shyness. It is habitual in Kahlil not to put himself in the power of others—but allow them only touch, so to speak—never *grip*. But he does put himself into my hands—seems to throw away all self-protectiveness.

[New York]
Friday, April 19, 1912

I went to sleep at 3:30 this morning. The air was so charged with the horrible sea tragedy* that I was not able to go to sleep earlier. At 6:30 I was up. Cold water and strong coffee brought light to my eyes. At 7:30 I was with Abdul-Baha.†

At 8 we began to work, and then people, mostly women, started to come, but they all sat quietly gazing at us with thirsty eyes. At 9 o'clock the drawing was finished and the noble Abdul-Baha smiled. Then the twenty-five or thirty persons in that large room began to shake both my hands as if I had done something for each one of them. "It is a miracle." "You were inspired." "You have seen the soul of the Master." And so on and so forth. Then Abdul-Baha said to me in Arabic, "Those who work with the Spirit work well. You have the power of Allah in you." Then he said, quoting Mohammed, "Prophets and poets see with the light of God," and he smiled again. In his smile there was the mystery of Syria and Arabia and Persia.

The followers of Abdul-Baha liked the drawing because it is a true likeness of their master. *I* like it because it is a real expression of my better self! It is as good as that of Rodin— perhaps better in some ways!

My eyelids are heavy and I am going to rest my head in yonder corner! Three hours of sleep are not half enough for children.

Kahlil

* The White Star liner *Titanic* had sunk April 15, 1912, with more than 1300 lost.

† Abdul-Baha, the Persian Bahai leader, was traveling throughout Europe and the United States preaching and winning converts to the Bahai religion.

[New York]
Monday, May 6, 1912

The last two mails from the East brought a huge body of literature about *Broken Wings*. I read some of the criticism and I found many surprising things! They all discuss the little book in an impersonal manner which I like, and they all seem to agree on its being "a wonderful work of art," "one of the most remarkable pieces of modern literature," "perhaps the most beautiful in modern Arabic" and "a tragedy of subtlest simplicity which the author must have lived a thousand times." But they disagree most dissidently on its *spirit* or philosophy. Sulma Karami, who is half Beatrice and half Francesca, is analyzed and examined in two totally different ways—gently by the radical, and brutally by the conservative. The ninth chapter, in which I tried to bring Christ and Ashtaroth* together, is looked upon as "remarkably beautiful" and "Absolutely immoral and irreligious." *Tawa* Efendi, a young, enthusiastic writer published a long article entitled "Modern Literature" in which he places Goethe and Balzac on the two highest summits. He said in the end of his article that *Broken Wings* is the beginning of a new era in Arabic poetry.

Two kisses for your hands and two for your eyes.

Kahlil

[JOURNAL]   [Boston]
Monday Night
May 6, 1912

Oh! Kahlil! I whisper it fearfully—but I really think I'm beginning to find it *easier* to hold my tongue and listen, instead

* Or Ashtoreth. Ancient Semitic goddess, counterpart of the Phoenician Astarte.

of wanting always to say what *I* think! I long to perfect that gracious art. The sneak in me longs for safety—and my safety is silence.

Six more weeks—and all stakes are left behind—I shall be in the West. I sorrow to leave *You* behind—for that great letterless country. And all your pictures of this half year that I have hardly seen or not at all—for even in February it was just a glance; I can't *see* them in a couple of hours! And with me is always the shocking fact that I don't know your language! This is ceaselessly *strange*—I gaze at my ignorance as at a circus beast—inexplicable.—Then again, I bethink me how far wider and deeper than language speech is—and that I might know Arabic and yet nothing of your wider and deeper speech—that is often so clear, and dearer to me than language however dear.

Nothing matters except what matters supremely.—There's the conclusion I always return to from flights after ease or Arabic or other delights—and I realize that through and through I am really full of the sense of blessedness. God put a light in your every finger-tip, and in your heart strength!

Mary

[New York]
Tuesday, May 7, 1912

Did you not smile after reading my letter of yesterday? Did you not say to yourself "Kahlil is just a little boy, and he talks so much of what the Great Santa Claus puts in his stocking." Did you not say that, Mary?

Mary, are you not going to let me spend a few days with you this summer before you go west?

May the blue wings of Allah enfold you, dearest Mary.

Kahlil

[New York]
May 16, 1912

Abdul-Baha came back to New York a few days ago. "The Women's Committee of The New York Peace Society" gave him a great reception at the hotel Astor Monday afternoon. There were many speakers and "Peace" was the only subject! Peace! Peace! International Peace! Universal Peace! It was tiresome, illogical, flat, and insipid. Peace is the desire of old age, and the world is still too young to have such a desire. I say, let there be *wars;* let the Children of the Earth fight one another until the last drop of impure, animal blood is shed. Why should man speak of Peace when there is so much *ill-at-easeness* in his system that *must* go *out* one way or another? Was it not the Peace disease that crept into the Oriental nations and caused their downfall? Because we do not understand Life we fear Death, and the fear of Death makes us dread strife and war. Those who *live,* those who know what it is to *be,* those who have knowledge of the Life-in-Death do not preach Peace; *They Preach Life.*

My only desire, Mary, is to *be* and it does not matter how or where or when. There is no Peace in the art of Being.

O' Mary, how much I want to kiss your hands now, and your eyes, too. And how much do I want to *be* with you and *in* you and *around* you.

Kahlil

[New York]
Sunday, May 26, 1912

The spirit is still willing but the body is tired out.
I am not well, beloved Mary, and my whole being is aching

for a green, silent spot where I can love God and Life and the Absolute.

When spring is dancing among the hills one should not stay in a little dark corner. It is such a beautiful day out, but I have not enough of physical will to dress and go for a walk.

You must be a little tired, too. *No;* you are never tired, never ill. Your body is like your spirit—always ready, always willing, always eager. You are like the Cedars of Lebanon, full of fragrant strength.

I wish those people were not coming this afternoon. I wish you and I were in the woods talking and walking and eating berries.

────────────── ◈ *MH* ◈ ──────────────

[JOURNAL]

314 Marlboro St.
June 2, 1912

[*Mary:*] "Is the expression you put into your drawing new, too, like the technique?"—It's hard, he said, to separate style and subject—What a man wants to say determines how he says it. If he has a vision of life he is always putting that vision before us—in different forms. We unconsciously contradict ourselves when we say we like a man's style and not his ideas. Style and ideas are one.

"Have I told you about my new studio chairs? Very beautiful. Roman curule back—wood all painted black—and a very dirty old cushion cover. For 14¢ a yard I got a very beautiful piece of silk—and covered them. I have four at a dollar and a half apiece."

Boston
June 5, 1912

We met at the Athenaeum—because it was raining and cold. "What do you say to the State House?" said Kahlil.—We entered behind the driveway under the mid-building—and saw the beautiful stairs—and then the warm rotunda, with its glow of yellow marble. "Doesn't this remind you of Napoleon's Tomb?" said Kahlil as we stood in the little circular balcony and saw the school children shown the cases of war flags beneath. "And you wouldn't want anything more complete than that"—indicating the tiled floor.

"Though Americans want public buildings to be glorious, and are willing to spend millions of dollars on them, they don't know how to choose artists. Having Puvis de Chavannes decorate the Boston Library was an exception."

"Hope," says Kahlil, "is laziness, hope that one will suc-ceed, I mean. We have nothing to do with hope or faith. We hope instead of working." And by working he means travail of being to give birth to itself — to Life that it knows—the completest, deepest, wrench of labor.

The Chinese are young of soul, said Kahlil. Their art is primitive: Egyptian art is simple but not primitive, for it expresses the soul, the essence. Chinese art expresses the ap-pearance of things, in a simple way. Arabs are like trees that bear fruit in the seventh year, compared with Chinese, who are trees that bear in the eightieth year. The Chinese vibrate slowly —they mature slowly. The Arabs mature and vibrate quickly. If the Chinese deserve to be eaten by Europe now, they will be: if they can prevent themselves from being eaten, they don't deserve to be. But as long as there are live souls in China she will not simply be food; she will be alive in herself. The

Chinese have no great conception of life. They are not a spiritual people. But they have a wonderful code of morality. To them life is a series of fine things, not an omnipresent vital principle.

[JOURNAL]

314 Marlboro St.
June 7, 1912

We met at the subway, and walked across Common and Cambridge St. Bridge to grass on the other river bank. "This cool warmth," said K., "is like summer in Mt. Lebanon. I love it."

He wants to study rock forms this summer. There is a wonderful relation between the human form and the forms of rocks. He thinks of Marblehead because it is near the art stores of Boston. Doesn't need anything so wild as Monhegan —nor even rocks very large.

We went around each of the bridge towers as we always do—for the bigness of it. Kahlil likes that bridge extremely— and would like it even more if the iron were covered with stone or cement.

Again he commented on the chance ignored to make the Common beautiful—and on the hard redness of the Hill and Back Bay—that need mist in order to be beautified.

"Yes, a bridge"—said Kahlil as we crossed it—"to build a bridge—that is what I want to do: to build one so strong and solid that it may be crossed upon forever."

"What is Imagination?" said I.

" 'Imagination' is a way of knowing," answered Kahlil.

For example, suppose a mummy in the museum. A scientist would bethink him of the manner of its keeping, the drugs, herbs, and processes—another of the inscription—an excavator of its exhuming from the sand-blown tomb—a poet of the princess or priestess whose body it is, with all the beauty and elaborateness and mystery of her life—and of the journey of the body from Egyptian sand and rock to the Boston Museum. Or all these associations, suggestions, radiations, might crowd into a single mind. All of them are the contribution of imagination to the thing actually present to the eye. Imagination sees the complete reality,—it is where past, present and future meet—where London, China, Chicago and the poles are present in the same moment. Imagination is limited neither to the reality which is apparent—nor to one place. It lives everywhere. It is at a centre and feels the vibrations of all the circles within which east and west are vitally included. Imagination is the life of mental freedom. It realizes what everything is in its many aspects.—Imagination does not uplift: we don't want to be uplifted, we want to be more completely aware.

"I want to be alive to all the life that is in me now, to know each moment to the uttermost.

"I don't want to be just a painter of pictures, or a writer of poems. I want to be more."

Kahlil said Nietzsche was the occidental mind most like Christ's to him—that Nietzsche hated Christianity because it stood for softness.—We talked too of Wagner, whom Kahlil called essentially Christian, not Christlike.

With Kahlil I feel as free as alone—and often I speak to children or smile with women on the street, as is my wont by myself. He never does—though he's never a damping presence. Something led me to ask him whether it made him uncomfortable to have me do it. "Yes," he said. "And I'll tell you why. I'm always trying to feel for the way it affects the other person—not you—and I think it gives a little pain." Then he went on, with that gentleness and yet that keen firmness of perception. "You are a lady. Neither clothes nor manner can conceal your social position. If you speak with another of your own rank, I see no harm. But with people of less position, even though they may smile or answer pleasantly, there may be the sting of that thought that you are speaking with the kindness that descends. You do not speak out of condescension; you speak from joy—there is no philanthropy in it. But these people do not know you. They only know that you have clothes and gloves and position beyond theirs—and not that you speak differently and are different from other women of your rank. We have a saying 'Do not limp in the presence of a cripple.' That is the principle. There is a natural dignity in the misfortune of poverty—a natural majesty. I might say—a right to privacy. Pity or philanthropy sets a little arrow in its heart."

[JOURNAL]

314 Marlboro–Boston
June 8, 1912

Kahlil came in with a headache—drew a little red sketch while I made a late supper—and decided to return to New York on Sunday 16th—for a promised speech to a Syrian Women's club for helping immigrant Syrian women. "Since I can't write them a check for a hundred or two hundred dollars a year I make them a speech."

We read much in Nietzsche. "Perhaps the greatest period in my life in recent years was when I got a new conception of Nietzsche."

He and Mary used often to come to the Reservoir—so that he knows it well. "Poor fellow, he has to get up," said Kahlil when the bicycling custodian reached a transient lying on the sacred grass.

Boston
June 10, 1912

We went to the Reservoir—and sat on a bench and read *Zarathustra*. First "Of Great Longing."

"This is the loneliest song that has been written," said Kahlil —"unless it be what one reads behind the last words Christ spoke after the last supper." That was when he told his disciples they should be persecuted for his sake—and he should die. He was saying, "I have given you all. I have no more to give."—When we read "Hath the giver not to thank the taker for taking?" Kahlil said, "You've so often said this." We read the thing twice—as we sometimes do when we love it very much. "We must read together his sister's biography of him," said Kahlil. He continually fills me now with that sense of together. We laugh over his mistakes of pronunciation. I never laughed so laughingly with anybody else. "I believe Nietzsche would like it," said he, "if he could see two people reading him and laughing so"—for we often laugh at Nietzsche's exquisite wit or his boyish downrightness of phrase, so fresh.

That night I put him on the rack, too—for I told him how I had become skeptic toward his own understanding of his own mind, when he mistook about readiness to marry.—And what he said in reply was but further revelation of his soundness, his insight, his complete sensitive tenderness, his greatness. Everywhere I touch him, I touch Reality. Life, Rock-bottom:

Nietzsche he has loved since he was twelve or thirteen. "His form always was soothing to me. But I thought his philosophy was terrible and all wrong. I was a worshipper of beauty—and beauty was to me the loveliness of things—the harmony and music and lyric qualities of them. What I wrote before I was

83

twenty-three or twenty-four was liquid and musical. I had not learned to catch a greater rhythm of life, that includes it *all*. So I thought the philosophy of destruction was all wrong. Then by degrees I found more and more in Nietzsche. Gradually, I came to realize, that when we accept a man's form, we also accept his thought. For they are inseparable."

Every work of beauty is a discovery of a rhythm that is in Life—is a part of Reality made manifest——

[JOURNAL]

314 Marlboro St. Boston
Tuesday, June 11, 1912

Kahlil looked tired. I was so conscious of wounds open from the fisticuff confession of yesterday—that without delay I told him my skepticism had been only toward him as regards me. "How could I think a man didn't know his own mind, who had created his own work out of nothing?" I said, "nor that he lacked courage when he had developed his work and his life as you had? The affair with me was but a detail—only I cared too much, to be picked up and dropped; and as for my ungraciousness, that was from pride, lest I arrogate to myself a nearness not really mine. I think I've known your quality. You said yesterday that there are seven heavens in poetry. There are seven heavens among people we cherish, too—besides all the people in no heaven at all. And you've always been in the seventh heaven with me and I've always known it. There've never been more than two or three or four others there—but you, always."

The shadow left his face at almost my first words—that wonderful responsive face. I was moved to go on presently.

"You know it's a test of a person—to say hard things."
Kahlil nodded. "Whenever I've tested you you've just been
more. So it was last night. And at these times a strange sense
comes to me. It came then again—a sense of a faraway childhood with you—very beautiful. I see bright fields and you
and I are in them, together, children."

Jack came in for the night, on his change from the Brook-
line Country Club to Mrs. Willard's camp. He asked about the
school. Gibran was interested to hear him condemn the over-
emphasis on prayer meetings and tell how the "professing"
boys sometimes curse and swear and utter profanity in the
dormitories. How two Turkish boys turned Christian also.
"What did they get from it?" said Gibran like a flash. And
when Jack said one got a scholarship—and perhaps the other
would when he came back after a term's expulsion for smok-
ing, "because all the Christians were so delighted at a Turk's
conversion"—Gibran's nose was high. Jack says many Greek
boys came over to avoid service in the Turkish army, which
is now compulsory. "But I wouldn't mind serving," he said.
"I'd go in and learn and know how to fight for Greece against
Turkey when the chance comes."

"Good," said Kahlil. "I like that."

[JOURNAL]

314 Marlboro
Wednesday, June 12, 1912

Today Kahlil got the first motif, for his Island God. He
has finally decided that his Prometheus exile shall be an Island
one. "I can put a mountain on the island. An island gives so
many possibilities—especially if it is near enough the main-

land for a city to be visible."—This first part is to have a name given in Arabic to the rising of the new moon. At the end of 7000 years from the shore near the city he puts off in his boat alone—and we learn why he had left the gods to be an exile among men, and why now he leaves men as an exile to solitude: because he must await a new race. This is the book he means when he says "My Book." There is a slowly growing body of material for the book—Similarly *The Madman* grows. "I have always six or seven prose poems on hand." When he has completed a thing he keeps it for months—and then returns to it. Then he revises—and may put away again—either to revise finally later, or never to publish, but just to keep for a few lines in it worth using in something he shall care to publish. Thus he has much he never will publish—and some now of old date that he may yet publish. He told me the story of the Bridegroom, "perhaps the most complete thing psychologically that I've done"—in which the man and girl believe each that the other loves not, and the girl therefore marries an older man: but sending for her lover on that night is told by him that he does not love her; kills him and then kills herself.—Theme: When we cease to believe the idea we no longer perceive it; we kill it and its death kills us. Unfaith the destroyer.

"I've talked with the gods today, and prayed to them," said I.

"What did you ask for?" said Kahlil. "I have been doing it too."

"What was your prayer?" said I.

"Oh! I asked you first," said he.

"I realized," said I, "that all the trouble I ever had about you came from some smallness or fear in myself. And I prayed that if more of that remains in me, as no doubt there does—it shall be burnt, torn, blown, killed, *out* of me—at whatever cost."

Kahlil said, "Mine was very different. I asked that things be made lasting."

"Our things?" said I.

"Yes."

The reality of a thing is sometimes different from our conception of it. I've always known our relation was permanent: that even if its expression went in this life, the real thing would wait to be resumed. I thought Kahlil might think it gone— but I knew he'd come to it again. I wanted continuity of conscious togetherness.—And since togetherness has so increased how increasingly I prize it.

We read in Nietzsche of August, of Paris, of Scholars. Kahlil reads to no one else in English—naturally: for he still makes many mis-stresses. But shyness with me is gone from him.—and I love to listen to him. His voice is as responsive as his face. He inflects enough; and I seem not to have heard enough of it before since—again some faroff bright childhood. What is that memory in me—of something perfect in breeding, in spirit and in form—that brings a sense of mother with it—and comes rarely except when I'm with Kahlil? Was there in early childhood a loftiness or a sensitiveness in me, since diminished? All that is musical and deeply bright in personality harks back to those days of gold.

We worked at defining snobbishness and aristocracy— apropos to American aristocracy.

Kahlil called aristocracy Breeding. Breeding he defined as an inheritance passed from father to children—indefinable but unmistakable—a beauty of spirit and of dealing, that permeates the whole man and meets everyone. Kahlil said Haroun Al-Raschid * was probably the best bred man in the world, and how he was at home with everyone and all were at home with him; and he could come near to even the poorest; and what a free simple dignity he had, and what joy in the integrity of the simplest subject.

He sleeps now seven or eight hours out of the twenty-four. No matter whether from 12–8; or from 4–11; just so he gets it

* (764?–809), most famous of all caliphs of Baghdad; was idealized as the caliph of *Arabian Nights*.

—though doctors tell him to choose the earlier hours. He does his best work between 12 and 4 at night.

He eats *very* little. "Work and food don't go together, I find." An orange for breakfast—and a cup of Turkish coffee —or only the coffee. No lunch or a bit of bread and cup of coffee—or just coffee—or a piece of fruit. A dinner that would be small for anyone else. And no more. Nothing between meals—just indifferent to it. And absolutely indifferent to every virtue of service except cleanness. It is his only stipulation. Katie's* casting of food on table suits him just as well as the service given at Miss Jean's. Actually, the less service the better. So only it be clean. You can't talk him into caring about un-essentials in anything.

[JOURNAL]

314 Marlboro St.
Friday, June 14, 1912

Kahlil to lunch. For the first time he volunteered a suggestion about my dress. "Have you another pin?"—I had my jet butterfly on a white waist.—"That one is so black, it makes a spot." Finally we chose Osiris on his bug chain.

To-day he had his laboratory look—problem beset, but it wore off. Golden Links met last night—"I gave them H——" said Kahlil, "about giving up their oriental reality for an occidental seeming." What is real and fine in America is hidden to the foreigner, he said. "Orientals love splendor. But splendor is beautiful thoroughness. Cheap, glittering brightness catches the oriental eye here, and the oriental thinks he is getting the real American in it. Sportsmanship attracts the eye of the young foreigner: but the real splendor of America is in her

* Maid at 314 Marlboro Street.

ideal of health, her power to organize, her institutions, her managements, her efficiency, her ambition. The immigrants eagerly drop what they brought here. What they grasp at are shadows. I want them to keep their orientalism till they know America better and can distinguish between the real and unreal."

314 Marlboro St.
Saturday, June 15, 1912

We met in the library. Kahlil was waiting—always there first!—reading by the table lamp—his head the most vibrant spot in the room—dark, domed, luminous—eyebrows like black lifted wings—The full high forehead—the burning star, and night quality dominant in his quietness. Lustre.—Katie, a fine dear girl, said of him yesterday, "His face is full of stars. There's brightness all over it. Look at him and you'd know there's not a dead spot in him. Anywhere you'd see him you'd know there was a peculiar power in him and a peculiar beauty."

We walked home—Kahlil loves to walk though not fast. "I've shoes mending round the corner on Massachusetts Avenue"—said I—"Will you walk with me for them?"—"Indeed I will walk with you!"—with the delicious warmth of a glowing child—I was so glad I had asked instead of suggesting that I run on alone for them while he tell Katie at 314 we longed for lunch. That would have saved him four blocks with my bag of stuff—but he doesn't need to be saved that—and he prizes each moment together. Little flashes like his answer then lay the beat of his heart suddenly against mine and I start at its fresh strength.

He was talking about English. "If I gave up six months to

studying English I think I could master it idiomatically"—after he had noted the idiom "in ruins"—"but how can I give up six months!" He hears very little excellent English.

Kahlil says we can only progress when we tread real elements—Life that is not real is actually *not* real and if we fill it with borrowed or unrealized elements we *fill it with shadows*. It is then a suspension, a postponement, a shunning of Reality. And if we call such hours and activity *real*, we are killing life; we smother and deny and banish it. He has been gradually electrifying my sense of Life, and scooping it bigger.

His own speed quickens mine. Every other life I know is low-geared in comparison. But he is so reserved that people see only his fruits—not his processes. He is as silent as a tree—his movements gentle as a leaf's.

At supper I said how much I often longed to let him know what richness he is to me. "You mean what we get together," said Kahlil, "or have together, or what being together opens to us." He spoke a little about his silence where he feels deeply—and I of the actual freedom to speak which I so love doing, which his silence gives me. And of my delight in absence of habits that can become forms—of all things that have to die away with time. Kahlil has had all his life an absorbed longing for the lasting—for eternities.

"Do poets wait long for recognition in Arabia—or Arabic-speaking countries?"

"No. Literature has been so long the sole art except music—and *the* chief art always—that all love it—all are alive to it. The language is the pride, the joy, the instrument, of all the people. But a small poet is hardly ever mistaken for a great one. The difference between poetry and verse is known."

"Do you love domes?" said he one day. "I love them so much, when you go to Constantinople you will have your fill of them. They are to me the complete form."

Nantasket [Mass.]
August 14, 1912

The great storm, for which I have been waiting, has just come. The sky is black. The sea is white with foam, and the spirits of some unknown gods are flying between the sky and the sea. I am watching it as I write. It is as wonderful as the one we saw together in New York. Do you remember?

Mary, what is there in a storm that moves me so? Why am I so much better and stronger and more certain of life while a storm is passing? I do not know, and yet I love a storm more, far more, than anything in nature.

And you, you are nearer to God. There is more freedom and more beauty where you are than this little place.

The storm is at its best now.

Love from your
Kahlil

Box 176. C/O C. T. Haskell
Wenatchie, Wash.
My beloved Kahlil,   August 16, 1912

Today I am out of California—with all that California means that I cannot express comprehensibly to you.—Subconsciously a desire concerning your coming year has hovered in me all summer—California means summer. I want to see you on September 7 and 8 if that is convenient for you—and then if I can I am going to get you to plan your next year for the West instead of for New York—dear Old Man. The constant battle against physical weakness is greater postponement and detriment to your work there than anything else can be. I believe the year I want you to take will make you physically fit—and I want to talk to you about it.

I have too much to say—I can't attempt to write it, and yet I don't want just to spring the idea on you when we meet. Your constant state of *under par* means constant leakage, so to speak, from both the present and the future of your work and your life and your self. I think you must change it, and by some means which will be not hopeful but sure.

Let me hear at once that I may know when and where. Love and blessing to you, dear,

Mary

Dismiss thoughts of expense. The year is already provided for with the money you have, and nothing is so ruinously expensive as your bodily incapacity's defeating your days and nights. I beg you *not* to let that consideration enter: it will be the mote that obscures the sun. I *know* whereof I speak. Trust me, please.

[JOURNAL]

New York
Saturday, September 7, 1912

Came three days early from Chicago to see Kahlil and beg him to go west for the winter, or even for a month—to live outdoors and build up. His grippe attacks every winter, his stomach attack this summer—his frequent under-par-ness—impede his production and his life. Got round to Kahlil's about eleven a.m.—the studio open and alone, with only *Consolation* and *Angele* on view—and the three beautiful black chairs purple-seated, and the two gilt and cutglass Louis XIV decanters he got at auction for seventy-five cents apiece and for one of which he has already been offered twenty-five dollars.

When he came in I was introduced to these new things—

and then we had a long hot talk—my observation of his failure to get the right physical thing and its detriment to his work—his wholesouled refusal to go west. Doesn't want to go away—doesn't want to go alone—or with anybody—Believes he can get well in New York with hygiene—and volunteered to live hygienically. That was more than I had expected: I accepted with joy——

I was to go on Monday. Kahlil said he had thought I was staying till Wednesday. And I had a sense that he was preoccupied when Monday p.m. came—and not sorry to see me go. Like a busy mother, who loves her child but sometimes wants it away.

"My life is an inner life. Little is 'happening.' I write in the morning, paint in the afternoon—dine and walk or see a friend. So-called big happenings are few. The three weeks of June 17–July 6 were my most productive ever in writing. I wrote *The Grave-Digger* then. It is the best thing I've done yet."

He read it to me—very fine. The earth spirit (strange new self) talks with a man and bids him turn grave-digger for the heaps of lying dead, who are thought alive because they are trembling on the Life Tempest. The spirit can tell the living from the dead, because the living follow the tempest, run and dance *with* it. "Divorce your wife and marry a djinia (earth spirit)." The spirit can't show him a djinia; if he could, he wouldn't say marry her. Next morning the man did divorce his wife, and to his children gave spades, bidding them be grave-diggers also. The oldest was playing ball—the youngest still chewing words.

"Nietzsche was probably the loneliest man of the nineteenth century and surely the greatest. He not only created, like Ibsen, but he also destroyed. The concept of Superman was not new with him, but the degree of realization of Superman was, although Ibsen wrote with Superman in mind. Christ was Superman."

Instead of saying "not at Home," he sees the visitor for ten minutes—"Don't send word by servant; that is sharp. To impertinent questions, hide facts or refuse to answer."

"Do you know my definition of Maeterlinck?—oatmeal and milk—but not meat. From fourteen to eighteen he was my idol. I mind now only his being taken for what he is not. He gives not his own thought or life but that of others! His life is not true to his writing. He says to the husband who is unhappy, 'Try to find the best in your wife and she will improve'—and himself divorced his wife to marry Mme. LeBlanc. He wrote *Mary Magdalene* on two weeks order; nothing in it. His last book is on autos. There is a discrepancy between his present life and work and the old days of the *Treasure of the Humble*, which is his masterpiece.—I hate writing that is untrue to a man's life; there's nothing in it."

It is dishonorable to permit people to speak to us about others what they would not say if they knew we knew the others.

Speaks of Island Man—Mustafa—as "my book." "It will be with me probably five years more—but it is complete now in structure in my mind."—"I shall probably get out two or three other books in the interim."

When we supped at Charlotte's new place, 529 East 77th, we sat out on a rock pile where they were levelling for the River Park. Kahlil would be sorry to live in that part of town —because he says you would live one day and the next would be just like it—nothing different. Greenwich Park and Washington Square have a richness of personality that makes them delightful and warm. "The older parts of the city," he said, "are full of exhalations from generations of human spirits. Something of them remains." He is always seeing—always looking.—Always feeling what surrounds him. All of consciousness is quickened by him. He is truth itself, and able to discern reality. I trust him absolutely—infinitely. And I have learned this is right. When I trust him not, all is confusion in me—and trusting clears all at once again. It shames me, too, for ever having lost my steadiness toward him—to trust seems almost impertinence—like trusting God: the very word *trusting* implying possibility of distrust. He is as real as the trees and stars.

······◄{ KG }►····

[New York]
Monday, September 16, 1912

Beloved Mary. I had two decayed teeth extracted on Saturday! Yesterday was a day of terrible pain! Today my face is badly swollen on the left side and it looks so funny!

Tomorrow a wisdom tooth must come out, and after that I will be quite right!

Love from your Kahlil

····◄{ MH }►····

[Boston]
September 22, 1912

What does the doctor do with you? And what changes have you made? And how have you got sunlight? Tell me what you have done and are doing for wholesomeness. There is nothing I love and desire that I do not find brimming over exquisitely or powerfully in you—except health. And I want that too. I want you perfect! I am so sure you have the basis for solid health—as well as the buoyancy and nervous endurance which are already yours.

95

God bless you, my Dearest—The same Life in you that is putting you among men's beloved Immortals, gives me a nearness with you. Nothing grows in me but this sweetness grows with it.—Do you feel Autumn chills? Love to wrap yourself round and round in—from your old

Me.

---

314 Marlborough Street, Boston
October 2, 1912

Off and on all day I have been looking at Turner—in Rogers' *Poems* and *Italy*, and in *Paradise Lost*. And then as I stood by the piano I looked up at your unfinished portrait of Fredericka Walling*—and seemed really to see it for the first time—with fresh eye, as an unknown face. It is very very beautiful, Kahlil—its light, its depth, its wet color, and the living personality in it. Finished or unfinished, it has you in it—and Freda too—and I love it a thousand times more than ever.—I am sending back the Turner books I bought. I'd rather put the money if I have it into some form of present life—and when I think how much more to me ten square inches of your painting is than all the prints and reproductions that could be offered—and that I have two of these treasures daily before my eyes, I feel richer than if I owned the whole Library. Nevertheless, I have learned something more about seeing, from these wee Turner prints—and my farewell to them is grateful.—But how incomparably more than reproductions I love the surface of paint, and its divine color!— star dust, music-molded in the twilight of earth; odorous! It

---

* One of Mary's sisters, who had married English Walling.

sings! The brush seems a feather dipped in pollen. And in yours, is always your spirit, Beloved.

If you will be strong, Kahlil—I see such addition to everything you produce—and to your consciousness. You must have that—to fulfill yourself. Your wings must have that open —to fly in—your feet that earth, to walk on.

I just wish that I could show you how sweet the thought of you is to me, and how I love to love *You. Welcome* to your Mary.

---------------- ---◈{ *KG* }◈--- ----------------

W. 10th Street, N.Y.
Wednesday, October 9, 1912

Just came from the dentist's chair, and I am somewhat dizzy. He worked for an hour and a half drilling and filling.

My general health is *fine* now. I feel as if a new force is running with my blood—I owe it to you, Mary, Mary, mother of my heart. What you said to me when you were here made me realize how helplessly one-sided I have been through all these years.

And am I feeling near to you? Have I ever felt far from you? Am I not always more than near? Am I not always hovering around you as a bird would hover around its nest?

Between us, Mary, there stands an unknown god whose feet are solid, and whose hands and eyes are always open, and whose mind is unchangeable. *Someday* you will hear me saying that over again in another world—a world nearer to the Sun than this.

Kahlil

New York
Friday, October 20, 1912

Your letter is marking a new era in my life. It is filling me with flames. I feel as though a war has just been declared between us and the world. But *we* will win in the end. We will conquer. I say that now with all the voices in my soul. I could not have said it a month ago: I am no longer a dreamer. The world of dreams is beautiful but there is a region beyond where Absolute dwells.

Kahlil

[New York]
Sunday, September 29, 1912

Pierre Loti* is here and I had a charming hour with him on Thursday. We talked about "his beloved East." He said he saw my *Broken Wings* and ended by saying, "You are becoming more brutal and less Oriental—and it is too bad, too bad!" I love my country too well to be like her other children. But he does not see that; he is too delicate, too sensitive. He has all the beautiful Oriental diseases in his artistic soul. And he will not be drawn. "Oh no, no! I, I sit before an artist? No, no, never, *jamais, abadun* (in Arabic), anything else but that; it will kill me."

Loti is sixty-two years old, but he is wonderfully powdered and rouged and pencilled—yes, rouged and pencilled—and he looks pathetically much younger.

I want to see him again. It makes me feel *good* to see such a dreamer of shadowy dreams, such an Orientalized occidental.

* (1850–1923). French novelist (*Pêcheur d'Islande, Madame Chrysanthème*, etc.) and naval officer. He had served in waters near Japan, West Africa, and Indochina.

I have extracted all the bad and decayed teeth, six decayed teeth, six, all together "6"! The pain was beyond words but the result is good. I feel so much better in every way. My stomach is in far better order than it has been for the last three or four months. More work is to be done before I think of bridge work and other things.

It is really surprising how good I feel now! I walk five miles a day in open places such as Central Park and Riverside Drive. I am eating nourishing food (beef and eggs and milk) and I sleep near the window. I work less but I accomplish just as much and everything goes well.

K

--◃{ *KG* }▹--

[New York]
Tuesday
October 22, 1912

The most wonderful thing, Mary, is that you and I are always walking together, hand in hand, in a strangely beautiful world, unknown to other people. We both stretch one hand to receive from Life—and Life is generous indeed.

Pierre Loti is gone back to the shadow of some temple in the East. He left New York disgusted with "noisy America and crude Americans." He can be happy only amongst the faint shadows of the past. I saw him again after the performance of his play *The Daughter of Heaven*, a remarkable series of Chinese pictures, but not great drama. He was nervous that evening and out of sorts—but he promised to pose for me when I go back to France. His last words to me were "Now, Gibran, let me tell you on behalf of Syria that you must *save your soul* by going back to the East. America is no place for you."

The War between Turkey and the Balkan States is a conflict of two different spirits, Civilization and Barbarism. Rich and happy people protest against the young Balkan States because they fear that they might "break the peace of the world." And why should they not break the hypocritical peace of the world? They have suffered enough under that one-sided peace. I pray to God that this war may bring about the dismemberment of the Turkish Empire, so that the poor crushed nations of the Near East may live again; so that mother Syria may open her sad eyes and gaze once more at the Sun. I am an Absolutist, Mary, and Absolutism has no country—but my heart burns for Syria. Fate has been cruel to her—much more than cruel. Her gods are dead, her children abandoned her to seek bread in faraway lands, her daughters are dumb and blind, and yet She is still alive—alive—and that is the most painful thing. She is alive in the midst of her miseries. I am writing something which may turn the whole Arabic world against me. But—I am prepared for it! I am getting used to being nailed on the cross.

My model is here. The light is good today—and my hands are hungry for work.

Here is a kiss for your blessed hand. And here is another for your bright eyes

from your
Kahlil

[New York]
Tuesday
November 5, 1912

Why, of course I will be here on Friday and Saturday! You don't think for a minute that I would leave New York when you are coming to it—do you? An hour with you in this little studio is better than a week in Mount Lebanon.

O I have a thousand things to tell you. But I'll wait until you come. I can say things better when you are nearer.

Au revoir, my beloved Mary. xxx and xxx and x.

Kahlil

[New York]
November 9, 1912

Got (in at 7 a.m. and went) to Kahlil's by 8:30. He has done little since September 9 because dentist and doctor have so engaged him—and for the three weeks when his teeth were being pulled and filled he was unfit for much. He has been writing rather than painting.

Kahlil is eating three meals daily and walking usually more than five miles—with none of the old weariness five miles used to sometimes cause him. Still in 51 West 10th—because can't find any good studio with a sunlight room or with bath for less than forty dollars. He says that if you find a room that suits, the rent is raised from thirty to forty dollars the moment you say you want it for a studio—and that any rooms built with a high light may be called studios and so let for more.

Artists seek vainly for a place to paint—while dilettantes are the only ones who can afford studios in New York.

I took him my blue-dragon Chinese kimono.

"Did you not tell me the last time I was here you had none?" I said. "Have you one now?"

"I had one—but very thin," he said—"and it was covering my dress suit from the dust."

I told him this was my best-loved—and that whichever of us first became well-off would get him a new one and give this back to me; I'd love it the more for his having worn it, and he'd like it the better now for my use of it. "O! but that's not fair!" he cried—"Whoever first can must get a beautiful one for *you*. I'll bring you a beautiful one when I go to the East." He loved the color—as I do.

Kahlil's face shows now so much strain and stress—shows privation and loneliness, and burden—and the most intense concentrated effort. I asked him if he had a cold—but it was only his morning voice; he says his higher voice is nervous. He was nervous then a good deal of yesterday—for his voice was seldom at its low pitch. He cleared his throat so often, too—a symptom I don't like, though he says his doctor says susceptibility to cold temperature is really his vulnerableness —and that if he *keeps warm* he ought not to suffer from throat or grippe. We talked, and I watched myriad lines go and come in his face—with tension and relaxation—the eyes narrow and then open, the nose sharpen and expand—gradually all smoothed and filled out more. Occasional free companionship—every now and then to talk about himself—response, and to be understood—to be loved and let love—he needs this relief in his loneliness. "What a release!" he said yesterday—and has said before.

We had supper at Child's. Kahlil goes there because the food is clean and wholesome—though "they are not generous." Their meats are tiny!—I can see Kahlil's wee sausages now, on their mashed-potato nest—and his three small biscuits!

"To me the picture is all one—from edge to edge it says *one thing*. The whole form of the picture and all the forms in it must say the same thing: Many painters do not think in form—they think in color. A picture may be in harmony in color, yet a discord in form. Its form may say two things. That is why we have so many painters and so few artists."

"Did you ever look upon the present through the eyes of the future?" said Kahlil at night. "I have become familiar with the human mind of today—in many parts of the world—its attitude toward things, its reactions, its tendencies, its modes of working and I know how it will look upon things a hundred years from now. I know the future—not in detail—but in the great outline—and I accept it. Nothing will stop my work. I may lose health—but my work will go on."

I have come to a sense of a larger I that has controlled the relation between him and me—and protected it often from this smaller me. My Buddha, I call that larger, longer-living self; and now I pray it to use my smaller self, and to teach my smaller self to lend itself to the Larger's purpose.—Not to obstruct or misexpress the Larger. There is, in Kahlil, a being longing simply to be allowed to love, to lavish itself, to speak its innermost, to be closer than inner souls can conceive —an unspeakable sensitiveness.

He seems to be adhering with great exactness to the bodies of his models, whatever they may be. In his technique I am sure I see also the technique of his poetry. What each stroke conveys is the result of its relation to all the rest of the picture —and it conveys something other than itself and exceeding itself. So does the whole picture. In his poems there must be the same interplay and interdependence of meaning—each word, phrase, line deriving from the whole—and expressing something other than itself and beyond and the whole expressing something other than itself and beyond. In neither good poetry nor good art does he feel that anything is there by happy accident: it is all thought out, realized, intentional, analyzed.

"Such a funny little face," he said of his own face when I was looking at him. He is far from as strong as I long to see him. He needs the tonic now of success—of freedom. Till he sells, the latter must gall; his strength leak while his heart aches.

In *Golden Treasury* work with my college preparation class this month I have realized how pre-eminently the great poet is the great lover—and now I see it in Shakespeare and Aeschylus and Homer and Job. No poet curses Sleep in sleeplessness—but woos her; Falstaff is Shakespeare's poor slight child—Aeschylus feels Clytemnestra's extenuation. Homer spends an epic on Odysseus—and Job champions God. This explains the gentleness of Kahlil—and his loneliness. Explains too the instinct I've had ever since we first met, to assure him of my personal feeling for him—my desire, in every degree of love I've borne him, to make him certain of it. Gradually I've understood that the value of such certainty is chiefly the freedom it gives him to love—since to Love only is Love welcome.

It explains too so much of the small direct emphasis on sex of great poets: it irradiates their work, as it does real life—but is not predominantly talked about. They love *all* the life of man; his asexual levels have no dullness for them; therefore they take sex-love as it comes—and every other miracle thread of the web as it comes. Hence they are so clean! Their souls are exercised like athletes' bodies.

I have been aware of a difference from the custom of lovers—in the infrequency of letters between Kahlil and me and the brevity of his at least, and their rather few love-expressions. I've always known that rareness of love-words with him arose from more love, not less—but I've never known why this was. Now I know it is because all his living is a loving, is Loving.—I know too why I so often wish I could just sit in the room with him and work while he worked—why I *miss* our never doing the daily round while we are together—and sometimes desire that more than special talk with him—if it were not that we meet so little that there is always more special talk that *must be*, than we can possibly finish.

"Engaged girls are always thin." Is it love of Man that saves poets from fat, and burns away excess flesh from my Kahlil?! I must be misanthropic—who have to cut down my diet so vigorously to keep down my measurements!

Is Love the explanation of the Whole, I wonder—is Love

the Core of Truth? For some years I have called Truth the core of Love—no doubt it is—but Love the core, the very being, of Truth too. But Love and Tenderness are not synonymous! Love is Oneness. As Kahlil once said, "I wrote to-day, 'Love says, "You are myself." ' " Hence it is not Tenderness or Helpfulness, or any of those services it renders or withholds in detail: it is sharing, understanding, setting free, answering; it is Being.

—⁓{ *MH* }⁓—

MISS HASKELL AND MISS DEAN'S SCHOOL
314 MARLBOROUGH STREET, BOSTON

November 10, 1912

I've been writing our diary—writing about you—thinking about you—until it has carried me through the fatigue of the earlier evening and I wish I might say it all over to you too. I love to talk to you, with you, about yourself and as I have sat here in this cloudless, soundless union with you and looked up at *The Three Women*, and at *Fredericka*, and at *Mary*, so much has taken shape. And your poetry technique which flashed on me in the studio while I stopped to see the strokes that made the *Breather*—I feel quite sure I know its living principle now—for there it is *pictured* for me, beyond mistake.

Mary

—⁓{ *KG* }⁓—

[New York]
Tuesday, November 19, 1912

Your last visit, beloved Mary, seems so much like a dream. It was too short a glimpse, and I feel now as though we had met in spirit. I had many things to tell you, but I never did. We did not have time to talk and to be silent. I love to be silent with you, Mary.

I have worked quietly last week, and before this week is over I will have two finished pictures. The man crucified, which you saw, and another smaller canvas which I call *The Silent House*. An English girl posed for it. She is a student of English poetry and devoted to Browning and Swinburne! One can never tell what those models are made of. They belong to the most mysterious class of people, perhaps the most unhappy class.

My life is quiet. There is little beside working and walking. I have no desire to see people, and I feel as though I am waiting for something new and strange which will burn the unburnt side of my soul.

I want to write more but I cannot. I am a little weary and the silence in my soul is black. I wish I could rest my head on your shoulder.

Kahlil

[Boston]
Saturday, November 23, 1912
12:30 a.m.

Such the school-marm life—to lift the hand to throw a kiss —and have it so job-beset that it is two weeks reaching her lips! I have been intensely conscious of your cloudy state, like those monotone skies, gray, uneventful. Inwardly something in me has been saying to you, "Never mind, Kahlil Gibran, if you don't produce right along,"—except that you shall continue to walk by your own light. I don't even want you to be a poet or a painter: I want you to be whatever you are led or impelled to become.

—"If you find yourself disappointing—drop self-expectations. *What* you are turning into you cannot expect to know, but you can trust it, and believe that if it is other than you planned, it will also be better than you planned—however different."

Nothing you become will disappoint me; I have no preconception that I'd like to see you be or do. I have no desire to foresee you, only to discover you. You can't disappoint me. In Lexington tonight the moon seemed to me north, so I corrected my inner compass, for I knew the moon moved true and my seeming north must be south because she was in it. *Et tu, Brute.*

You do speak and you are silent, to me, whether you are aware of it or not—and you said a great great deal to me in our few hours together in New York, irrespective of words.

You owe me a big letter. Before I came to New York you said you had much to say, but would wait to see me—and after I go you say you had much to say, but did not say it. Therefore I have had but my own observations to depend on, and you are "bearing none of the expenses of the entertainment." To a wise mind the unspoken is recognized as chiefly unknown, surmised perhaps, but not sworn to. I hear much without ears—but how much more hear not!

And the moral of that is—no moral at all! I like you letterless, if letterless you are, and am contented to hear the more or less, as You or you convey it to me. Last June meant rockbottom for me, I think, in oneness with whatever is between us. And sometimes when I talk I'm "just talking," because you are my freedom and my dear all-understanding One, and I love you and am happy with you.

Mary

[JOURNAL]

[Boston]
December 1, 1912

Kahlil has a cold! I reproached him frankly about his room at 51 West 10th and begged him to set eighty dollars, not thirty, as limit for his room, because it is less costly in the end than doctors and need of doctors. And debated the old question of adjustment of dependence. Why not feel enriched by one another as by God, when bread and drink are received, and isn't the guest and host relation *sweet*, viewed eternally, rather than bitter? If work and independence are incompatible, and he chooses work, *give up* independence. He is *not* well. He is a candidate for consumption right now. His *cold* fled before me, as it so often has before. But he looks *thin*.

"But I shall see you soon again," he said at parting. Planning to come to Boston for Christmas, in confidence that I'd be there.

———— ⋯❦ *KG* ❧⋯ ————

[New York]
Thursday, December 12, 1912

Never have I met so many people as during the last ten days. And I have never received so many invitations for so many different things. It seems as though the nice people of New York are beginning to know of my being somebody! And it is all so strange and so funny, Mary. But why is it that the more we come in contact with people the more remote we feel? Even the kindness shown to us makes us feel different, and alone and sad.

Miss Alice Bradley is a wonderful little woman. She wrote *The Governor's Lady*, which is running now with such a great success at the Belasco Theatre. I made a drawing of her and it is successful. Last night I dined with her, and she is coming on Sunday to see my pictures.

Mr. Arthur Farwell and his mother came last Sunday and spent this afternoon with me. Mrs. Farwell is one of the most appreciative women I have met for a long time.

Mr. and Mrs. Winch are coming on Saturday with friends.

Mrs. Martin said she is trying to get Davies* to come and see my work.

I have two new pictures that are nearer to my heart than anything I have done.

The picture of the English girl is going to be a success. I shall call it *The Little Tame Fawn.*

May the gods be with you, my beloved Mary. And here is a kiss from your

Kahlil

--- ⋆{ *MH* }⋆ ---

Miss Haskell's School
314 Marlborough Street, Boston
December 14, 1912   Night

The room is chilly. I wish you were here, nice warm thing! In default of you I take out your sketches and letter with its good news.

I rejoice in each one who comes to you, because any work of art is like something made for a mirror, and that mirror is Fellow-Man. Your tribe is at once the loneliest and the most dependent on people.

Allah be praised that love, heaven, earth, interests, understanding, desires, draw me but nearer to you. Therefore, dear Kahlil, if this most desirable accession to your acquaintance

---

* Probably Arthur Bowen Davies (1862–1928), American painter, whose New York studio was well known.

leaves you free to come here at all in the holidays, which with us begin on Saturday the 21st and last through Sunday, January 5th, will you not bring with you one or two canvases for me to live with during your visit? Express your suit case and bring these by hand. That will be both safe and light-weight.

Let me not be more of a stranger than is necessary, but bring them if you come. And if your stay is to be very short, tell me ahead about your days that I may plan to keep for you those you plan to keep for me. Lovingly

Mary

--------------------------- ⁕{ KG }⁕ ---------------------------

[New York]
Thursday, December 19, 1912

My plan, beloved Mary, is to be in Boston late on Monday. But a little *business* which I am trying to see through may keep me here until Tuesday.

I had twelve visitors on Sunday! Just think of twelve people in this small room. I felt all the time the keen desire of pushing the walls away.

I do not think I will stay more than a week in Boston. Just now there are many elements working for me, and I do not want to lose certain chances which may benefit my work. There are certain people who like to do certain things at certain times. When that time passes they lose the desire of doing anything.

I believe, Mary, that the future will not be unkind to my work. I will not be able to interest those who worship old gods, follow old thoughts, and live with old desires. But, thanks to the Ever-new gods, there are people who could be free from all the chains of Yesterday. Those who are capable of living in this *Now* are rather few, but they are the most powerful.

I will surely bring two pictures with me. I will bring the two largest paintings in this studio! Sometimes the largest is the best!

Kahlil

[J O U R N A L]

314 Marlboro Street, Boston
December 25, 1912

Kahlil came last night, and I looked at him as I have looked much at people lately—as with a fresh eye. He is electrifying —mobile like flame.

[J O U R N A L]

[Boston]
December 25, 1912

"I wish there could be a constant interflow of pictures between 51 West 10th and 314," said Kahlil. "Why didn't I know you at fourteen? I ought to have been painting in oil all these years. I stayed naive so long, so long after I was a man in writing." I said I had always been told he ought to study but that he refused lest his individuality, his "genius," be destroyed. Yes, he said, so it was; but only because that idea had been drilled into him. Mr. Day and the other friends who seemed wonderful people then to him, told him not to study, that he would be spoiled. The whole stress of his environment was not for training but for self-admiration.

The exhibit where I first saw his work, in Mr. Day's studio,

III

"was the worst thing that ever happened to me," he said. "Some really big people actually bought things: Mrs. Buxton, Mr. Charles Peabody, Mrs. Montgomery Sears. And of course I thought I was big, too, and all right. Had I been in New York, I should have heard the truth. People are cruder there and less careful not to hurt you."

Asked me to feel wholly at ease about his health, apropos to one talk in New York about his taking a costlier studio for sun. "I'm not careless about my health." But he confessed he had not been careful until this year. "I've told you before, my life was not right as a boy. Had I been brought up according to my father's ideas it would have been better for me. Then came the change to this country, and at fourteen the return to Syria to college, where I did eight years in four, worked terribly, and had only riding in vacation for activity. But I am well, I have never been really ill or had any disease.......I am attending to one big thing in life: I can't stop for details alien to it. I can't plan the hours of sleep and exercise and food every day. One hears people say they rise and eat and tea and go to bed at the same hour every day, and priding themselves on it as regularity. It seems dead to me. Such a man may be said to live One Day. 'It is four o'clock; stop work and walk an hour,' he says. I can't do that. I have to let details happen as they happen." Yet he [Gibran] made a *general* plan for hygiene, eating and walking practically regularly, and is better than ever before.

"If I can open a new corner in a man's own heart to him I have not lived in vain. Life itself is the thing, not joy or pain or happiness or unhappiness. To hate is as good as to love—an enemy may be as good as a friend. Live for yourself —live *your* life. Then you are most truly the friend of man. —I am different every day—and when I am eighty, I shall still be experimenting and changing. Work that I have done no longer concerns me—it is past. I have too much on hand in life itself."

314 Marlboro Street
December 29, 1912

Kahlil was here from 3 to 10.

He was impressed for the moment at the rumors I had heard about him and women in Paris and New York. "Do you realize the actual amount of work I've done in the last ten years? About fifteen volumes the size of *Broken Wings*, if the things were collected into volumes as someday they will be —and not of watered stuff, but of the condensation of poetry. Besides the painting. Anybody knowing that, would know that it would leave me no time for romance. I have been too busy." He is physically shy, too. Kahlil is not sexual-minded, but absorbed in bigger things. As he says, sex-energy is transformed with him into art-production. It is not "virtue" that keeps him "chaste," but temperament. He has no code about sex except honesty, reality. "Should you say," asked I, "that if a man or woman loved seven and lived sexually with seven it was all right?" "If the seven were all willing, yes," said he.

Of Love, Understanding is necessary, says Kahlil. To love, I must understand—even understand with the body, too. When for instance I see a beautiful flower, my body understands its beauty, is drawn to it.

His love is as restful as Nature itself. He has no standard for you to conform to, no choice about you, but is simply *with* your reality, just as Nature is. You are real, so is he: the two realities love each other—voilà!

❧ 1913 ·❧

---❧ KG ❧---

New York
Friday, February 14, 1913

There is a chance of my getting a fine, large studio here in this building. It is three times as large as mine and it has north light, south light (sunshine) and sky light, very cheerful and good for work.

The rent is $45.00!

Now I have been debating with myself for the last few days and I do not know what to do!

I shall have to spend some money to make the place look nice and clean—about $50.00.

May I take it if they would let me have it?

Just write a little note on one of your cards. I know you are busy.

Love from Kahlil

Miss Haskell's School
314 Marlborough Street
Boston
February 15, 1913

The only thing that could have given me greater pleasure than your note of yesterday would be the news that you *had* that forty-five dollar studio! Go straight downstairs, upstairs, or wherever, and take it, Beloved, before it escapes!

And something else. I was thinking how, if I were rich, I'd buy all your pictures so that they should be separated only as you might please, and it suddenly occurred to me that you and I can do a good deal even as it is toward retaining control of your output. Will you settle now for all that you have borrowed from me—with pictures? Whatever of yours is legally mine is, you know, spiritually yours, and my will is yours concerning it. The only aspect of possession that I can ever grasp anyhow is *control, authority*. My owning your picture means your controlling it—which is desirable. The actual price of your work is something that must someday begin to be determined. That is hard, but let me ask you to do it, because certainly I can't do it myself. Choose from all you have done, what at first sales price (you see I suggest taking that advantage, which is in itself right and fair and would be any other first buyer's—and it will enable us to hold unbroken a greater number. If you were unprolific that might disadvantage you, but it does not matter to you whether a customer takes six or eight.)—take what first sales price will repay your full debt. Then add for a thousand dollars more—mortgaged to the future. Choose what you want as nucleus for *the* collection of your work. We shall talk about it when we meet again, but I think that will seem to you as to me assurance of your will's being carried out always, as concerns at least an important part of your work. For my own part, it will be a better financial thing than money, because your pictures will multiply their first price times over as years go on. And for the delight it would be to know that the ones I prize most for themselves and for their expression of you would not be shut from my sight in Jones' house in St. Louis and Morgan's in New York, I've no words. Nor for the satisfaction of knowing that their disposition now and for hereafter would be your own. Then, indeed, I shall feel something accomplished after my heart's desire. Of course, the pictures would remain with you perforce—also an advantage.

Will you do this, K.G.? Or is it really not the advantage for your pictures that it seems to me? I know I may be all wrong, though I can't see the flaw in this. Financially I know it is sound, for if I can afford to wait for increase it is the biggest investment I can make. And I can afford to. I *think* this school can succeed. I see things practicable ahead which will help it, and I believe this is its poorest year. I shall need no other money, and say carefreely, "grind the face of the poor" artist to lay up riches for my old age.

If you do not see greater advantage to your work in not selling to me, you know advantage is what I want, and you will act for it. But if you do sell to me, and if you do want to sell to others then, just let them know you have made sales of so and so many in Boston, and things may move the faster. But if you do it and let it be known, not my name to anybody. Nor should I tell of it. It would be a disadvantage to our object and turn alien eyes upon my inmost joy.

To me this looks so lovely I could cry—you freed—at least some of your work rescued from chances—and myself endowed without harm to you or it with the preeminent riches of this planet. Then never more lending to you, but only buying from you if I can, your own selection. All this is real, too—solid—not formality only. Maybe you thought of it years ago, but considered I might not choose pictures rather than money, and so did not offer them.

Love—love—love—Mary

Friday, New York
February 18, 1913

I have already chosen ten pictures (some of them you have not seen yet) as a part of a body of work which should be kept together, if possible. These paintings are legally yours and you control them with absolute authority.

There is nothing more difficult than putting a price on a picture: but if these ten pictures represent ten dollars today they should represent fifty within ten years.

One of my dearest dreams is this—somewhere, a body of work, say fifty or seventy-five pictures will be hung together in a large city, where the people would see and perhaps love them.

And I want also the series of drawings to be kept together. Someone said to me not long ago that the New York Public Library should buy the series when completed. He said that in twenty-five years most of these big men will be dead and the value of the drawings will be great—not only as works of art but also as documents.

My getting into a larger studio is a fine thing. Putting aside the physical comfort, I know it will mean a very great deal to the work. Humanity is afraid of the work of a starving artist who lives in a "dark little hole." *Respectable* people can really be themselves only in respectable places! To be a victim of the respectability of people is a fine thing from the *artistic* point of view, but somehow, Mary, it is not in me to be a victim of anything or anybody; and I am *not* artistic.

I shall write soon of other things and shall also send some little drawings. Whenever you and I are alone in this little studio I draw and draw. And I always feel that you are looking on and smiling.

Two kisses for your hands—and love

from Kahlil

117

51 West 10th Street, N.Y.
Monday, March 16, 1913

I have been as busy, beloved Mary, as a little bee, and the outcome is not honeyless.

Every year, about this time, my soul goes through a volcanic eruption. It is a sort of civil war between *me* and *me*. The old me is always conquered, or rather put through a process of elimination. I find my better self expelling and discharging old thoughts and old ideas and at the same time forming new ones.

Why should not art in general go through the same fire which I go through? If we are all marching towards the Absolute, which is a simplified vision of Life, art should not stay where it is now.

These ten pictures will form a part of the Haskell collection:

> *Let Us Rise Together*
> *The Seed*
> *The Beholder*
> The Paris *Study of a Nude*
> *Rose Sleeves*
> The two pictures which I brought with me to Boston
> *Medusa*
> *The Heart of the Desert*
> *The First-born*

The last three are new and I feel sure that you'll like them.

I have seen you many times in my dreams during the last two weeks. We are always talking about wonderful things and you are always so gay. The night before last you laughed as only a sea could laugh, and I liked it.

Two kisses for your eyes and two for your hands

from your Kahlil

[New York]
Sunday, April 6, 1913

Spent the day with Kahlil in New York. The "arrange-ment" is that whatever money has been used by Kahlil in his work, he is to give pictures for, and thus start a collection of what he thinks it well to keep together. He put in ten pic-tures at once: *Angel, Rose Sleeves, The Beholder, The Saint, Let Us Rise Together, The Silentest Hour, Morning, The First-Born, Medusa, The Heart of the Desert.* I proposed now to invest for this collection the Securities I have with Moors and Cabot. Kahlil will add from time to time the pic-tures he wants not to have separated, and this money will make it unnecessary for him to sell any picture he would rather not sell, for two or three years more, till he shall be established. Prices are being asked about now, and when he has said of one of the Ten, "It is no longer mine," the ques-tioner, asking further about others, has returned to the sold one and said, "But I want *that* one!" I believe he will soon sell enough to make needless any fund for protecting the col-lection.

"Here is one I wouldn't part with for *any* money," he said as he set it against the chair for me to see. "This has come from the very depths of my being. For two or three days after the conception came to me I could think of nothing else—and I was actually nervous about it—I was so afraid I shouldn't be able to express it, to get it out of myself and into sight."

He asked whether I'd like to exchange any of the Ten for others. I said I thought *The Silentest Hour* and *Morning* were not in the same class with the others. For answer he brought out *The Silentest Hour*, and it was big, majestic, finer far than seen in my house.

He showed me a pencil portrait of Jung.* Jung he saw several times and was invited to visit him in Zurich for two weeks whenever he goes abroad. "And of course I'll go to Zurich." Bergson† will pose for him any time they are both in Paris, but here he was too worn out. Edison he waits for.

The friends or potential friends Kahlil has made are legion.. He has had to form the habit of refusing. "There is a set of women who do this: they plan a dinner, for the twenty-seventh of May, say. Weeks ahead they think of nothing else. Twenty guests.—If they meet anyone a little different, a new flavor of their social dish, he is invited. He goes. If you talk about anything real, to an issue, you are spoiling the dinner party, unless you are so remarkable a mind that you can dominate a table of twenty.

"And perhaps you do succeed in holding the twenty: it means twenty more dinners. For all of the twenty want you at their tables. It is an endless chain.....I confess, I tried it for a month, then I stopped.....Most of those people are very kind. They have beautiful houses. You go—you can't entertain them in return. What can you do? Simply pay with yourself. I have only my life to give, and I need that for my work. It may sound ugly, but I can't help thinking it: that all that those people give takes nothing away from them, but I have only what must be taken away from myself, my life."

But there is a set he loves to see once a week or oftener, dropping in to tea on their days. Winches, Griffins, Mortons, Sterners, Miss MacChesny.....

"The people are intellectual, with a sense of humor. They are real, warm and genuinely interested. When I go in with vague conceptions I often come out with them cleared and definite. I *like* this—the friction is refreshing and stimulating."

* Carl Jung (1875–1961), the Swiss psychiatrist and founder of analytical psychology.

† Henri Bergson (1859–1941), the French philosopher and Nobel Prize winner, was Professor at the Collège de France from 1900.

When he speaks thus, the pleasure he tells of glows about him
with almost sensible warmth and light."

"Everything is unique, if we have the ego to perceive its
uniqueness."

Lunch on the tray—Syrian cheese, olives, graham bread—
peanut butter—eggs—and wine in the little bottle Mother
filled with honey for me in 1898. But first Kahlil read a little
Arabic of his to me, lyrics, without any translation.

Kahlil has power to refresh himself by talking. The morning had tired him a little, so I got him to lie down by me for
a siesta after lunch, and then without rising started him talking—and presently he was up for a walk on Fifth Avenue.
We branched off to the Pennsylvania Railroad Station and
the new Post Office behind it. Kahlil questions whether in
Europe such fine buildings have been put up recently. Their
size and perfection fills him with delight. So does the rebuild-
ing of the church near the Park which we entered and saw
the original structure of under the new, which was being
built around it so that services need not be stopped.

Kahlil's superbness, his simplicity of underlying structure,
and his completeness of endowment and more-than-me-ness
are so vivid to me that I find all storms gone from my heart
concerning him. Joy floods me at the thought, sight, touch of
him. Dining at Gonfarone's* I told him how near I have felt
God this year. Tenderness kindled his eyes. "I too have felt
that this year," he said, "more than ever. It is so real, sweet
and wonderful, especially in the one or two hours just before sleeping. Do you know, Mary, I talk to you about everything in me except just that. And it isn't because I don't want
to, but because I just can't talk about God." I said I had become so much more aware of expression other than by speech
or any sense-means. "Do you know," he said, "I want to talk

* At the southeast corner of MacDougal and 8th streets, Greenwich
Village.

to you about everything, but not write. I am talking to you all the time within myself, but when I come to write it it is so hard to have to translate it from the Arabic. I do write a great many letters to you that I never send. (Protest from me.) No, they aren't me, they don't represent what I want to say. But I never write or paint without you, and when I think, 'She won't like this,' I destroy it and do it over again." I confessed I know now I am near to him, but it had long been hard for me to know it, and I had had to use "the will to Believe" because I had received so much true love from other people, and he was so much less expressive tangibly than the others, that I had had to learn to understand his non-sense expression. But how glad I am he let me learn, gave me time, did not try to express for my sake! He told me, too, how often voices say to him from earth and air and little plants: and deep within him, "Just give yourself time! Give yourself time," so reassuringly, quietly, suddenly. And while he talked of these things, tenderness deepened like the night sky in his face. When we got back to the studio at nine o'clock and I said, "Have we two blessed hours here?" I long to remember always the sound of his "Yes." (It is twenty-four hours ago that I heard it, nine o'clock on Monday.) I tickled him, and he was ready to scream. I stopped.....Walking to 14th Street for a subway to Grand Central, we heard a caterwaul. "She tickled him!" said I to Kahlil. "No wonder he made such a noise then," said he.

Jung's woman secretary wants some of Kahlil's work. She finds his prices high, so Kahlil is thinking of not lowering prices but just giving her *The Valley of Delightful Dreams*. He questions whether she will be offended, but I say it is an *honor* to her that he has the privilege of giving to anyone and having his gift an honor, because an artist is universal, impersonally intimate with everyone who cares for him.

He goes into the big studio upstairs on May 1st—longs to go earlier. Yet how deeply this little room glows, what spaciousness it radiates, arranged by his hand and containing him!

[New York]
Sunday, April 20, 1913

Do you know what it is, beloved Mary, to have seven heads and two hands? Of course you do. Just now I have seven heads and only two hands, and these two hands are burning like fire. When my hands burn I become wordless.

So you see I am dumb. But I am singing your last letter with all the mouths of my heart. Yes, Mary, my heart has many mouths and they are all capable of kissing your hands and singing your letters.

These spring days make me restless. They fill me with a hunger for something unknown to me. I wish I could go to the fields and grow with the flowers.

Kahlil

[New York]
Wednesday, April 30, 1913

The "psychology" of selling pictures must be simplified. It could easily be simplified if all buyers of pictures were lovers of pictures. (Love is the simplifier of all things.) But most buyers are not lovers, and those who are made lovers, by the Spirit of God were not given the power of buying!

I received this morning a blank order for the payment of dividends from The American Telephone and Telegraph Company, Boston, which I have signed and returned to the Treasurer of said Company. Now for the first time in my life I find myself a stockholder, and it all seems so strange. Only God, who lives within us, could tell you how I feel about these things, and He *does* tell you.

I am getting ready to move into the new studio. Tomor-

row will be the beginning of a dusty-tearing-down-and-hang-
ing-up week. I know I shall be well and happy in the new
studio, but I shall always remember the silent spirit of this
little place. I shall always remember it with love.

Kahlil

[Boston]
April 30, 1913

Those last two hours on April 6th added another to the
lights by which I see. Kahlil takes me so near: without intercourse he yet gives me the joy of being desired, loved,
caressed. This night it was a new completeness of touch that
most stayed with me, and it took me long to know into how
much beyond itself that touch has led.

And it conveyed to me more than ever the sweep and rapture of his consciousness, his expansion into many heavens,
and his tenderness and presence through all flight and sky
wideness. Do other men put themselves to such self-control?
And tired though I saw he was at the station, I knew he would
set to creative work after we said goodbye.

Kahlil is so honest with me: regards no conventions, because neither of us accepts them, save as conveniences; does
not try to spare my spirit by lying "for my sake"; gives me
share in his life by taking means to it from me; doesn't pretend I'm self-sacrificing, but *knows* how vital his work is to
my life; does not pretend to love me otherwise than as he
really does, but gives me the freedom of himself.

The same spontaneous acquiescence I feel toward Kahlil
fills me now towards God—about all things, Kahlil included.
And so, I am sure, does he feel me included. Our union has

always rested, I believe, on our conscious love of that ultimate. This was our last meeting in the little studio; on May 1st he moves to the top floor studio, which is three times as large with south and north windows—five!

It will be beautiful and he can paint large canvases.

—◆{ *KG* }◆—

[New York]
Thursday, May 16, 1913

I have been everything since the first of May from carpenter to a *scrubman*, and now the place is clean and delightful, but not beautiful enough to satisfy the eye. It will be made beautiful and without my spending money on it. O Mary, Mary, I am no longer in a cage. I move about without touching the walls with my wings! I am physically a free man. It is a resurrection. I have air, sunshine, and space.

The International Exhibition of modern art is a revolt, a *declaration of independence*. The pictures, individually, are not great; in fact, few are beautiful. But the spirit of the exhibition as a whole is both beautiful and great. Cubism, Omissionism, Post-impressionism and Futurism will pass away. The world will forget them. But the spirit of the movement will never pass away, for it is as real as the human hunger for freedom. Turner, seventy years ago, was the only free soul among the artists. Today we have hundreds of free souls whose only desire is to be and not to follow. These free artists may not be as great as Turner, but they are as independent as he was. We can not measure freedom as we measure greatness. A man can be free without being great, but no man can be great without being free.

And of course the Bostonians are hostile. The children of *yesterday* can not hear the songs of Today nor those of Tomorrow. To them the Laws of the past are the Laws of the future. They live in the past; they eat, drink, and sleep with the past. They dream the dreams of the dead. I pity them.

-···❧{ *KG* }❧···-

The divine Sarah Bernhardt is here. I was given the great pleasure of seeing her off the stage last Tuesday. She was most gracious—gracious is the only word. She spoke with more than delight of her visits to Syria and Egypt. She also said that her mother spoke Arabic and that the music of that language lived and is still living in her soul. But when it came to posing for a drawing she smiled and said, "How can I do that now? I am so tired. I am giving two performances a day—even Sunday." After that she said, "I will try. Come and see me again next week." So there is some hope, Mary.

Love from Kahlil

-···❧{ *KG* }❧···-

At last the divine Sarah is caught! The drawing which I made of her yesterday, though it does not show her *real* age, is a great success. But if I am to go through the same process with other great men and women, I might as well give up art and become a diplomat! She wanted me to sit at a distance so that I may not see the *details* of her face. But I *did* see them. She made me take off some of the wrinkles. She even asked me to change the shape of her huge mouth! Sarah Bernhardt is hard to please, to understand, and to be with. She has a temper.

She must be treated as a mighty queen, and if you do not treat her as such you are done for! I think I understood her yesterday, and I behaved accordingly; and perhaps that is the reason she liked me a little, for when I wanted to leave her she gave me her left hand to kiss.

The question of Home Rule in Syria is filling the mind of every Syrian. We shall get it eventually. But if Turkey wishes to play the old trick with us there will remain one thing and only one thing to do. *And we will do it,* Mary.

Kahlil

--- ◆{ KG }◆ ---

[New York]
Tuesday, June 10, 1913

Well, beloved Mary, your Kahlil came very near to going to Paris!

A conference will soon take place there. More than thirty Syrians will discuss Home Rule in Syria. Diab and myself were asked to go as representatives. The idea is fine, but after talking things over with a committee of Syrians, I found that we do not agree on any point. They were to pay my expenses and I was to speak their minds—not mine! And since their minds and my mind are so different, there is no way of representing them without being insincere.

Diab thinks I am mad—others think so too; and because I am mad I must work alone. Praised be the mighty merciful gods who give me this lovely madness.

But tell me Mary, when will school be over? Could we not spend a few days together before you go West?

Kahlil

June 22, 1913   Sunday   In New York

Kahlil and I met on Fifth Avenue. He came down as appointed, and I saw him in his light brown suit before he saw me looking into a window. Firm and well-colored he looks, no more delicacy of physique. The sun and space of the new studio have done that. It is beautiful and his own handiwork. He painted the floor, washed the white woodwork and stained it with yellow the color of natural pine, covered the walls with burlap, hung his purplish curtains, his two yellow brocades, his gilt pieces. Light in amber shafts upon the walls. Space is multiplied. But it was not a picture day with us, for Syria is filling Kahlil.

There is a conference of Arabs and Syrians in Paris to work for Home Rule. Kahlil was asked to represent New York but could not because he disagrees with all the Syrians here. They would appeal to the Powers of Europe and by diplomacy seek Home Rule. Kahlil knows they will not get it by diplomacy, but their very asking for it diplomatically obliges them to accept Turkey's consent diplomatically given. And Turkey *will* consent; will promise; and will not keep the promise. Kahlil wants Revolution. Arab military strength is enough for revolution. It need not be planned. Revolution even failing will be met with Home Rule, succeeding, will free Syria and Arabia. Kahlil can't represent anybody; he must be alone. He ought to have gone to Paris, but bearing his own expenses.

"A mistake, I lose a big experience by it. But it is not a total loss." For he plans now a July conference in New York of some of the men from Paris and the leading Syrians in this country. The Damascene Eresi (or some such name) is the most important, for he can command Arab troops at bidding, and he has said he will come. General Garibaldi* is here. He

* Giuseppe Garibaldi (1879–1950), grandson of the popular Italian

and Kahlil are twins in mind. Garibaldi can't take part in the conference, but he will be great in carrying out the revolution. But Kahlil speaks to no one of this— He seems entirely alone among the Syrians who have influence. The Oriental poison of safety, of patience, paralyzes their eye. They cannot *see* themselves fighting, starting a revolution. His plan is simple and direct. Honest and good—yes. Kahlil would appeal not to the governments of Europe, but to the *people* of Europe. *They* would be with the Revolution. Kahlil has written a great deal in the matter. Has met with storms of abuse. This battle with his own people, his sense of their waste of time, his *not* going to Paris have made it a time of great anguish—sleepless, unspeakably solitary.

[JOURNAL]

[Boston]
June 26, 1913

The new studio is perfect, big windows on both sides, *high* ceiling. Kahlil will build a partition by the washstand for his tub and his cooking; and for winter he will look up a Sears Roebuck stove. Heating is hard. The air and light and space are hardening. Every other day he buys a ten-cent cup cake and eats half of it for breakfast. "It is fine to get up here in the morning, so pleasant that you feel like getting up. Sometimes when I sleep I have a big fight, and wake up tired with fighting. Then I sleep again, three or four hours, and wake in the morning feeling fine. Then you get up and make your cup of coffee, and it tastes good, and your cake tastes good too." He eats two good meals a day besides the morning cake. He

---

patriot and general, served as general of a brigade in the Greek army during the Balkan Wars (1913) and was with the Italian army in 1915.

used to eat less than I, now more, though not at all heavily. He burns it all up, adds no flesh. Smokes less, drinks perhaps less coffee, gets less tired in the evening. He has long walked in his sleep. In the old studio he once found himself 'way at the other end of the corridor, and not infrequently outside of the studio. Here is space enough, so that though he goes all over the room, he stays within it. Dreams much, as ever. Sometimes a flower opens from a dark speck like a pinhead to a white rose three feet wide. "It is like seeing heaven open, the sun open." This evening he dozed a moment and dreamt. "I was moving a sphinx, a big black sphinx, beautiful, shiny surface. It was heavy, but I was moving it just the same."

Kahlil refused to dine at Mrs. Sheridan's. "I don't like the people. And I don't want to see uninteresting people now. My mind is full."

"I can think just the same, with you. I can be silent with you as long as I want to. When I am with you I am working." And again when he said, "I think I should have gone crazy without you now."

"Where shall we go?" for dinner our last evening. "Gonfarone." "Oh!" said he, "I was hoping for that word." We get a wonderful fifty-three cents worth there: space, air, music, plenty of pretty good food, and better wine than is common, leisurely service so that we easily spend one and a half to two hours at table.

Kahlil always gets back to Michelangelo and Rodin for illustration. "They sought to express Life—Life itself—nothing less."

He is always seeking companionship. He still makes many mistakes, he says, in thinking that the interest women show is interest in his work or thought, as, of course, it sometimes is. "But they want to give generously all they have. They do not want to receive. To give their best, but not to receive your best." Sometimes with women it is just weariness with their good husbands and desire for distraction elsewhere. Then Kahlil says, "Excuse me, I'm busy."

Beloved K.G.,   June 28, 1913

Every year in the Sierra I pick laurel for you from the first bay-tree I see. Here are last year's and this year's together! I wish I could send you the berries too—they cluster so beautifully. This is the very laurel of all the centuries, and when you crush it, fragrance flows like wine.

The rough thick sticky leaves the natives call "balm." "When your mouth is full of dust," they say, "just chew this balm, and it will sweeten you."

The trees with these round-heart leaves are fringed every bough length with these seeds. And perhaps you have at home, as I have, these thick, sweet shrubs that are blood-brown and dear to children. We used to warm them in our little hands till they were delicious.

I send you laurel because it is always on your head, and balm because it is in your heart, and fruit because your hands are full.

Dear K.G., it is not my mind that when you have freed yourself from others you are to have to guard yourself from me: I have no thought to try to share your desert, your travels, your studio, your "daily life," your space or time. This is what I meant in 1911, and have meant ever since. "Solid griefs," and real longing after you, and any other pains that come are but like the trembling of light, whose big movement is nevertheless steady. I tremble, but my course does not. And I love my course. I choose it because it is beautiful to me. Pains are no more than the pains I have had in these mountains, when every step has been on raw flesh, but the walk has been a glory. So is my way with you, beloved Kahlil, a glory.

As for your freedom—with your remoteness, your loneliness—from which I do not except myself, but mean your
absolute aloofness, it is You, to me.—Why should I not love
it? A star is dearer than a glow worm.—And I have One Wish
for you. I want for you what you want for yourself. And I
tell you so lest this too you should not know—because I want
you to know it.

These things let me add, Kahlil, for however I seem, these
are my structure and do not change. I want to be near you,
but the only essential nearness is the nearness of understanding.
I want to be with you, in will and desire. And I can give you
many reasons, but I care for only one, that I love you. I can
always say these things to you, to God, and to myself—they
are between me and each of us. I can live by these. They can
always grow and need never end. And now you must hear
me without words, as you do Blessed Twin. Good days and
nights to you.

Love from Mary

--❦ *MH* ❦--

[JOURNAL]

August 29, 1913   Friday   New York
114 E. 10th Street

Here for five days with Kahlil. He has loved his summer—
first holiday for years. He looks older.

I went in, full of electricity from the summer. "Why," he
said, "How brown you are! And fat! I never saw you so
brown before! I like it!"

He has been writing a good deal. The Madman's sayings
are increasing, and when he gets seventy-five to one hundred
he is going to have them typewritten and sent to me for revi-
sion. He read me a soliloquy of a suicide in Arabic as well as

in English and *Leaves from a Grave-Digger's Journal*, how a priest journeying to sacrifice is called aside by the wounded devil, who implores and when priest refuses reminds him that the devil is the basis of the priest's sin, rebuking job and priest-prestige. It ends with a silhouette of the priest against the horizon, bearing the devil on his back to cure. "Do you know I am called the Grave-Digger in Syria now?"

Going to Child's for lunch, we saw the noon stream of workers. "This procession is of slavery," said Kahlil. "The rich are rich because they can control labor for little payment. Control conception and the working women will bear fewer children; employers will have to give more; employees won't be slaves. Now people are slaves to sex. It rules and the children come."

Another time Kahlil said he would gladly kill a vast proportion of the race to prevent their reproducing their kind. "You would *have* them killed," said I. "Would you *yourself* kill them?"

"Certainly."

"Have you ever killed anything?"

"Certainly. I've hunted, I've killed chickens. I've killed a sheep." Having seen him turn away from the sight of extracting things from eyes, I had fancied he had shunned blood-sides of life.

He is much loved because to each he is her release, and people feel his sensitiveness, his strength, his mind and surpassing understanding. Women naturally long for him. He rests and stimulates, and everything about him is better than anything about others. If more got a sight of his real self, more would suffer for impossible longing for him. Each wants to appropriate, to become the chief object of attention; she does not want less, or other, than this personal awareness and reciprocity—and that Kahlil has for no one. He is *seeing* and *creating the future—and destroying the dead things in the present.* He can't make loving his object—as they long to do.

Most of us live in but two or three rooms of the house of our being. Khalil lives in *all* of his. This intensity irradiates him, as companion for everyone, and they love him in their rooms.

His friends urge him to exhibit. An exhibit is like a trap, he says, baited with good food, to get people there. Then he can know them a little, and knowing them will give him by degrees a chance to tell them his truth. As he knows people he can do this. Sometimes when they get a deep taste, it is great suffering to them. Occasionally some will have the waste of their lives appear, the years spent worthlessly. "And then it is very terrible." People tell each other least where telling is most needed. People conceal from one another what should be told.

For exhibit, shall he hire a gallery, or have the dealer exhibit and charge a commission? The existence of the Collection is a drawback for a dealer because it contains so much of his best. But he is inclined to try the dealer first. If the dealer is willing to exhibit with so much sold, take the dealer; if not, hire his gallery. The cost of renting has to be considered, because the frame bill will be large anyhow—probably an average of ten dollars per picture.

I said we spent not more than fifty dollars apiece per year at utmost seeing each other—and surely we earned it, he said. "We don't spend enough. We ought to spend more."

He left me after dinner—9–10:30. When he got back, an electric storm was beginning, a shadowy likeness of the one we watched from Charlotte's window two years ago. "It seems such centuries ago," said Kahlil. We watched this now from Kahlil's window—playing and muttering quite high and far with rare bursts of terror in fire and explosion. "I am my most real self in this," said Kahlil. "Why don't men write and speak like thunder and lightning?"—"I should like to be on a mountain top in a great storm, naked. I should like to die in a great one."

"You are food to my mind. You speak of chicken, and I hear bird of Paradise. Days later I hear new worlds of flight and new worlds open. I am always hearing beyond what you say."

"When I was a little boy, five or six, or seven, I had a room all my own, filled with things I collected. It was a perfect junk shop, old frames, and bits of clear stone, rings, plants, pencils. I had hundreds of pencils and little ones that I wouldn't throw away. Later, it became colored pencils. I drew swiftly and covered dozens of sheets of paper. When there were no more sheets, I drew on the walls of the room. I was the busiest person in the town and everybody knew it. I had water wheels at the big tank, one wheel connected to another with ropes. And I wrote compositions. I remember one on a poor old man, cold and miserable. And I said over and over again how old and cold and miserable he was and then how another man came and helped him and did him good—a real good Samaritan story."

[JOURNAL]

[New York]
Saturday, August 30, 1913   1 p.m.–4 p.m.

Kahlil had waked with hard pain about 3:30 a.m. Later he got something from the druggist and was better, but still a bit depressed. I showed him the pieces I had got at Toby's in Chicago for cushion covers, soft rose, blue and green tapestry, and gold-moire with heavy neutral stuff for backs. He liked them as much as I had and consented that I should make them, which I noted as an advance, since he had never before allowed me to do any "work."

I spoke of my desire, in case of his death, to go to Mount

Lebanon with his body—go authorized by him. "Any friend could go, and it would be just a token of respect," said he. But I wanted to be other than just any friend, and though I don't know how I said it he understood and said, "You know what people would say." I said I did not care, and that anyhow, whichever of us died first, the terms of our wills would make people say the same thing. Kahlil was much moved to my surprise. "Why, Mary, why are you talking about it? I'm not going to die for a long time. Why do you care about these matters of the body after death? Why?" Then the tears filled his eyes. "I *do* care," I said. "I love the things after death. They seem to me just done with the person I love. I don't want to be shut off from them. I don't want to just stand around like anyone." My tears finished his upset. He is not willing to see me cry when he sees no valid reason. He talked about caring or not caring whether people talked of our intimate affairs and whether they knew or did not know, and about dying. I knew pretty soon that the time would come when I should see my going with his body as a detail, and should know it did not matter. I told him frankly how I used to wish people might know he loved me, because it was the greatest honor I had and I wanted credit for it, wanted the fame of his loving me. He wants it known that I had faith in him and made his start possible, that I backed him financially. And he has no desire to conceal our friendship. But he does not want it to be called a mistress-and-lover affair, as it might be. Somehow he got me into at least no more tears, but it had taken it out of him.

His friends' misconceptions of him rushed naturally upon him in this talk of what would be said. Here he is living without sexual intercourse and is considered to be full of affairs: hungry because he is passionate and is lightly regarded as freely at feast. He had even thought when I told him last year that I had been told he was being "kept" in Paris by some older woman, because he had no money, because a woman was likelier than a man to supply money, and because such things weren't done without pay,—he had even thought *I* had thought this—that I had thought I was buying his *friendship* (not love) with money. He can't talk freely. People want only his old self. He is the man, and the former man is dying. Four or five years more and the former man will be dead. Then Kahlil will leave this life for some hermit life. People bore his other self. He lives in two worlds, Syria and America, and is at home in neither. He is free only when alone. With more people he must wear seventy veils. With me even he must wear two; if he wears only one, he shocks me.

Leonardo was the most wonderful personality in the world, Kahlil thinks. His picture of S. Anna, Mary, Jesus and the Lamb is to him the most wonderful picture in the world, though not the most wonderful *painting*. Michelangelo was a great painter—he painted superman—superman physical and male—his God is human and bearded. Leonardo painted *mind*. He wanted to paint what men could not understand.

We were at table in Gonfarone's when he said this. I can see him and his half smile. "Nietzsche took the words out of my mind. He picked the fruit off the tree I was coming to. But he is three hundred years ahead—I'll make a tree and pick the fruit for six hundred years ahead!"

"If you had to make your living as a laborer" (we were still at table), "what would you be?"

"A mason or a carpenter. Because I'd always see something growing under my hand. It is constructive."

"If you had to be a professional man?"

"A scientist, probably a chemist. A doctor I could be right now, with about two years study. Geology would tempt me, perhaps next to chemistry. But I think on the whole I'd like to be a research chemist. I was an ardent botanist once. In my college days I loved Botany and I wrote a fifty-page manuscript on Mysterious Plants, those that are affected by sound, by touch, by color."

[New York]
Sunday, August 31, 1913

We had a sort of relaxed day. Rode to the Museum and saw the Arabic and Persian collection. Then we walked up on the Reservoir, new to us both, sat on the grass to wait for sunset.

At Gonfarone's we had white wine. Kahlil prefers it, and I did not know it. It was very delicious.

[New York]
Monday morning, September 1, 1913

Living artists are so few; Kahlil is the only great one I even know of, though I know of other great minds. Kahlil's rich friends, even, like his poor ones, are far from his inner being. As for money's making the bond possible between Kahlil and me, the bond made the money possible. I had reversed things, and unfairly to him, as if he would give friendship for money that he would not give without, as if money would have anything to do with friendship with him. In my depth I knew it had not, and that he protested against my implication. I would tell him so.

I did tell him, and received a revelation indeed. I have three times before, he declares, said that money made the bond between us, and Kahlil has understood me to mean that money had bought his friendship. Yet when I gave it I called it impersonal—from time to time again I had called it impersonal, had said as I said now, that I gave it impersonally. One thing contradicted the other, and I said both with equal earnestness. What was he to believe? He often questioned whether he had not made a mistake in going to Paris in the first place. Was his whole acceptance of money not a blunder? He has suffered inexpressibly under the uncertainty. What should he do? If he stopped taking the money, he disappointed my desire for his career for which it was designed; and repayment might take longer even than if he kept on and became a "profitable" artist. He was like one who has undertaken to go to the bottom of a hill and must finish before he can change. Again and again he would have "had it out" and said all must be ended; and then when he saw me next, I would be the other person in the other attitude and he would wait. When we made the collection arrangement last spring, all seemed settled and he was light at heart. But last night it became uncertain again, and now he does not know what to do. "Just tell me what really was your idea in giving me the money, and I shall know where I stand. Tell me simply and so that I shall not make a mistake. Was it a gift? Was it a loan? Was it meant to make a bond between us? Tell me. Whatever your intention was, whatever your attitude is, I will try to meet it. But I can't stand the uncertainty. It has been one of the hardest things of my life. You have said opposite things with equal earnestness, and I really do not know which you mean. Months at a time I have suffered terribly from it," and his face spoke with him.

Since 1908, I saw, I had embittered him. I had said I was buying him, I who said also that the money passed impersonally through my hands, and that I felt about it as if it were a bundle left in my fence corner addressed to Gibran, because money beyond my personal needs did not seem to me mine. I only wondered that Kahlil had so long preserved so much nearness to me. I told him I had given it in 1908 as a gift, yet knowing he would think of it as a loan. I considered it a gift because I thought he would be long unable to pay it back, and that when the time came he would allow me to cancel the debt, if it were heavy on him. Or if he came suddenly into wealth I would leave it to his pleasure. That I looked on it as a gift is proved by my not even keeping record of amounts. I did not consider it necessary in 1908 to work out this point with him. I still felt now that it were a justifiable gift, because I feel young people have a right to their training without being saddled with debt thereby. But since he is himself I prefer that he repay it because it is his nature to; and I prefer pictures in repayment, because I love them and do not care for the money. But when I suggested pictures, I felt presumptuous, and was surprised and delighted at his consent. Now, I'd rather have him pay as he preferred to, in pictures, or, in course of time, with money. Was that clear?

To keep the collection from hindering the spread of Kahlil's work, because sales will greatly help that, and we *want* it to spread, and spread now—and to keep the collection from loss that would lessen its absolute and its historic worth, we decided not to increase its number further, before Kahlil exhibits, but to shuffle pictures freely in and out of it. For instance, if *The Heart of the Desert* proves saleable, sell it, and replace it by something not so saleable, but to us of more worth. For his really, completely best, people "are afraid of," he says. "They don't want to live with them. They admire *The Summit*, and may even call it my best, but they don't want to hang it on their walls." So when he sees a picture popular, he knows that in it he is nearer to them, and less himself; and it puts him to the question, Is it as much of a picture as some others? *Passion* would be loved, but a woman would not dare put it in the drawing room, but would love to hang it in her bedroom.

Sitting as usual in the window after dinner, we heard the French family in the white house opposite. "I think they are all a little deaf," said Kahlil. "They go to bed, and then they keep on talking to each other for a long time. . . . Do you know the story of the deaf family?

"Once there was a family all deaf. The husband came in one day at noon and said, 'I hope we are not going to have that same stew that we had yesterday.' And the wife answered,

'I didn't pay too much for that bonnet. It's a lovely bonnet, and cheap at the price.' Just then the daughter said, 'Yes, I will marry him. I love him and I won't have anybody else.' And the mother-in-law said, 'But I've already made my will, and I don't want to change it.' Everyone spoke what was in his mind, and seemed to hear the others speaking to that, never mind what they were really saying."

Kahlil was speaking from a heart lighter than before, for our long talks about money had been accepted by him. "K.G.," I had said just after dinner, "if ever I trouble you again as I did about money, just cut me off. You've given me chances enough. If I'm so dense and careless, and can so hurt you, it is not worthwhile to stick to me. Why should you be troubled? I don't deserve it. And I shan't complain if you tell me. I know justice when I see it, and I know mercy too, when it is shown me." He just looked at me and smiled and patted my arm. I believe he has no hanging to a past grief or injury, but that when I tell him I see my mistake, and will do better, he simply accepts, and that is the end of the past.

That night too I said something else evil. I said I wished I were a married woman or an actress, a free lance in the sex world, accustomed to sex intercourse and to preventing consequences. Next morning I knew that was dishonest. I don't wish I were either, and I had implied that Kahlil made much of our not having sex intercourse or took the fact other than simply. He never has done either. It is his will that we have no intercourse, and he has never been other than simple and direct about that will, nor made much of it.

I wearied of myself in relation to Kahlil, of my club-footedness and the confusion and pain I created so needlessly, always complicating things, always rubbing at the bloom on something so beautiful, always pulling at its roots.—*What* was the wrong in me? I looked directly at it, at Kahlil and me, and my answer came.

It was Kahlil's face (the answer), a look on it that I know well and love. And the look told me, and I knew it had always been telling me and I had never listened. Now, what it said ran through me. He spoke so simply, Kahlil through his look. What he said was only: "I have met you as a little child. I have become as a little child to meet you." And I knew he had said it to me a thousand times, and I had not heard. I knew I had not known what "as a little child" meant. Now I seemed to know. And it seemed the key. There seemed nothing simpler to find, nothing truer.

Kahlil is self-protective only in sheer self-defense. Where he loves he remains buoyantly generous. With me, he would let me touch the very quivering strings, if I would, if I would not thrust at them or ignore them. He has no holding back, no keeping to himself save as he is *made* to have. He is like the Sun who will shine through any chink allowed.

[JOURNAL]

[New York]
September 2, 1913

Fresh from my vision I went to Davies' studio. He had said in a note he would like to make a sketch from me, and now suddenly he asked to do it with me as a regular model. I was surprised, but it never occurred to me to suggest waiting till we were better acquainted. It seemed wholly impersonal. I said Yes. He sketched—it still seemed wholly impersonal. We talked, it was over, we arranged that I should bring Kahlil at three next afternoon, and I went. It still seemed wholly impersonal.

I was late for lunch, but we went first to the Bank. I told him that I had been dishonest in saying I wished I were a married woman or an actress, that I saw at last that he had always been simple in his sex attitude and had made little of it, that he had always told me to be, and I thought I was, but I

had never been. And that henceforward I would be. That if
the sex element went out of our life I'd take it simply and not
make much of it; if it increased, I'd take it simply and not
make much of it; if it remained as it is, I'd take it simply and
not make much of it. He was silent, as so often, but I think
he approved and believed.

We were waiting for the teller. I then told him about Davies.
The simplicity of my deed vanished. I felt him astounded. It
was my ignorance of Davies that made it so impossible for
him to see how I could have posed, the very thing that had
made it possible. What Davies might be thinking, or saying,
filled him with anxiety. He told me frankly that Davies was
thinking me either very big, or a fool, or a woman seeking sex
experience.

"You are too impersonal, Mary. And in some ways you are
very ignorant about the world. In some ways I know it better
than you. That is natural. You have seen very little of it. It
is good to see it and know, but you have not had the chance.
After all, you live very much out of the world. Sometimes I
have thought of that, and have almost wanted to advise you.
We must know the world, and meet it with its own weapons.
We must not be victims or martyrs to it, but we must master
it." All through lunch he thought, behind his talking, and after
lunch we started out to see the stuff he had found that might
do for curtains in the studio. On the way he said, "We don't
want to make too much of what has happened, but we do
want to make sure that it shall do you no harm and that Davies
shall not misunderstand you. I think a letter will set it right,
a letter that he will get tomorrow morning. I think I know
what you ought to say. You ought to say that since the world
is what it is, and not what we wish it were, you feel on second
thought about our delightful work this morning, that it may
not be altogether unnecessary for you to make yourself clear.
That you know him to be an artist of the future as all real
artists are, whose work is a strange and beautiful gift to the
world; and this gave you a strange and beautiful freedom from

the narrowness of the world and let you be for an hour the woman of the future. That question about such a matter will of course some day seem absurd, but since that day has not yet come, the deed needs explanation because it was before its season. I think that is enough to say."

I felt saved, as if suddenly my clothes had been restored to me.

We looked at curtain fabric at Arnold Constable's. The color was good, but the design too large and lifeless. We found velvet of purple-grey, most beautiful in the sample, but too purple in the piece. Then we looked at Faulkner's and found a noble purple velvet and took a sample home to try. It proved *very* dark, and we recalled a gun-metal grey that we had thought less beautiful and much lighter than the purple. Kahlil was tired, and I blessed him unspeakably when he yielded and let me go back alone for a sample of the grey, while he stayed to make coffee and block out my letter to Davies. The grey proved right, among the handful of samples I brought back from both places; and to my speechless pleasure again Kahlil let me go back to Faulkner's to fetch the grey, that we might see it by day-light. It was a *big* bundle, fifteen yards fifty inches of velveteen on a roll.

"Why, Mary, you are sweating. Why did I not know it would be so large? Aren't you good?" And then he took the pleasure in the beautiful stuff that it deserved. Then we wrote the letter to Davies and mailed it on the way to Gonfarone's.

After supper we cut the curtains, three yards and twenty-one inches each, laying them on the floor. "I'm so nervous doing this," said Kahlil. "Not a bit," said I. "You're steady as a rock. That's just your quick *tempo*." And we laughed. We had a fine time with it and got a sofa cushion left over from it at the end. We were so glad to have the curtains there and cut.

Kahlil had been growing less tired. When I went I said, "Oh! Kahlil! You are a tower of strength! I don't know what I should have done today without you. I should have been bathed in flames. And I've felt so shielded, so protected. And the letter really seems to me wise and sufficient." The extremest beauty filled his face and he said, "My heart is light about it now, and it was very heavy today. I do think it will be all right." And he kissed me as he has a few times before when I have been in trouble, with a tenderness beyond dreams, as God might kiss a child in his arms.

⋯❦ *MH* ❧⋯

[JOURNAL]

[New York]
September 3, 1913

I went out on Wednesday morning (September 3, 1913) for cushions, curtain rods, rings, cords, brackets, thread, and in my own mind to look for a couch cover. I did not like the old blue and silvery cover Kahlil had bought for eighty cents. At Wanamaker's I found a tan that I *liked* at two dollars a yard, and a stylish basket weave whose color I did not *quite* like at a dollar fifty.

We went, Kahlil and I, to Fourteenth Street for lunch, but first we wrote to Mr. Moors asking for a list of Kahlil's securities and saying that if Kahlil could sell without loss to the amount of fifteen hundred to two thousand, Kahlil would like that much by 1914 but would prefer not to sell if it must be at a loss.

From lunch to Davies and I was wearing my Bulgarian waist with a little Bulgarian collar I got on Sixth Avenue five minutes before lunch. "I like this waist," said Kahlil. "I don't know but that I like it best of all your waists." His shoe hurt badly and we stopped on Fifty-seventh Street to have it stretched by a real Hans Sachs of a cobbler. Davies welcomed us with a royal completeness of display. He ran through his pictures from youth to now for two hours. Neither man spoke much, Kahlil hardly at all. Davies said nothing of theory, of which he has spoken so much each time that I was there. At the end he showed a lot of drawings from life on colored paper, and when Kahlil asked about his Rodin drawing that he had lent the Exhibit last spring, he brought out two Rodin drawings that he has. I could not have had a better object lesson in what Kahlil talks of as the life, the reality of great art. Kahlil's Rodin drawing burst with *growth*. Davies' is simply decorative, by the side of it "tapestry work," as Kahlil briefly put it. I enjoyed the time very much.

When we went, Kahlil said, "I am disappointed in that work. His other work that has been bought is much better. What I said of him as an artist of attitudes is true. It is all too obscure, too broken up, too mixed, too unclear. The man is very strange, a divided personality. Something is morbid in him, something peculiar." He kept on puzzling. "He is uneasy, restless; he doesn't belong here."

We got out at Wanamaker's, just at closing time, to look at tan velour. Kahlil liked it, had liked the sample, and we bought it on the spot (Sept. 3, '13), three yards at two dollars a yard, and took it home, going out with the employees at the back door. On the way, I went by for tan silk thread and Kahlil straight home to change his shoes.

We put the cover on the couch at once. It was supreme. And we put all the yellow cushions on it, and it was like sunlight and moonlight and palpitating Life. The curtain rods are too long, and the rings too large, but Kahlil can have those made right.

The doorwoman is sewing his curtains, Christine. "I do not like to call her just Christine, so I do not say her name." She is a great fat soul, who loves to sew while she sits. She seems fond of him and interested in his studio, and he likes her.

No stove ordered yet. "We have three months yet," said he, optimistically. "What!" said I, "no heat into December here?" "O yes! we have two months," said he. So it was decided I should write from Boston for Sears Roebuck's catalogue.

Then we settled accounts—$5.59 for curtain findings, eighteen cents for thread. The curtains cost, all told exclusive of sewing, $40.93, the couch cover $6.09, and the "curtains" include a cushion cover also. Kahlil forgot to ask about his grey cushion. That gave me purest delight because it is so rare a thing in a human being to genuinely overlook a financial item. Kahlil is intensely practical because he is intensely real. But the practical is *difficult* for him. Curtains and couch cover were the main needs in the studio—a chair can wait. "If you hadn't been here," he said, "I might have been six months about it." And I think he was glad we had got them together. Of the couch cover I was very proud, because I had found it. It is really enchanting.

He was anxious about my money situation, says he has long been. I thought I had long ago made it clear to him that he must not be uneasy.

He told me my sense of touch seemed my strongest; and that I would be called both sensuous and sensual for kissing or touching affectionately things of beauty that I love. I took it as a warning not to do it, and shan't hereafter, except with him or intimates.

"I can't hide anything in my face," he said once when I spoke of seeing something there. But he *can*. He hides a wound at the moment of receiving it; he hides surprise or curiosity or intense interest. He does not hide *memories* of pain, or pleasure, unless the pleasure is of the deepest and most personal.

His sensitiveness, vibrating so far beyond ordinary intensity, responding so far above and below the vibrations that most of us catch, so aware of the most latent or even unconscious hostility or critical disagreement, so boundlessly free under accord. So crippled and diminished under discord, unless the disagreer is an enemy, so soon fatigued by dragging one wing, so alone to the real self of all he meets, so readily agitated and depressed and strained, so soon rested and refreshed and relaxed: how beyond measure this sensitiveness is, and how it lives in consciousness of all time and the universe, as well as in such detail as the above, I seem to have learned for the first time, to have *realized* for the first time. His loneliness and his suffering I know as if never before. And my own brutality to him is new to my knowledge. Marriage! The wonder is that we are friends! He has said to me, "You have hurt me as nobody else ever hurt me. Nobody else has power to hurt me as you have. You have said the most bitter things to me. You have made me suffer more than almost anything else in my life. But I know what is fundamentally in you. And I have waited." Had he not begun now to speak more of what is in his mind, perhaps I should never have had my eyes opened and might have worn out our friendship by unconscious outrages.

"Since I look forward to leaving 'the world,' " said Kahlil, "I feel a new freedom in it and from it. I am independent of it, for I have my hermit-home before me. And about painting I feel differently, too. Now that I have mastered it enough to know what I am doing, I know I could lay it down for a period and work in an office and then take it up again when I became able to, and I should not have lost it. I could go on."

Spirits Rebellious, published while Kahlil was in Paris, was suppressed by the Syrian government. Only two hundred copies got into Syria, secretly. Long since, of course, it has entered, and the edition been exhausted, but the Church considered excommunicating Kahlil. Practically he was excommunicated, but the sentence was never actually pronounced because of his family. He comes, especially on his mother's side, of a race of priests and scholars and church rulers. When the two representatives of the Patriarch, however, came to Paris, they invited Kahlil to dine along with them. He did not want to, but, urged, he stayed. One Bishop had a sense of humor, the other none; humorous, I believe, was kin to Kahlil. Non-humorous took him aside: "You are making a grave mistake. You are using your gifts against your people, against your country, against your church. The holy Patriarch (I forget the phrase used for him) realizes this. But he does not condemn you. He sends you a special message and loving offer of friendship, and I am sure you appreciate how greatly you are honored in that the holy Patriarch sends you such a message. Give this up, return, and the holy Patriarch's own arms and the arms of the Church are open to you. Your future is assured. And now, destroy every copy of the book and let me take word from you back to Syria to the Church and to the holy Patriarch."

Then Kahlil told his Holiness that far from "returning," he was working then on a book to be called *Broken Wings*. He hoped his Holiness would read it—he hoped the holy Patriarch would read it. They would see in it how entirely he disagreed with them. And he said Goodnight. Did not stay for dinner.

As he passed through the outer room where the reception was still not over (he had been taken for conference into a private apartment) and stopped to bow farewell to the humorous bishop, the latter said, "Well, Effendi, have you had a good talk with his Highness?" very cordially. "Yes, your grace," said Kahlil, "delightful. But I am only sorry I was not able to convince him." The Bishop laughed. He understood the case was hopeless.

-----------------------------------※❦{ KG }❦※-----------------------------------

Beloved Mary—

[New York]
September 12, 1913

I am being visited by an ancient friend, the Grippe! Now don't be angry with me. The Grippe and I have been friends for so long and we understand each other so well that we can never be serious. We both laugh things down! And please don't tell my sister.

149

I am not able to work just now. But I can close my eyes and think. I think of my madman whom I love and honor. He is in spite of his large smiles a sort of comfort, a refuge. I go to him whenever I am ill or tired. He is my only weapon in this strangely armed world.

I received a stove catalogue from Chicago. Most of the stoves are fancy. The one which they suggested is less fancy ($14.60). I shall send for it just as soon as I am myself again.

Kahlil

Friday

--- KG ---

[New York]
Thursday, September 18, 1913

It is all over with the Grippe and I am feeling much better. Just a little tired—that is all. I simply need both physical and mental rest: physical rest is quite easy, the other is almost impossible. You see, Mary, I am in a strange mood. I am always digging, just like a mole, and not always in the clean earth. There are times when it is so muddy that I feel disgusted with my own vision of life. And yet I cannot thank the gods enough for the little mole in me.

And now for the stoves! First let me tell you that I have kissed your hands a thousand times for writing to Chicago for a stove as I have kissed them for bringing the beautiful things for the studio while you were in New York. The giant size (number 18 on back of the order blank) is *too large* for this place. Even number 17 is too large. Number 16, from what I read about it, seems to be *the* thing. But one can't tell. Perhaps number 17, the next largest size, is better but we don't want a huge pile of iron in this studio—do we? At any rate the largest size is out of the question, is it not?

Mr. Moors wrote saying that he will be able to sell fifteen hundred dollars worth of shares without any loss.

Kahlil

Will you not forgive my supreme stupidity? I thought the illustrations on the back of the order blank are there to show the relative sizes and not the different kinds of stoves.

Giant Cannon number 22N725 is what we want. The studio is twenty-one by thirty-three feet, but I think number 22N725 will be large enough, if not we'll get the drum afterward.

Mr. Moors has already sold fifteen hundred dollars worth of shares.

Mary, I am so tired of being indoors. I feel like a helpless bird in a cage, and it is such a fine day out. Perhaps I shall go and sit in the park and watch the tired and the ugly faces. I must have worlds of ugliness in my eye, for I see so many ugly, soulless, characterless faces; faces without a mark or a note or a quality.

Kahlil

Beloved Mary, I have lived much during the last three weeks. I've crossed an ocean and I am now in a new land. Things seem so strangely different. I am tired of the world.

Why should any lover of life put up with such a stupid, soft-headed world? Someday I'll take a paint-box and a bottle of ink and go off and be a hermit. A true hermit goes to the wilderness to find not to lose himself. One can find oneself anywhere, but in large cities one must carve a way with a sword in order to see a shadow of himself.

Just now I can't work for more than three or four hours a day. After that I need rest and space and silence. There are times when I can't work at all. Too *busy* to work. There is a form of thinking, or rather *being*, which does not permit one to do any physical work.

A volume of my earliest prose-poems is coming out in three or four weeks. I've corrected some of the proofs this morning. I hate to correct proofs. Is there anything more wearisome than examining carefully the work of one of your dead selves? It is good to be a digger of new graves, but not an inspector of old ones!

My new book is almost ready. They tell me that it must not come out too soon after the other book.

The stove hasn't come yet and I need it badly for my models.

Now, Mary, please don't think I am slow in doing things. You see, I am alone and I can't do more than one thing at a time.

Kahlil

[New York]
Sunday, October 19, 1913

Of course I shall be here on Saturday the 25th, Sunday too. Do you think for a minute that I would go off as if *no one* was coming to see *me*? You want to assure me that you will be with me while looking at the pictures. But what about *my* wanting to be with you? Have I no desires of my own, beloved Mary? Perhaps you think that I could look at you from behind these canvases. No, Mary, I want to see you with my own eyes and touch you with my own hands.

The stove is here at last, and it is wonderful. It will make this place most comfortable no matter how cold it is outside.

I am not seeing people in these days. The "no" in me is working well, as well as the "yes" of my former self, my dead self. Thank God for the little undertaker in me! But I must not speak of these things now. Saturday is not so far away.

And will you not tell me at what hour you will come on Saturday?

Kahlil

--◦❦ *KG* ❦◦--

[New York]
Sunday, October 26, 1913

Well, Mary, I was frightened to death yesterday. The three hours that passed between the two telegrams were among the most terrible in my life. When your first telegram came I put a few things in a bag and began to walk to and fro in this studio. It was eleven o'clock. The train leaves at three minutes after one. I wish I could tell you of all the wild things that went through me. And then I read the telegram again. The two last words "getting better" gave me a clue. I began to think hard! A certain process of reasoning changed my terror into uncertainty. Your little note of Friday gave me another clue. I felt somewhat different, but not less frightened. And then I wired you.

You see, beloved Mary, it was the thought that you are being nursed secretly that complicated things. 314 is a semi-public place. My being there while you are ill (and I am not a doctor) would open the blind eyes of people. In getting into 314 one *must* go through the door!! In getting out of 314 one *can't* very well fly through the window!

These and many other thoughts struggled in my mind before your second telegram came. O what a relief it was. I was calmed and fell asleep with my clothes on!

And now I am thanking Allah for your getting better and better. I believe everything you say and I will not permit myself to read between your lines, although there are times when one can't help it. I have been reading between the lines all my life, Mary. It is a mental habit with me. When people talk to me I hear what they don't say and when I read books I see what is not written. But I promise never to read between *your* lines in time of illness or sadness. I shall read just what you write, because I know now that you would not hide the truth from me no matter how bitter it may be.

If you don't come to New York on November 7–9, I go to Boston. But I hope you will be able to come.

Kahlil

[New York]
Thursday, October 30, 1913

Why do you explain *some* of the things you say to me? I *do* understand the spirit in which things are said. Will you not trust my understanding?

And there is another thing I must speak of: please, *please* do not think that I am easily hurt. A real knife may cut me, but knives made of wax do not. Harsh words and harsh looks are apt to make me take care, but it is the iron hand that hurts. Unreal things erase themselves. So please be absolutely *comfortable*, for your Kahlil is not made of whipped cream!

I am so glad you will be able to come on November 8. We could have a much better and much *longer* time here than in Boston.

With love,
Kahlil

———————— --◄❧ *MH* ❧►-- ————————

Miss Haskell's School
314 Marlborough Street
Boston
Saturday, November 15, 1913

When I saw your letter in this morning's mail, I was so surprised to get it already, and so glad I was to have news of you. As I read your note, it was like seeing in words the image of you that has been with me this week, unspeakably unhappy.

I am only half here. I want to take the train to New York and see you with my own eyes. You would not have to talk; you could be silent; you need not even smile. I should just be with you instead of two hundred miles away.

I think, among many things, about how you could get a change. That is such a deep longing, the longing for a change, when we are sickened. We do need it. It gives such a peculiar release. We are refreshed so effortlessly. Since you have been in New York you have had hardly any change. You would probably be the better for a big one. But I know how many things make a big one, a "complete change," matter for long thought; and I wonder whether meantime something smaller cannot be had.

[Boston]
Sunday, November 16, 1913

How I blessed you for answering me so soon and telling me you are not well. And of course I never speak of your illnesses to Marianna.—It always moves me when you are willing to say to me that you suffer. And I am very conscious of your suffering, even when you do not speak of it. When I think of the burdens you carry, the work that hurts like childbirth labor and never stops, the two arts, the two tongues, the two worlds (hemispheres), the two eras, of present and future, the loneliness, and of the handicaps under which you must live the life that is enough for two geniuses; lack of means, lack of robust health, lack of the aids of home and background and native surroundings, lack of opportunity for either art to influence acknowledgement in the other—and occasional stabs out of trusted darkness, like this *et tu Brute* blow we had—so that your life moves from one set of pains into another and from less pain to more:—when I think of all these things, it hurts beyond hurt.

At last I remember God. And oh! what it is to know there is strength more than enough, and love more than enough! Measureless as are your pains, and vast the outlines of the work you feel growing in you, the pains are small in proportion to what is being born—and the real work is beyond what in this generation or perhaps for many generations even you can realize. Only the future can show its scope.

For there is nothing surer than that man will grow to the stature that now you singly are. You are surely for Him. You are pace-maker to the worker of the future. The burdens you carry, what you do, will some day be no more superhuman. And in that day, when man is calling the twentieth century an embryonic stage of himself, he will call you *like* himself. But you when that day comes will still be creating tomorrows.

156

Perhaps there will be more joy in it then, Kahlil. We do not know.

To you now, what you write and paint expresses mere fragments of your vision. But in time the whole vision will appear in it. For man will learn to see and hear and read. And your *work* is not only books and pictures. They are but bits of it. Your work is You, not less than you, not parts of you. You do not need to give yourself up to your work; you cannot do it; for you *are* your work. These days when you "cannot work" are accomplishing it, are of it, like the days when you "can work." There is no division. It is all one. Your living is all of it; anything less is a part of it.—Your silence will be read with your writings some day, your darkness will be part of the Light.

To think of these things wakes so many other things in me about you that pain is no longer all of consciousness. For that future that I see is so dear to me. It is like the resolution of greatest dissonances in great music. You know the use of that word *resolution* in music, don't you?—so deep and beautiful. —And it is like the reconciliation of life. And do you know *Reconciliation* used in that way? To me it is one of the profoundest and fullest of our words.

God bless you, my dear near Kahlil.

Love from
Mary

⚜ *MH* ⚜

[Boston]
November 27, 1913
Thanksgiving

Indeed, dearest K.G., I understand with all my heart your desire to be alone, your *need* to be alone.

Even when two people are actually together, is it not a pulse-beat of meeting-and-parting, meeting-and-parting like that? Sometimes the parting from a person needs to be very long, but however long it may be for you and me, meeting will come again and with new Kahlils and new Marys.

Meanwhile, forgive me that I have not been able to stop casting about for something easier than your "pulling yourself up by your boot-straps," will you not?

And the other night, just before dawn, in bed, something flashed into my mind. Now I have looked it up, and it still seems good. So I tell it to you. But I am not urging or begging, dear Kahlil. You know that, do you not? I know you have your own guidance, not I, and I don't want to advise.

The West Indian cruises are what I thought of for you. I have heard so many people speak of them with delight. I knew you would hesitate at expense, and this is no time for you and me to talk about money. But I have found that you can get into those mild islands without much expense. You can go to Cuba for two or three weeks, having four days on the boat each way. You can go to Bermuda and stay two or three weeks for seventy-five or eighty dollars, two days each way on the boat.

There is a sailing for Bermuda each Saturday. If, by barest miraculous chance, you should feel it would be a relief to go this Saturday you could do it, for the Bermuda trip is as simple as coming to Boston; you simply telephone to the office and ask if they have accommodation, and if they have, pack your trunk, including your wash if you need it, for a Bermuda laundry! The Quebec Company's folder gives a list of boarding places, and you can avoid hotels and go to one of those women-kept places for fifteen dollars a week (some say twelve), which is moderate in this day for comfortable living anywhere in America.

Bermuda would cost little or nothing more than to go to a comfortable boarding place in New York climate, for the round trip at lowest first class rate is twenty-five or thirty dollars, and Bermuda is so sweet and mild and sunny!

You will say—How about leaving the studio and pictures? If you would be willing, I will gladly insure your things in your absence. It will be no trouble to me, for I can easily find out what companies are best for it, from the business connections I have; and such things, being in the line of much of my daily thinking, are easy for me to attend to. If you are willing to let me do it, it will take me but little time, and will be only a pleasure.

I do not beg or urge you to let me do this. But you will forgive me again if I say that if you were paying me thirty-five cents an hour for clerical work, you would not object to me doing it—and if you are unwilling for me to do it unpaid, it were a happier thing to be an employee than to be a friend. I would let you do it if our conditions were reversed; would let even other friends do it.

If Cuba draws you, Kahlil, I think you will not regret what you spend for it, if you will go. Perhaps you would rather add a little, however, and cross the Atlantic for two or three weeks. But the advantage of either Cuba or Bermuda is in the semi-tropical climate—such a relief to the body-energy all poured in instead of all going out.

I do not want to prolong this letter. Had it not been for this "inspiration" with the sailing for Bermuda on November 29, Saturday, and December 3, Wednesday, I would have written only a word, or nothing at all, for I too have been in deep waters, according to my measure, strange and terrible to me. But one more thing I will say. A big enough something has come, in regard to money, since I saw you for me to say to you that you can not only take a Bermuda trip, but you can go to Syria if you like, at present, without sense of extravagance. You do not want to receive, nor I to make, explanations just now. But I know what I say, and if you will trust me and believe me, you will say in time that I wrote the truth.

Perhaps you will not be attracted to go on any of these trips. Please then, dear Kahlil, do not let my having looked them up annoy you with a sense that I have been taking trouble. How can I help thinking about you? You do not want me not to. Do not notice little things like looking up steamboats or insurance. They are so matter-of-course to me that in a few hours I forget them. But when they concern you they become warm to me, and a pleasure. Good night, and God dearly bless you. Love and blessing from

Mary

---◆{ *MH* }◆---

[Boston]
November 29, 1913

Beloved Kahlil, I do feel anxious about you, very very anxious, and I do want you to go away and get a real change. I want you to go to Bermuda.

So much that is difficult still lies ahead of you, my beloved Kahlil, that you *must* do the thing you see that looks like the best physical and mental relief and rest. You must seek strength. And you must leave your cares about it with God and let your child-self in you guide you to do what is the simple and evident thing to do. You can do that so beautifully, beloved Kahlil. You always do it, finally. Things come to us from God, not from people, but only *through* people; or from that in people which is beyond their limited humanity, from their god-self, *through* their limited human self. This comes to you from God, and you will take it, will you not, Kahlil?

I have been daring. In reply to inquiry I made about accommodation for the December 3rd boat and the December 10th boat for Bermuda, I received the enclosed letter. I telephoned to New York and said I was asking in your interest, who were out of town and could not be got at before tomorrow; that, therefore, I did not know on which of those dates you could get off—and I could not even say positively that you would go at all; but that if it were possible I should like both chances held for you until you could telephone the office on Monday morning; and that I would send a special delivery to reach you tomorrow, with their letter to me, and explanations. They were very courteous and said to ask you to telephone them the first thing on Monday morning; and to mention my name, since, because I wrote, the reservations are made in my name until you are heard from.

You will notice twenty dollars difference in the price of the two round-trips, December 10th being the cheaper. But if you can arrange to go this Wednesday, it is so much better not to wait, that it would be penny-wise to delay because of the twenty dollars. In the end it would not be economy, but the contrary.

Everything you ever did, or said, or looked, or were, that showed me you loved me, gave me pleasure. And you must let everything I do because I love you give you pleasure too.

I know God is all about you, yet I am always praying for you.

Goodbye.

Love from Mary

You understand, do you not, that to try to push you into going would not be possible for me, and that I took steps with the steamship company only lest everything be taken if we waited and decided before inquiring? You need not answer this question. I know you understand.

Mary

[New York]
Saturday, November 30, 1913

How sweet you are, beloved Mary, and how wonderfully considerate. You are always doing things for me, always, even when you think you are not. You keep me in your mind as I keep you in mine. But listen, Mary; it is not really necessary for me to go to Cuba or Bermuda. I am well now, and if I need a change I shall have it without going far. It is not the physical change that I need. Bermuda will not make me think differently about things. But I feel better now, and my heart is not so black. Your way of seeing things is a change in itself, and the spirit of your last two letters makes my life brighter and clearer. I want to be sure that everything is well with you. *That is what I need.* But I want the truth. You see, Mary, I fear that you don't tell me everything. I fear that you want to save me from pain, and that makes me imagine all sorts of things, more so during the long nights. Do you see?

Mary: please don't think that I always hesitate at expense. Your godly hands have given me the best possible life that any artist would wish for. Yes, Mary, you have given me a *life* and I know it, and I want you to know that I know it.

I only hesitate at expense when things are unnecessary. My going South now is unnecessary, for I am sound physically.

And now, beloved Mary, I am going to read your letter again. It makes me feel good.

Love from Kahlil

[New York]
Sunday, December 7, 1913

Beloved Mary. Are you angry with me because I did not go to Bermuda? Please do not be angry with me. When winter comes one wants to think and work, regardless of how one feels. And besides, I am naturally stupid about going to a *different place*. I always feel as though I am leaving my reality behind me.

I have been trying all week to know what you are thinking about, and now I don't know. I wanted to be sure that everything is well with you. Can't you tell me?

I am feeling much better. I do a little work every day. Each day things seem less cloudy and less gloomy. Perhaps when we meet again we both will laugh at clouds and "glooms."

I shall probably go to Boston about the 18th. I want to spend ten days with my sister. Can't I see you before you go south?

Love from Kahlil

[New York]

Beloved Mary, Friday, December 19, 1913

I shall be in Boston Sunday morning, and if you let me I'll come and spend Sunday afternoon with you. I shall phone Sunday noon. You are always near me. There are times when I talk to you by the hour. There is telepathic communication between us. I knew that ages ago. How could two beings, such as we are, understand one another without *that* silent communication?

Until Sunday, beloved.

Love from Kahlil

December 21, 1913
314 Marlborough St., Boston

Kahlil is in Boston for his Christmas visit to Mary—arrived this morning and telephoned at noon that he'd come at two.

His voice sounded joyous and eager. He looked better than on November 8th, and had a new brown overcoat that I liked.

I had twelve hundred dollars from last year's school. I asked him if I might give it to him. And I told him how sure I am that our money relation is simple to our larger selves and happy that I give because I love him and his work and he takes because he loves his work and me, and that any basis of buying and selling, lending and borrowing is illusory, a failure of our smaller selves to see the simple final truth.—We talked more frankly and freely than ever about the suffering of our lesser selves in the money relation, mine because it is a barrier to the sort of love I want, his because he is not sure I shall have enough in my years to come and is sure I deprive myself now. He said his work in Arabic, no less than his painting, was my gift. "You have *literally* given me life. I should have ceased to exist, if I had not been able to do this work." But if he had died, that would have been no calamity to him, said I; whereas if he had not been in my life, I should yet have lived a life so much less that it would have been a calamity. We both see that apropos to the collection it is wise in a larger way. I *think* money heartaches are probably nearly over for us. Since that talk—for it *is* simple—just the working out of our inner partnership, which we discover more and more fully as we grow toward our larger selves that are so at one.

It was a heart-rending talk. I confessed my recurrent desire to marry him, and the happiness of my larger self in *not* marrying him, and the struggle I still have at times before the larger self dominates. This desire has troubled me almost none this fall because I have loved and understood Kahlil so much more, and to tell him about it made me feel as if perhaps it might even cease.

"You understand my sensitiveness about money, don't you, Mary? Sensitiveness means a sense of what we lack. No doubt there is a man who could paint three or five hours, write four or five more, and make a living. I can't. Four or five hours a day is all I have strength for." I *do* understand, I believe, his whole gamut of suffering about taking money. This took all supper time—strawberries and egg salad were untasted—perforce. We were choked with intensity.

Kahlil took the twelve hundred dollars. I told him my desire was that he be independent, my plan to give him all the money I could, if he'd let me. He spoke of what independence means to him.

"Do you grow through it?" he asked when I said it was my desire to give money to secure his freedom. "More than through all the rest of my life," I said. "Very well," said he.

I wanted him to will me his tan velour couch cover that we bought together in September, and his coffee pot, for their personal associations. He was pleased and added the coffee cups. "Mary, that coffee pot is the nearest thing to my life," he said.

When we were speaking of money, Kahlil asked me "not to give away large sums on the spur of the moment.—I would say that about other things too," he said. "Don't do any *essential* thing on the spur of the moment."

About 11 o'clock we sat down and ate the supper we had not touched at 7—hungry!

—— ⊸❈*MH*❈⊶ ——

[J O U R N A L]

January 10, 1914
New York

The afternoon, 3 to 5, with Kahlil.

I never felt his peculiar *glow* more, embracing and deep. His consciousness no longer has moments with Reality, like the rest of ours; he *lives* with Reality. It is that that he is always perceiving. His times are all superlative, his retina seeing freshly, his thought moving on.

And never was I more enveloped with his simple lovingness when he had kissed me.

"Mr. Macbeth the art dealer will probably come here on Tuesday to see the pictures. I don't know whether anything will come of it. And I shall not give up anything of my real personality to make something come of it. I am *not* an artist struggling for recognition. I do desire it. I do want to know that my work reaches other minds. I do not need anyone else to tell me about my work. Macbeth says frankly that he must handle what will sell as well as what is art."

I asked Kahlil to tell me his last dream of Jesus. "Do you remember the ruined pillars about three quarters of a mile from

Bsherri where I have told you of meeting him before in my dreams?—Near this is an old Phoenician tomb. You know the Phoenicians cut a chamber in the solid rock for a tomb; and in each of the four walls of the chamber there are two niches for coffins. Near the tomb is a Franciscan monastery. One of the Italian monks there was a great friend of my grandfather, Bishop Suptianos. They always talked Latin together, as you and I speak English. Everyone in the town knew the monk and loved him. He was very venerable—stout and short, with white hair and bright color and large bright blue eyes. I remember him perfectly but I had not thought of him for years. And it was he that I was talking with in my dream. We were walking towards the old Phoenician tomb—and he motioned me to notice an axe that was lying by one of the big walnut trees. It was the biggest axe I ever saw. The strong old monk picked it up and swung it with a smile and then he began to hit the big walnut tree with it. The blows made a tremendous sound that filled all the valley. I remarked to myself with surprise that they sounded not like steel on wood—but like a great bell—as if the tree were made of metal. I walked on slowly—and rapidly the sound grew less. With each step it was so much less that I was very much interested—and in a moment I was saying to myself, 'I am only fifteen yards away, and near at hand those blows sounded through this whole valley. Now I can hardly hear them.' And in a step or two more I did not hear them at all. Then I saw Jesus coming toward me down the road. The walnuts and weeping willows arched over the road, and I could see the patches of sunlight falling through on his face. It was the same face as always—an Arabic type of face, aquiline nose, black black eyes, deepset and large, yet not weak as large eyes are so apt to be, but as masculine as anything could be, with his straight black brows. His skin was brown and healthy, with that beautiful slight flush of red showing through——" [*Mary:*] "Was he bearded?" "Yes, with a thin beard like the Arabs—and his hair was abundant and black but not well kept, head bare, as always. He had on the same brown robe, loose, with a cord round the waist, and a little torn at the bottom—and the same rough, heavy, common kind of large sandal on his feet—they were as usual a little dusty. But he was not walking as usual. His staff was longer than in former dreams—and he was walking proudly, holding his head high, and with his bosom projecting"—and here K. stood up and faced me with the royal mien he indicated. "Staff held in front—eyes piercing—and he walked like a peasant who deliberately walks like a king. When we met he turned and walked back with me toward the Phoenician tomb. There is a large, large rectangular stone in front of the tomb, carved with inscriptions. We sat down on it and talked. There is no noting of time in dreams, of course—but when I waked I had the sense that we had talked a long time. And yet I can't remember what we talked about. Only —the same old thing. Mary, as we sat he took his staff and marked in the sand with it—just as any of us would do and often do. And one thing I remember that he said, in Arabic— 'Yes, it does sound like copper' (nahass). And when he said this, though for some time I had not been hearing the monk chopping the walnut tree—I now heard him again—and it did sound like copper.—But there was nothing striking about the conversation. We simply talked."

Today I was unusually aware of him.—It is my joy of joys that he never hides from me. "With you, Mary," he said today, "I want to be just like a blade of grass, that moves as the air moves it—to talk just according to the impulse of the moment. And I do." I told him my delight in that—and how it seems to me the highest honor one can do another—to be free and himself with her. To be this, is to treat one's friend as one's equal.

I have not the time to learn Arabic. But perhaps as a being I grow more through school than I should through such study, I trust—therefore, I take this state from God as a lover's gift, and love it. And if it shall be that I must wait till K.'s death before I read him—still, how precious the reading!—I often think of his death and of myself after that. This Sunday night before I left for my train I lay by his side on the yellow couch, and in the dim light looked at his profile as he lay with face straight up—and thought again of the day when it will not turn to me. Beautiful face! That this realest being is so beautiful, tells me all is well—always.

We talked of what we have learned about preventives of conception; for we have spoken before about intercourse and did not know what could be known about preventives. Facts to date confirm us in refraining. A safe and sure preventive is not yet known. Abortion is illegal, and discovery of intercourse without marriage ostracizes a woman so the price is too heavy for us to risk. If that were all we could have, or the chief thing, says K., it might be different. But we have so much together and this union has grown up without intercourse—and so proved itself not dependent on intercourse. "You rouse me physically," he said this afternoon, shaving. "And that was so, ever so far back. When I used to sit on your sofa in front of the fire, desire was often a great pain" (one reason why I now see my absence as a repose!).

While we were talking about intercourse, K. said, "There is nothing indifferent in your body. You are alive, and vital and loving and you are so strong and well. Safety would be peculiarly hard to secure for you.—And I too, have great warmth sexually. I think a great deal of sex power goes transformed into my work."

[JOURNAL]

[New York]
Monday, January 12, 1914

When I came in for lunch at 1—as we had agreed—K. was reading on the yellow couch, in undershirt and old coat and trousers—unbrushed, unshaved—and jumped up big-eyed. "Just waked?" said I.—"No!" said he. "But what time is it?" His watch had stopped as usual; it practically does not run. "I thought it was about 8 o'clock in the morning," and he laughed. "What a beautiful gown!" he said, the moment I took off my coat. It is pretty—the blue and black dress Natalie found for me and fixed last night, bless her! I asked him for a photograph to take the place of the one of him that he gave me and I gave Mary because she had none and liked it so much. (Mary told me, by the way, that he saw it in her room, and when she said I gave it to her said, "I wonder whether she didn't like it?" (!) He had only one of that kind left and I wanted him to keep that because it is the best for publication. So we looked through the rest and he showed me his choice—a very noble head—with the light above. To off-set its blond look, we added his blackest one—the handsomest photo—graphically, I remarked; "You know if I have it it's just being kept for you." "Oh! now you've spoiled it! You've spoiled it all!" cried he—despairfully. "Why are you, who are giving, giving, all the time, so sensitive about taking even a hair, a straw? Is it so hard for you to receive?" I told him I always see the little hole that is left when I am given something. And I told him I don't mind receiving; it is *asking* at which I hesitate. I love to receive. Had I ever refused anything from him? He laughed—said I'd had hardly anything offered me. I said there is little I really care about—but what I do care about I keep jealously and eagerly desire. And with his pictures (photos): as far as other people save Mary are concerned I don't hesitate to take the best, because however much the others care for them I care more. But if a time came when he could *use* his photograph that I have, would the possession of it be as dear to me as his use of it? See? That was what I meant when I said it was being kept for him.

When we came out of Gonfarone's, I took his arm, in a gale of fun, and started off. But on Sixth Avenue I said, "I'll drop your arm. This is your home district, and mightn't it be pleasanter if I attached no lady love to you?" "O," he said, "You are allowed *one*—and I never have anybody else on my arm—so it's all right."

Miss Haskell's School, Boston
January 17, 1914

Dear old elephant-eared partner! Dear old man! Blessed and beloved Kahlil! All week I've looked in wonder at your beautiful big photograph. I can't tell you how glad I am I have it.

K.G., did I leave my big watch on the studio table? If it is there, won't you send it to me in the box in which I am sending you my little gold one? Please don't be shocked at receiving the gold one. This is one of the things I am always forgetting to do—to carry my watch to you. For with my present clothes I've no fit means of wearing it—and I have therefore not used it for fifteen months. And it is not good for a watch to be unused. Yours is out of commission—so you are free to exercise mine! I prefer the big cheap one, because I never carry a watch in a pocket, and outside it collects so much dust— especially in my western summers, that to keep a good one in order I have it cleaned at considerable expense every year. Whereas the big one lasts several years and dust does not affect it.

And now, dear old Darling, I laugh—because I'm going to ask you to try something for physical benefit! Turkish baths. They do so cleanse and eliminate and fortify. And they are cheap—there is one on 29th Street, I think. Good night! Ah! Kahlil Effendi! It is good that my heart can harmlessly clasp you and my soul harmlessly kiss you and visit you—and I harmlessly love you!

Be a good Daddy and take a Turkish bath just to spite your vile tormentor! See how it works with a woolly Lamb! Did your stove warm the studio well, these freezing days?

When you are painting again, will you send me, when you write, a little sketch of what you are doing? I can't help knowing that not these two past months nor anything else mean anything less than increase, with you. They too have been painting months.

Mary

----------------------------- ⚜ *KG* ⚜ -----------------------------

[New York]

Beloved Mary,   Wednesday, January 21, 1914

Turkish baths are wonderful. I had one last night and then I came home and slept well.

Ruth St. Denis* danced for me yesterday afternoon—almost nude. I made a few little drawings of her while she was moving and whirling in her fine, large studio.

The big Ingersoll watch is on its way to 314. But why—why—WHY—Why did you send me this lovely gold one? You need it more than I do and you should have kept it. You are always giving me the best things you possess. Your hands are always full for me. Listen, Mary: I shall keep this gold watch until the means by which you could wear it is found. We should soon find the means.

And the bottle of Lotion, too! It is a fine stuff for the face —indeed it is.—I have used it ever since it came, and the result is wonderful. You are a fountain of joy, Mary.

I shall see the insurance man tomorrow. I think we should not pay more than $100.00. This building is one of the safest in town in spite of its being old. Everybody is so careful.

Love from Kahlil

* (1877?–1968). American dancer who had a major influence on interpretive dance.

Miss Haskell's School, Boston
Dear old Belovedness: February 4, 1914

I was so glad to hear from you!

The reason I want you able to exhibit now is that I feel as if you were only waiting for such sales as would come, before you will go to Europe and Syria again—and I long to have you free in mind to go; and free too to give Mary what you want to give her.—Oh! free to give anybody what you want to give! For I know how strong that desire is in you. You say I am always giving:—how well I know why *you* are not always "giving!" I have taken up a thousand of your giving impulses, as you paid them down, and kissed them in my heart—and kissed them and kissed them—and these things I keep, Kahlil. You have made me rich within.

Great things do not make us despise small things—they make us want greater things, and show us what are the greater things. That is why I would not change places with any woman in the world.

A great deal, K.G., of what you are to me you are to other people. It is all in proportion to their understanding you. Between you and me is understanding—but to its present richness it has come by growth. And so it will come from other people too, to you—through many years. It *is* coming, already—and it will come perhaps more and more quickly as time goes on.

How much exhibiting this year will advantage you above exhibiting next year we really do not know at all. Do we? If that guidance within you, which I know you trust absolutely, leads you to further efforts now—it is for your increase, even if next year is the result. If your guidance says, stop, and just work—*that* will be your increase.

Yes, Kahlil, I too do trust God—and that you suffer deeply and long and terribly, does not make me trust him less. Everything hard for you makes me love you more. It feels like a nail being driven through both of us. I have a sense I am being riveted to you—and that we cannot be shaken apart. Perhaps, however, it is simply that I am growing aware of rivets which have, through many existences, joined us.

Now I have a wee bit of business to add. The skin craves *variety*. Ma Belle Lotion may lose its virtue unless you have other things to change off with. Won't you get Hind's Honey and Almond Cream, 35¢ at all druggists. Leigh's Cold Cream, at Leigh's Chemist, 158 Madison Avenue, between 32nd and 33rd. It is the best I know. If you will use these two, and drink ever so much water, and take turkish baths sometimes, I believe you will have no further trouble with my cheeks!

Mary took supper with me last night. Your old Syrian doctor is giving her what seems right and sound treatment, for a terrible vaginal state dating back to the lifting strains of her sick-nursing—abundant hot medicated douches night and morning. The poor child will be healed probably in two months—and is already soothed and refreshed. It is wonderful to see her native strength seize the chance. I seem to see a smile begin all over her body. The doctor said that if she had waited another year, tuberculosis might have caught her.

Love from Mary

--- ❧ *KG* ❧ ---

[New York]
Sunday, February 8, 1914

I wish I could tell you, beloved Mary, what your letters mean to me. They create a soul in my soul. I read them as messages from life. Somehow they always come when I need them most, and they always bring that element which makes us desire more days and more nights and more life. Whenever my heart is bare and quivering, I feel the terrible need of someone to tell me that there is a tomorrow for all bare and quivering hearts and you always do it, Mary.

Love from Kahlil

[New York]
Tuesday, February 24, 1914

I have worked yesterday and today as I have never worked in my life.

I do not need a larger stove, beloved Mary. This stove warms the place wonderfully. But on very cold days, such as we were having, no stove is enough. When I wrote my last note everybody in New York was shivering—and I must have been a little angry with the sky! So please, *please* write to Chicago not to send a larger stove. If I needed a larger stove I would just as soon say so. I always ask for the things I need—and there is no one else but you whom I ask for anything. Do you see, beloved Mary?

God bless you, beloved Mary. God be with you always.

Great love from Kahlil

[New York]
Sunday, March 1, 1914

A mighty snow storm is raging outside. The studio is *nice* and warm, and a keen desire for work is in my soul. A storm frees my heart from little cares and pains. A storm always awakens whatever passion there is in me. I become eager, and seek relief in work. I often picture myself living on a mountain top, in the most stormy country (not the coldest) in the world. Is there such a place? If there is I shall go to it someday and turn my heart into pictures and poems.

Now I am going to work. With your blessings in me, and the storm outside of me, the work is bound to be good.

This is not a letter, beloved Mary. I only wanted to tell you that you and I are going to work while the storm is singing a wild song and dancing a passionate dance.

Love from Kahlil

––––––––––– ⊸❦{ *KG* }❧⊶ –––––––––––

[New York]
Sunday, March 8, 1914

This is a calm Sunday, beloved Mary.

The Friday dinners at Mrs. Ford's are most enchanting. I always feel there that I could say what I wish to say—and I say it.

W. B. Yeats came to one of Mrs. Ford's dinners. He was more than charming—and there was a sad, sad look in his dim eyes. To my great surprise, he remembered our talk in Boston three years ago when I made the drawing of him. And we disagreed on Tagore.*

The past week was a fruitful one. There was a storm in my being, and I worked night and day, painting, writing, dictating and loving God. Oh, I cannot tell you, Mary, what it is. There are times when I feel as though I am carried by his great winds to meet the Lord in the sky. Then I forget my pains and the bitterness in my heart and become like you, large and free.

My "Open letter to Islam" created the feeling which I wanted to create. But there are some friends in the East who think that in publishing that two page letter I have signed my death warrant with my own hand! *I do not care.*

Love—and love from

Kahlil

* Rabindranath Tagore (1861–1941), Hindu poet. He received the Nobel Prize for literature in 1913.

176

[JOURNAL]

314 Marlboro Street
March 10, 1914

Mary Gibran supped with me tonight and we talked, as we often do, about the life when her mother and Peter and Sultana were all alive. The doctor has just told Mary her lungs are sound—she had had violent indigestion and had spit blood—and she had been anxious, because Peter's consumption had begun that way.

Peter died on March 12, 1902, at 6 a.m.; Sultana, April 4, 1901, about 9 a.m.; Mrs. Gibran, June 28, 1902, at 6 p.m. In fifteen months the three had died.

Sultana was 14. When she was 12 glandular swellings came on both sides of her neck. The doctor gave her medicine. He said she would not live long, anyhow; therefore he would not operate, since she might die under the operation. Peter had taken her to the hospital—for her mother spoke no English. He did not tell Sultana or Mrs. G. what the doctor said—but simply followed instructions as to treatment. Consumption of the bowel set in and after seven months in bed Sultana died. Two months before her death, when Mary came home one day, Sultana showed her her feet and legs, swollen to the knee, and said with bitter tears, "Now I can never get up at all." And she never did again. It was a terrible illness in every possible way and felt, in every possible way, by the child and all who loved her and nursed her.

Kahlil was away at college. He knew Sultana was ill but not how ill. Shortly before her death, he wrote to his mother that he had finished at college and wanted to come back. She answered, Come. He started at once—they had not expected that—and in Paris he read in a paper of Sultana's death. The family, meanwhile, had written him the news—but to Beirut. For sometime before her death, Sultana had said she longed

only to see Kahlil and her father and then to go. When he
came, she had been dead nearly two weeks. It was the second
Sunday afternoon after her death when a telegram came for
Peter, about 4; he was out walking, till 6. Then he got it.
" 'Mother!' " he cried, " 'Kahlil's coming!' " and for very
joy wept as if his heart would break. "And my mother didn't
speak for two hours—she was crying so for joy Kahlil was
coming and for sorrow that Sultana's not here."

Kahlil was coming by boat. At 4 a.m. they were all up.
Mary wanted to stay at home from work, but her mother
said, " 'You'll have plenty of time to see your brother at noon
and maybe Miss Tehan can let you stay at home for the afternoon.' " But Miss Tehan was too busy and she gave her only
a whole hour at home at noon.

"Lots of company were there to see Kahlil just come from
home." When Mary got in, [her] mother was getting dinner.
The aunt was with them. The company were invited to stay
for dinner, but did not. Peter could not control himself, but
all through dinner was running out to dry his tears. Kahlil
talked of everything else—but did not mention Sultana. "Because he knew if he began to cry he couldn't stop," said Mary.

Two or three weeks later, Mary said to him—"as children
will say, talking to one another"—" 'Kahlil, I think it was aw-
fully hard, you did not even ask about your sister that day.' "
" 'Why should I,' " said he, " 'I knew she was dead; I knew
my mother loved her, and my brother loved her, and you; and
I knew all their hearts were aching. And they knew I loved
her and my heart was aching. I didn't want to make it just
harder for my mother.' " "He got a black suit and a black
hat and black shoes for mourning. I remember. For all the
clothes he brought back from college were light—with a
brown hat and tan shoes."

The night before Sultana died had been very bad. They
had been up all night. In the morning Peter went upstairs to
rest. Mary asked Miss Tehan when she got to work not to
keep her but to let her go back home—and Miss Tehan

did. When she came in again, Sultana said, " 'Why aren't you going to work?' " " 'You know we were up all night,' " said Mary, " 'so I thought I'd rather sleep this morning.' " " 'All right,' " said Sultana. Then she said, " 'Call Peter' " —and Mary did. The aunt was in the room. Peter tried to make Sultana take a little hot beef wine and after a great deal of coaxing she did. Then she asked for her mother and Mary went to get her. She was helping a woman who had come in to wash and she told Mary to hang out the basket of wet clothes while she went to Sultana. In little more than a minute Mary heard her aunt scream. She ran back to the room. Sultana, who had been resting on her aunt's arm was dead. Mary started to scream like the aunt. She had never seen anyone dead before. " 'Hush!' " said her mother, " 'that is not a right thing to do.' " "Then I cried quietly, like my mother. Peter had gone into the little room. For three days and nights he cried. He couldn't eat nor sleep."

Peter had been consumptive for some months at the time of Sultana's death but he had been taking care of himself and building up. "It was Sultana's death that killed him, and it hurried my mother, too," said Mary.

He was wonderfully careful about guarding the others from contagion. Now he got worse and in the fall the doctor told him to go to Syria. Instead, he decided to go to Cuba, where he had friends in business. He took some samples and left on December 13. "In two days he was ill and he was never well again. He kept losing and losing and all the time he wrote to my mother that he was gaining and to me that he was gaining, and to Kahlil that he was gaining. Only to the fellow who worked for us he wrote how sick he was."

He left on Sunday. On Monday, Mrs. Gibran went to the Massachusetts General Hospital for a tumor. Smallpox developed in the hospital and no visitors were allowed for six weeks.

When they were allowed at last to visit her, Mary said to Kahlil, " 'I'll go the first day, because it is Sunday and I am free; then we will each go every other day.' " Only one daily was allowed.

" 'Oh, Mary!' " said her mother when Mary got there, " 'my tongue feels thick in my mouth—for someone to speak to,' " for she could not speak English. And her first words were, " 'How's Peter?' "

" 'Peter's fine,' " said Mary—for she thought he was.

In six weeks Mrs. Gibran was operated on. Minnie was staying with Mary and Kahlil. She went with Mary the day of the operation, and the doctor told Minnie the mother would not live. He told her it was cancer. Mary overheard " 'will not live,' " and got Minnie to tell her all. "I did not know what cancer was, so when I got home I asked Kahlil to explain it to me in Arabic. And he did, and when we knew there was no hope we cried together and consoled each other all that night. And Minnie cried with us. And Kahlil said, 'Let us bring our mother home as quickly as we can so that she can be with us' —and we did. We brought her home in ten days."

In one more week Peter came home. It was 6 o'clock in the morning. "The cabman rang the bell, and my mother said to me, 'There is the bell. You'd better go to the door.' So I went down—and Oh, how Peter had fallen away! I didn't know him. I said to the cabman, 'What do you want?' and he said, 'This man wants to get in.' And I said, 'We don't have any furnished room' and I shut the door. Then the cabman rang the bell again and when I opened the door Peter said, 'I'm your brother, dear. Don't you know me? Tell Kahlil to come help me upstairs.' He was so weak he couldn't walk by himself. So I ran up and got Kahlil out of bed and he came down in his nightgown and slippers, and he and the cabman got Peter upstairs. Peter went to mother's room, and he said, 'Mother, will you get up and let me stay in your bed 'til sister can get mine ready?' Then I said, 'Mother can't get up, Peter dear.' And he said, 'Why? Is she ill?' 'Yes,' I said, 'she's ill.' And I explained to him. So he got in my bed 'til I fixed his.

"Peter was in the front room and mother was in the back

room, and I put my bed between the two, so that I could hear if either of them moved. Peter lived four weeks. And every morning, noon, and evening when I'd take him his food he'd say, 'Mary, have you had your breakfast?' and 'Mary, have you had your dinner?'—'Mary, have you had your supper? You know you must take care of yourself now, Mary, because you are all we have to take care of us. What would happen to us if you got ill?'"

All the night before Peter died, Mary was anxious and fearful. Sultana had not changed in appearance, before death—but Peter's look grew different. "His eyes were larger and his face had a dead look, and he looked at me differently. And I said, 'What's the matter?' and Peter said, 'Only a little pain, dear, and it will pass. Don't be afraid. Just go and try to get a little rest.'" The aunt was there and she said to Mary, about 3 a.m., "'Get your brother's clothes out, his black suit'"—Peter always dressed extremely well. She did not realize he was dying and she thought it absurd to get out his clothes when he could not dress and get up. Mary questioned, so her aunt took his closet key and got his suit herself. Several of Peter's friends were there, in a friendly way, and they and Kahlil were in the room when he died.

All through this double illness Kahlil was in the store.

Their mother lingered until June 28. That day she was incessantly restless, "'Mary, lift my head; Mary, turn this way; Mary, turn my foot; Mary, fix my arm.'" She had not tasted food or water for a week. Now she asked for something. "I always had chicken broth ready for her and I brought some. But when I put a spoonful in her mouth, she said, 'Mary, take it out!' She couldn't swallow it and she couldn't get it out by herself. I was frightened and after I had helped her, I ran for the doctor. Then I told him how restless she was and I suppose he knew it was the end. He gave me some things to give her and then she was quiet and went to sleep. Kahlil was going out to dinner and said to me, 'Mary, do you think I ought to go?' And I said, 'Yes, Kahlil. Nothing will happen to mother. You see she's sleeping now. Go, but don't stay late. Come back at 6.' Neither of us had any idea she would die soon now. So Kahlil went.

"My aunt was there. And late in the afternoon two friends came in to help with mother. They were so glad to see her asleep. They said, 'How nice to see your mother better!' And I was glad, and I was telling them about her day—how the doctor had given me something to quiet her. My aunt said, 'I shouldn't think you'd be talking now. Look at your mother.' And mother was so..."—(Mary breathed a moment like one who is dying very quietly)—"then she was gone. And then I felt I didn't have anything in the world. About five minutes after that Kahlil came in. He saw his mother dead, and fainted."

[New York]
Sunday, April 5, 1914

I have been silent, beloved Mary. I have been working hard and sleeping much—sometimes ten hours—and I feel as though both work and sleep had robbed me of the power of speech. Some days I do not go out at all. I simply eat whatever there is in the studio and then I go to bed with a strange quietness in my soul.

As I grow older, Mary, the hermit in me becomes more determined. Life is a vision full of infinite, sweet possibilities and fulfilments. But people are so thin, Mary; their souls are thin, and their speech is thin. Life is mighty. Man is small. And there is a gulf between life and man. One cannot abridge that gulf without twisting his soul and becoming contorted. Is it worthwhile for an artist to be an acrobat?

Personally, I can get along only with the two extreme links of the human chain, the primitive man and the highly civilized man. The primitive is always elemental and the highly civilized is always sensitive. But here in New York I see and talk only with the *normal*, educated, polite, moral man. And he is so thin. He is hanging in the air between heaven and hell—but he is so comfortable there that he is always smiling at you!

I saw you in a dream the night before last—you were dancing with a tall man and you were laughing.

Are you not going to send me that photograph of yourself?

Kahlil

--◀{ MH }▶--

[Boston]
April 16, 1914

Have I ever told you, K.G., that you and I have been to a folk dancing class every Wednesday night this winter? This Wednesday is our last—oh woe! to jump, slide, run, turn and be hot and merry and forgetful and gay for two solid hours— with forty others. You may have been unaware of escorting me!

I do all my Sierra days with you because the Sierras would be dear to you. The one pain in the transport of my California summer is your physical absence—that your eyes do *not* behold my Superearth. It hurts to see with my eyes only; feel the air on me alone and singly catch this planet's hum.

--◀{ KG }▶--

[New York]
Saturday, April 18, 1914

I am so glad, beloved Mary, that we shall spend next Sunday together. It is so long since you were here and I must see you in order to be sure of certain things in life. The days that follow your visits are always clear, honest days. I always know what I have done and what I have not done, what I am and what I am not, what is and what is not, after you leave me.

I am so glad you are coming.

Kahlil

--------- ⋘ *MH* ⋙ ---------

[J O U R N A L]

April 26, 1914
51 West 10th Street
New York

With Kahlil from noon until the midnight train today.

He kissed me. "And I suppose you are hungry for lunch." But I said I'd just had tea and an orange and he said, "Then would you rather see pictures now or after lunch," and when I said, "You decide," he said with that same swift softness, "then I'll show you some pictures first."

My soul walked softly. I was listening to Life in the picture —in the studio—in Kahlil, and I was sensitizing myself to him.

I realized what complete solitude had broken itself to admit me. His agitated consciousness was all about mine like an eagle's by human presence, even though of a beloved human. The past two months were in his face. It was pale and tense.

I told him I was really trusting him about his health. He was pleased, and pleased that I will really not try again to "look after" him in any health matter.

The studio was so full of life and silence. "Yes, I love it," he said. "I wish it were somewhere else just as it is, with its light and space." His new pictures are coming on slowly— slowly, I mean, for him. He works on half a dozen or so at a time.

I watched Kahlil move about the room—so slight his frame

looked; his shoulders beginning to stoop; his beautiful hair thinning. His face at 31 often nearly 50 in agedness; his hands branded all over their fresh full warmth with lonely toil and grief; his movement like flame jets—swift and swiftly extinguished. The infinite suffering of sensitiveness opened like a scroll before me. My heart opens to receive and soothe that sensitiveness as my body would if we could have intercourse. *To perceive it is to receive it.* In my life has been no such day before.

And just because in will I said to him, be yourself without anything but welcome from me, whose delight is yourself— his whole self gave itself. Around our quiet talking day became an added world. Often we have suffered intensely from sex— longing and abstinence. At our last meeting, pain was so racking that without words we knew we should have to become free from such strain. His sketches had told me, during our following separation, that he was thinking, living it out. So was I. I learned by chance what are sure preventives of conception. But I did not provide them today. I went to him with no resolve save to be *with* him as completely as I could. His suffering is the greater, his being the more shattered by it, and he is always guided to his healing if he is left freely to that guidance. And my health is to be in union with him. When I listen to him, believing, what I hear is always from God.

So today I went simply with an open mind. How easy everything was! At once I knew and never came a moment's uncertainty. At once I felt his happiness that I knew and all day I felt thanks of his living body for peace. Freely we touched; often he kissed me or I him—never with more absolute sweetness and nearness of heart. We were soothed and comforted and refreshed. It did not seem hard to leave the door of torment shut and there opened as never before an intangible intercourse. The lack of physical union did not seem a lack— did not obtrude. Once it came to me—how sweet intercourse would be now if we could have it and I fancied the same thought flashed upon Kahlil. But it came tenderly; there was no pain and once in the day I felt a threat upon him, but I felt it dissolve and I have never felt so loved. All day he was not called upon to struggle, to be careful, to suffer. There was something of holiday for him and what a day he created burned into me.

Such infinite thanks for simply being let alone to do what he pleased! My bones turn to tears at it all. He cannot go too soon into hermit life. People are a scourge. They are all strangers to him confessedly. The chief thing they can see of his real self is what they called strangeness.

Kahlil spoke of his old feeling about money. "I have been ashamed of myself, that I took it as I did. Again and again I questioned whether I hadn't done all wrong to take anything from you in the first place. All the time it was a barrier and a check. Whenever I would have run to you, the thought would come. She has given me so much. It will seem to her I am doing it out of gratitude. It was a perfect curse and torture. But that's all past now. I ought always to have taken it as you gave it. You gave gloriously, but I could not accept gloriously. I seem to have had to grow up to it. Now you may give me money and it's all right; or not, and it's all right; or you may take it back and it's all right." I told him that the only thing that had surprised me had been his idea that I ever thought for a moment of buying his friendship with money. But that part of his suffering was due to my carelessness in speaking. I was crude and insensitive. "No," he said, "I was blinded, because the whole thing hurt so."

I said I too had had to learn to share life with him. False pride and the habit of being more loved by men than I loved in return had made me continually mortified by his undemonstrativeness and silence when we were apart—feeling as if I had thrown myself at his head. I thought he cared much more for me than he knew and it hurt me that he did not know. But all that seemed very far away now.

The small sketches of Ruth St. Denis are *beautiful*—full of nebulae-curves. "She is very remarkable. She couldn't dance as she does if she were not. She wants to come here and dance for me but I don't want to see her." The sketches are almost all nude. "She wore some gauze but I just didn't see the gauze. She was delighted with the sketches and wants them but I told her I'd make some more for her. I won't let her have these."

In the studio, standing in front of the window and sitting on his dresser, I said, "K.G., do you realize that all that has happened since we were here last April, when we bought the curtains and couch cover, has been in a single twelve months?" —"It has been a tremendous year," he said—"tremendous in every way for me and of all my life the best." "I have lived thirty years in the last five," said Kahlil. "And you gave them to me. You've given me my life in a literal sense. I could not have lived—except that you gave me life. So many actually die for lack of some such person as you to save them. It was not just the money but the way you gave it, the love you gave with it and the faith, the knowledge that there was somebody that cared. I wonder sometimes whether ever in history one soul has done for another what you have done for me. "No one knows of you and me," said I. "It has probably been done— and is being done—again and again but it was not and is not known."

While K.G. was at the Brevoort I had changed to my little India cotton waist and absent-mindedly left the final pinning. I was putting it in after he got back and he said, "Did I get back too soon?" "I fancy I shan't ever feel shy about putting on a waist in your presence," said I. Then I added, "Oh! K.G.! Isn't it wonderful to know somebody you are never afraid of and never shrink from." "*I* know *one* person," he said, "and *only* one." And he kissed me.

"Have you any ideas yet about summer?" I asked. Said he, "I want to do a good deal of writing. I've not written much for sometime and I've still these paintings to finish."

Being shown the pictures is an intense experience. There seem several Kahlils about me and I am eager to hear all that all of them say. A little he talks, and I always want him to talk more. "The big person in this country is Ryder.* There is so much *in* what he has done. The *man* is the great thing. He's very hard to see. If he says you may see him next Thursday, he will be a week preparing for the visit—he is so sensitive preparing himself, preparing his place. He was moved, by some people who were interested in him, from where he was living, oh! so poorly! The floor was so nicely painted and he spread newspapers all over it and lay on them instead of on the bed. I hope to get him for my series but I have to approach him carefully."

The republication of his early poems is now just ready to come out. He showed me specimen sheets—there will be three paper bindings—black, gray and soft brown. He is pleased with everything about it. I kissed him for joy.

---------- ⸙ *KG* ⸙ ----------

Beloved Mary,

[New York]
Sunday [May 3, 1914]

The blessings of last Sunday are still upon me. I have lived those few hours many times. I have repeated to myself, over and over again all the things you said to me and each time I felt the absolute joy of absolute understanding. You always make me see, whenever you talk to me, the reality of life and all the dear things in it. Whenever I open my lips to talk to you I become strangely clear to myself. You always make me put my hand on the brightest spot in my soul.

I am going out now to mail this and eat lunch. After that I am coming back to work. You and I shall work together.

Love from Kahlil

---

* Albert Ryder, the American painter, was at this time in his early sixties; his studio was in New York City.

[New York]
Sunday [May 24, 1914]

This is a wonderful day, beloved Mary, a warm-cool day, and I must go out to some lonely woods with your blessings and a book and some paper.

I want to do a great deal of walking in the open country. Just think, Mary, of being caught by thunder storms! Is there a sight more wonderful than that of seeing the elements producing life through pure motion? Now let us leave these four walls, Mary. Let us go to the woods. I shall talk to you there; I always talk to you when I walk in lonely places. I can never make anything clear to myself unless I talk it over with you. I have said that to you before and I shall say it again and again.

Love and blessings from
Kahlil

[JOURNAL]

June 20. Sat. 1914—51 W. 10th N.Y.

As I knocked at his open door, I felt his hand on my elbow, from behind—and we went in together. The studio looked large and cool. The emptied middle made the walls seem far away—as if we were tiny things within the air-space of a big flower. But the color had almost a sadness, as well as glow— as if of labor and of difficult life.

We were gay—both full of Montross's having undertaken to exhibit his work and be his dealer. "Mr. Morten brought Mr. Montross. He had given him a strange idea of me beforehand, which, I have since learned, is what people have generally felt about me. 'That fellow will consider himself to be doing you a favor when he shows you his pictures. He doesn't care whether he sells or not!' he said. And it was amusing to see Mr. Montross go about it when Mr. Morten left. 'Of course,' he said, 'I understand that you paint these pictures for the satisfaction of expressing your poetic imagination. But after they have passed out of your vision and you are on other things, I suppose you have no objection to selling them.' I said, 'Certainly not.' I thought his 25 per cent pretty steep, but I find that is usual.

"He asked me about my prices. 'What would you say for this, for instance?' I said, '$1500.' 'Very good, very good,' said he, 'but we can easily do a little better than that. That is very little for it—but this is only a beginning.' "

"He is shrewd. He called *Let Me Go* the biggest thing I had done. His whole idea is business."

Dealers apparently are pretty autocratic—decide what a man shall sell. Kahlil says if Montross proves impossible, he will simply not stay with him. He must remain free to not-sell what he wants to keep for his collection and to be his own final arbiter. I gathered that Montross will feel his way with Kahlil and not give him trouble.

When I said I wished the exhibit could come in Christmas holidays so that I could see the pictures a great deal, Kahlil said Montross would probably exhibit some of them in Boston.

Montross said, "I suppose you'll be ready in October?" "October's too early," said Kahlil. "Right," said Montross. "The golden months are December, January, February.—I guess we'll have something to surprise New York."

"Now I'm going to show you the biggest thing I've done, Mary," said Kahlil, "a memory portrait of my mother. It was begun when you were here before." He brought it out. His face and each of her children was in her face—and what had made her his mother—and gave her her love. Story of life with his father—and her death with such pains in poor Edinboro Street of Boston—it was too much. I was moved beyond speech. "That is a portrait of my mother's soul—done without tricks, without artistry. I have done what I wanted to.

Kamilah, Gibran's mother

Marianna, Gibran's sister

The soul is there, the simple majesty. And it is a likeness, too, the likeness to each of her children and to her. An old serving woman from Bsherri saw it and she cried out, 'Why, that's Kamilah Rahmi.' [His mother's name.] I see her only with my eyes almost shut. Perhaps I shall do no more on it. I should fear very much to spoil it."

He spoke about our working on his next book together. "You do my thinking," said I. "Think what years you've saved me, speeding me." "And think what you've saved me!" said he. "You've been my exhibitor, my agent, my editor." I was puzzled: "I'd have thought I was your cook, your laundress," said I. "Oh!" he laughed. "I was putting it in a nice way. I mean you've saved me from having to be all these."

What is poetry? "An extension of vision—and music is an extension of hearing." And later, when in his *Madman* he was writing the bit about the soul of a city, he said, "I want to make a man say when he reads this, 'there are other worlds—remote, lonely, silent, far—of strange delicious life. Let us go.' "

We worked together at putting some of the Madman's sayings into English. Again he said, "Though with you I use English, sometimes I think things that I don't get at by myself in Arabic."

Kahlil's craving for solitude is a great growing thirst. Dinner parties are tasteless to Kahlil. He loves people and if they could meet *him*, the real him—if he did not have to give himself in crumbs and weakest dilutions—they would know how surpassing most love his is. But as it is, he loves them in crowds. He hardly ever goes to Syrian restaurants—for "everybody comes to my table and I have to talk all dinner time—and it is no pleasure."

After lunch we always go back to the studio, unless for a bus ride—usually on Sunday—to Grant's Tomb—or for a walk on Fifth Avenue. This Sunday we were both tired. We got front seats on the bus and sat a long time up by Grant's Tomb, overlooking the River—while Kahlil talked.

This visit was personally momentous to us. It ripened our common understanding of sex in relation to our two selves. I had never ceased to think of sex and Kahlil told me this time that he never had either. We saw that intercourse must be permanently given up. We must keep sex emotion down.

My last visit had been so clear of desire. It was beautiful. But afterwards I had thought, "There will come so much more separateness if we have not that feeling. Gradually we shall cool to each other. There will not be that rush of the heart—that delicious glow." There was a grief about it to me.

Today the atmosphere was different. Early in the day I felt that presence of unconscious desire in Kahlil. It was very lovely. But it did not mean to me that we should be moved. At night, however, Kahlil *was* moved and afterwards I learned he had thought I wished him to be. The excitement—and no intercourse was keenest suffering to him—was agony, I knew. "This means a month's sickness," he said—and again, "This is a mistake, Mary." It was indeed a mistake and had I been on guard or understood, it need not have come. And the price—which *he* pays—to lose strength for days—now, when he is just beginning and has no time to lose! I left with fear heavy on my heart.

It was Saturday evening that made us so tired on Sunday—for Kahlil ached and my heart ached. On Monday though, he had said he would paint so that I could watch him, which I have not done since he lived in Boston and which I long to do. Now he could not. He did work on *The Madman* with me. On Sunday we talked about Saturday and about the impossibility of intercourse. I had said what a difference that feeling made to me in our whole day. He had said, there are three centers in everybody—head, heart, sex. One or another or two of them lead, in each person—not in the same equilibrium at different times perhaps in a given person. "With me," he said, "head and heart led until a few years ago. And then sex—with you." Then I said, "Dear Kahlil, we must have no intercourse. For the rest, how can we determine? We have to leave tomorrow to the morrow." I said it—leaning on his knees as he sat under the gas. He looked at me—so oddly pale and intense—a sort of flame-paleness. After a minute he said, "You make me feel so small and young. You do big things as if they were nothing."

That had been on Sunday. On Monday we were at *The Madman* about dusk and a hurdy-gurdy began to play, and suddenly I noticed a beautiful something in the sky and the real grief of the limitation on us returned to me suddenly. Kahlil noticed my face and said, "Why is your face so sad?" I had not known it was sad but thought my silence would go just as natural to our thinking on the phrasing we were seeking. I asked to evade answering, if all faces weren't sad in repose. Kahlil said yes, quietly—but in a few minutes I told him the truth.—"It is a solid grief to me," I said. "You surprise me again," said he. "You are always surprising me. You do a thing lightly and twenty hours later you look at it so differently."

Then we talked further and even at dinner. "If we could be free, do you really think it would be best?" Then he talked on. "I love you. I desire you more than you do me. The moment you come in I feel you all over the room. I love you. But physical things have their day. They pass. I don't want anything between us to pass—anything great. And we have had little physical experience. We don't know what it would mean, nor what it might take with it when it passed. Our relation is very strong. But whether it could stand *any* strain we might put on it we don't know." "I need your help. I put myself in your hands. I never had such an experience with another. But with you I want to show my whole self." I said, "I don't want to work against you. Here you are in New York fighting for life—and all alone—and I'm fighting with you, not against you—and I want to stand with you, whoever and whatever is against you. I want to help, not hinder."

"That's the biggest thing you ever said to me, Mary, and what nobody has ever said," said Kahlil. "I *am* fighting for life—and never anyone but you to stand by me." He was much moved. I was astounded. "Have I never said that before? I've always meant it." "No, you never said it, and I never knew you knew it," he said. "But now I put myself in your hands. You *can* put yourself in another person's hands when he knows what you are doing and has respect for it and loves it. He gives you your freedom."

"What I *want* for you is your freedom," said I. "Most of the time I know you must stand alone. But if there's room for a foot by you and you need it I want my foot there. And when you need to be by yourself I want you to be by yourself."

I was surprised. I saw he had not always felt safe from even me—and I remembered the old talks about marriage and wondered whether he feared after success came that he'd have that to get out of! What a nightmare! I was touched by his strong feeling, his joy, his release, at realizing that his Key was realized by me. And I was *so* glad I had happened to *say* he was fighting for life. For it has been so fundamental in my thought of him that I had never dreamed he did not know it, and I might never have said it.

This made our last evening glorious. He said, "This has been a great visit. These last two hours have made my whole life different. I feel nearer to you than ever." He said this so simply—standing like a child against me. Nothing ever made me feel his loneliness more and the suffering of it.

I asked him if he desired other women. "Of course I do, sometimes—though only when a woman is congenial, but I don't think about it." He wants his life now undividedly for his work—for his vision of life—and he wants companionship in that. And I want to be with him in that—and I want him with me in my life of vision, too.

I said to him—I've forgotten how I happened to—"Everything in me loves you. I believe the tips of my hair and the ends of my nails love you." His face whitened in a flash—his eyes looked black—nostrils dilated, chin lifted—lips parted.

It was joy—and it seemed to break out through him like a flame.

When he said he'd work at a painting when I came on Monday, I danced round him for joy, then swung him round in my arms. "Oh! my dear giant!" said I. He laughed and repeated the name—what he always does when I use a new pet term for him. "You throw your giant all around," he said. "Only because he lets me," said I.

I told him I had actually hesitated to suggest coming this June, because *he* had always suggested it in other Junes, but not this time, and I had thought perhaps he didn't want me and I hated to ask. But that I realized finally that this hesitation was a remnant of the convention so strong in me of the man always the seeker and that in asking this time I had about got free from that convention.

He hates to spend the night away. "I want to wake in my own place!" And when he visits, too much is apt to be done for him. Syrian dishes cooked—"and often badly" and special things because they've "heard you liked them."

About liking people of various ages, "There is one age I hate—about eighteen to twenty-two. There is nothing in it but absorption in the empty shows of things."

Nietzsche's belief in eternal return rests on assumption that there can't be *unlimited* changes though there may be for untold billions of years—that after limit is at last reached there is nothing to do but to repeat. Kahlil does not assume this impossibility of the unlimited—nor the eternal return.

July 8, 1914   New York

You have the great gift of understanding, beloved Mary. You are a life-giver, Mary. You are like the Great Spirit, who befriends man not only to share his life, but to add to it. My knowing you is the greatest thing in my days and nights, a miracle quite outside the natural order of things.

I have always held, with my *Madman*, that those who understand us enslave something in us. It is not so with you. Your understanding of me is the most peaceful freedom I have known. And in the last two hours of your last visit you took my heart in your hand and found a black spot in it. But just as soon as you found the spot it was erased forever, and I became absolutely chainless.

And now you are a hermit in a mountain. To me nothing seems more delightful than to be a hermit in a place "full of beautiful hidden places." But please, beloved, do not take any risks. Being a hermit once will not satisfy your hungry soul, and you must keep well and strong in order to be a hermit again.

The laurel-leaves and balm-leaves are filling this place with the most enchanting fragrance. God bless you for sending them to me.

Love from Kahlil

Yosemite, California
In the "Little Yosemite"
Monday—July 13, 1914

It is big and sweet and peaceful these days here, Kahlil—moving and calming, natural, wonderful. You understand. You are like my hands and eyes—as truly here as I, as these trees and rocks and sky and the sound of the river and the three naked mountains in the meeting of whose feet we are. We are all that is apparent, except a few jays, a mouse, a rat, a harsh little squirrel—and many insects. Sometimes voices seem to come from the old trail below—for I am at the end of a valley.

Where mountains become too steep and there are great rapids and a few people come up to fish or see. But they do not see me, nor I them. And often in the mountains come human sound—without humans.

I live in the clefts of a pile of boulder—like five fingers and a palm. We fancied such places for robbers when we were children.

Once a day I leave it—when the sun goes down I run down to the river. Below the rapids it widens to a big pool, dashing, but at my edge without current—and straight from the rock I dip in breast high. A dozen times in that iciness is equal to a good walk—and then I fill my bucket, and run up again. There is no one near, so late—so I wear no clothes, either—and that too takes the place of exercise. For breakfast and for supper I cook or heat something. At midday I eat from my knapsack —hardtack, dried fruit and chocolate.

Many things come to me here. Many things that we have talked about come, like living things. And our fellowship is clearer than ever—and fuller of life and power.

And what might have been here, Kahlil! I have waked in broad moonlight—and not night, but Nights, are crowding the forest—and though it is still, they walk and float and stand depth within depth—multitudes and choruses of nights —the majesty of them, Kahlil!

How I wish you too might have such a release as this. Beside its peace, all else seems uneasy, and while all else drops away from me, it but leaves me more companioned by you than ever. And while I seem to radiate all round into space, everywhere in space are you—and the meaning and blessedness of this fills me. To catch the movement again and again, each of the other, and be in rhythm with it and to catch other movements, and share them—this is very great. There is no human being I would exchange with—with you I *do* exchange.

You are our hands and our mouth—and you are speaking and painting of what I cannot say or paint or often even know save that with you I know it. It all seems so fertile—living does—when it issues at last in your voice—when with you it burns to such a heat.

I leave here at the month-end. After that straight to Wenatchee—and from there I shall ask you whether we can meet the first week in September.

God bless you—God bless you—Love from

Mary

---- ❦ *MH* ❧ ----

[California]

My beloved Kahlil,   7/17/14

I too was in the storm last Sunday—morning and afternoon, driving five miles each in a tiny open sleigh with a good horse —in howling wind and rain—wishing for you and knowing how you would love it. I am never in a storm now without you.

I wrote you a long letter on Monday—but did not send it —because I was under clouds—when life clears I will write again.—But you know how different writing is from talking, and how incoherent restlessness and how untrustworthy it may be.

Always at least I am *not without you*—even when all else is vague or ghastly. And this I should feel, even if you were for days without thought of me. Because thought is only a small part of us. We are more together than we *know*, even though our knowledge of it grows.—And when I turn to you, Kahlil, something loosens and dimness clears—and something is sweet and there is warmth.

Please don't take my state of mind to be important. It comes sometimes—only I've rarely written while in it. And it passes. I just wanted to write to you—and all I can say is that I can't write.

God bless you and be with you and fulfill you—precious Soul of Souls!

More—always more to you, beloved Kahlil—and love from

Mary

Yosemite, California
Sunday, July 19, 1914

A great storm is darkening high up in the East beyond the immediate mountains toward my higher valley—I want to get up there to meet it with you alone. Thunder has been rolling there a long time. There may be something big before night. And I shall not come down again before I go. About eleven days remain to me—and those shall be mine and yours.

Those are deep times for me. I see many receiving life from you because you have suffered. I see through the fire the pure gold—I see that which has no ending, which can be met not with words, but only with an uplifting of the heart. A woman suffers to bear one child and feed it. You bear many children —and you feed the World Heart, beloved Kahlil. Someday, you shall have the sweetness of physical solitude too. You sow your heart, beloved Kahlil—you withhold nothing—but many, many hearts shall come up to you for ages from that seed.

Your innermost is entering man's. Wherever life burns deep for centuries you shall meet it and it will love you.

I have found a treasure for you—a tiny Indian arrowhead —what I have wished for you every year in the Sierra, but never saw before. I love it so much—I climbed the rocks to get this for you. It grows only in certain limits and where it can climb a mountainside.

Love and love to you
from Mary

July 22, 1914   New York

Your letter is a wonderful message, beloved Mary. It thrills my heart—and makes me see the stupidity of any other way of living. How refreshing to be free from all that is not real and to live so simply and directly. You picture it to me even more clearly than my dreams and you make me hunger for it. But I am with you, and it is almost as actual to me as it is to you. And some day I shall go to a mountain and your great spirit will be with me as it is always.

I am in a silent, thinking mood, and there are many strange new things in my heart. I want to give them forms, but just now my hands are not working—I walk much in the woods. Yesterday I went early in the morning and did not get back until late at night. My luncheon was not unlike your midday meals on your mountain. How wonderful it is, beloved Mary, that we can both leave the world behind and seek the real world of absolute living and absolute being!

It is a mighty thing to go with love to those regions beyond these days and these nights. But how much more wonderful it is, beloved Mary, to know you as I do. You have freed my life.

Goodnight, beloved Mary. God bless you.

Love and love and love from

Kahlil

July 23, 1914   New York

I had such a strangely beautiful dream last night, beloved Mary, and I want you to know it.

You and I were standing on a high green hill overlooking

the sea, and you turned to me and said, "We must throw *her* back, Kahlil, we must throw her into the sea."

I knew you were speaking of a beautiful marble statue of Aphrodite that we had just unearthed—and I said: "But how can it be? She is so lovely. The rosy tint is still on her lips, and there is so much blue in her eyes."

Then you said, "But do you not see, Kahlil, that she would be much happier and more comfortable in the sea?" And I sadly said, "Yes."

Then we carried the large goddess as if she were a light thing—and from the top of a high white rock we threw her into the sea. And we were both glad.

Just then a flock of white birds flew before our eyes. And as they came near us they caught fire and were changed to flying flames. Then you said, "Do you not see I was right?" And I said, "Yes, you are always right."

Is not this a strange dream, beloved Mary?

Love from
Kahlil

August 1, 1914
San Francisco

I have left the mountains now—but I am not what I was those few days ago. And it has been so much—this wonderful release with you into all the paths of the soul world— that I have spent hours trying to tell you about it, but cannot. I need to be face to face with you—I cannot write. There has been death in me of old things—death so complete that I fancy the womb-life is not dimmer to the baby than my three years' shadows now to me. Three years ago I merely saw with the eye these things in these few days I have at last realized.

It is a long way sometimes—often with me—from perception to realization.

My soul folds you to herself for your beautiful dream of Aphrodite. Your spirit made it pour what has been in both our hearts. We *have* found a sea, Kahlil beloved, beautiful enough for her—and great enough to hold her. And with all my heart I know too that we are glad. We are not denying life: we are seeking it—and we are finding it.

I have no sense of time for those last ten days. Only a sense of death and birth and of so much that shall unfold in the new spaces. And the mountain is a Being with us.

God bless and love you
Love, Beloved, from Mary

—⊰ *KG* ⊱—

Beloved Mary,   Boston—Aug. 7, 1914

I have been in this strangely damp city for more than a week. I cannot work, no matter how hard I try. I cannot even think. I am tramped upon by good people with whom I have little in common. I enjoy being with my sister—but we are not left alone for one single hour at a time. And it has been so cold that it would be absolutely foolish to go to the sea or the country.

There must be something the matter with me, Mary. I am becoming like my Madman. I see people and I *know* they are good souls: and yet whenever I sit beside them, or talk to them, I feel a demoniac impatience, a kind of a desire to hurt them mentally. And when they speak, my mind takes frantic flights beating away like a bird with a cord fastened to its feet. The Syrians, after all, are less disturbing because they are simpler, and because they do not know how to *be interesting!* The people who are always trying to be interesting are the most ugly lot.

We must spend a few days together on your way back. I shall go back to New York about the middle of next week. My sister will go to the country with her friends to stay a month.

Now I am going to reread your last letter. It was full of voices and wings.

Good night, beloved Mary
Love from Kahlil

Sister sends her love to you.

⚜ *MH* ⚜

Aug. 12, 1914
Wenatchee, Wash.

I want to lie in this beautiful sun—and to study—and dream —and feel; and what I do, is to cook very nice simple delicious food and wash a year's wash—and recover the buggy seat— and see a little of the kindly neighbors—and get so sleepy that I am forced to sleep eight hours a day—and mend, and gather fruit—all worth doing, well worth—only, my heart remembers a life so much simpler than this which is so much simpler than most—a life so much richer too—and I am always wanting to fly away to it.

Life is real here—but only muffled music to me—because I have had it so intense—so supernaturally clear—so skylike.

I get to New York early Sunday morning August 31 and shall come round to the studio between 10 and 11 unless I hear from you not to. I'm so glad we can have a while together.

Love
Mary

Wenatchee, Wash.
Sunday, Aug. 16, 1914

Sometimes, I feel, K.G., as if I had little sturdy wings and you great sweeping ones, and that often when you open yours and I lay my little ones to them, I know their whole mightiness as we fly. And we fly to so many places I should not reach alone; and my heart fills every feather of your great wings, and goes out with your heart to God.

Evening. Between sunset and night I walked up on the irrigation ditch that makes this valley grow, half way between the big Columbia River and the top of the desert foothills— and we are just below it, above the other ranches. Below us are the young orchards and the alfalfa field and little houses, the wide river and the road white like moonstone—and above are the mounded sagebrush and dust of the ages. That is what you and I love best, in the strange beauty of dusk—that desert against the sky—twilight's gray body, the gray air, her sweetness.

So much has come to me! You know how the sun is not just his fireball, but all his light and heat and how the flower is not petals only, but its fragrance too. So You and Your whole scope have more fused in me—and as on earth I am "in the sun," so here I am with you—am anywhere with you— more actually than before.

Bless you, bless you, bless you, and love to you from

Mary

Beloved Mary,　　　　　　New York, August 20, 1914

It has been extremely hot during the last few days—more so at night. I go every day to the woods and lie under huge trees with a notebook. I almost live on buttermilk.

I have not been able to work in this studio. Only my mind is at work. The giant war in Europe robs one's soul of its silence and quiet songs. The air is full of cries, Mary, and one cannot breath without getting a taste of blood. Do you remember my telling you about two years ago that "within two or three years the mightiest war in the history of man will take place in Europe?" We were talking of the Near East question and its relation to European powers. It was on Riverside Drive, on a hot day—and I remember being very thirsty. We both looked for water and could find none!

It is a terrible war, Mary, but it will surely decide the fate of the human race for at least a hundred years. I am certain that it will give the world a better and clearer vision of Life.

May God bless you and protect you, beloved Mary.

Love from Kahlil

--------------------------- ⋯❦ *MH* ❧⋯ ---------------------------

[JOURNAL]

Sunday—Aug. 30, 1914   New York

Came from Wenatchee—for a week with Kahlil. A strangely new first day—that makes me think to spend probably much of the week *not* with Kahlil. He has so stripped himself to his Reality, that I feel how partial only my companionship is—how alone he remains actually and, therefore, may be better alone bodily. During the summer I have understood him with absolute newness.

His loneliness seems absolute and there's no sadness or regret in it. Pain is his by right—it makes no need, for comfort or healing. His Madman is "thirsty for his own blood" and so is Kahlil. He believes Jesus wanted to die, wanted to be crucified—as an *expression*—the only expression that would satisfy him—and that if he is now in another planet he may be being crucified there and will "be crucified" until he is satisfied—however often that may be.

His Madman has a dialogue with Night which is tremendous. This, and Intensity as a "life-form"—and his remarks about what we call this "force" or that "motive," as if they had individual existence—made me realize that his sense of existences, of forms established, far surpasses what we call human.

I asked him what books he liked best. He said Shakespeare —Job—"I think that much of the Bible is great—and *The Book of the Dead*."

Mary has made him a beautiful Syrian costume of her pongee and abba, and the under-robe—with his silver buttons from Paris on that. He has a silver chain-and-ball piece that with a bit more for extension will make a wonderful girdle for it. He wore it after dinner—"I shall finish out this girdle —and then I'll wear these things all the time in the studio."

He asked me about my experience in wearing no clothes during the warm hours, in my canyon solitude this summer. I told him how great it was.

Wish he could find a device for repelling people from sitting by him on the train, as my wearing a veil keeps people from sitting with me. For he is always sat with, and always talked to. "When I went to Boston, a monsignor sat with me. He was an interesting man—of wide experience—had been much in Syria. Knew Arabic.—He showed me much kindness. But before we parted I had him talking to me like a little boy."

———————————— ⋅≼{ *KG* }≽⋅ ————————————

[New York]
Beloved Mary   Wednesday, Oct. 14, 1914

We are living this great war; you and I. All those who live the collective life of this world—are struggling, like you and me, with the nations of Europe. And it is a noble struggle.

Man is a part of nature. Each and every year the elements in nature declare war on each other. The strife of every winter for a new spring is infinitely more terrible and painful than any *human* war. More *life* is destroyed in one winter day than in all the human wars put together. Man is elemental. He must fight and he must die for what he does not fully understand. And it is the fight and the death of any seed in the fields. Those who work for an eternal peace are not unlike the young poets who wish for an eternal spring. Man fights for a thought or a dream. Who can say that thoughts and dreams are not a part of the elements that once came together to make up this planet? This war in Europe, Mary, is as natural as any storm in any winter, but not so terrible nor so destructive to life. The early races used to weep over the death of Adonis (Jamooz), and rejoice in his coming to life. Adonis, as you know, is Nature, or the God of the fields. Today we do not weep when winter comes nor do we dance when winter is over. In fact some of us love winter more than spring or summer. And how would it sound if I say to any of those who are apt to be happy on a stormy winter day, "You are heartless, man, you see life destroyed before your eyes and yet you would not weep. The beauty and the glory of summer is crushed to death and still you are indifferent."

Well, Mary, if God the Power, God the force, God the mind, God the subconsciousness of Life, is in all the struggles that take place on this planet, He must be in this war of nations. *He is this war*, as He is all wars. He, the mighty one, is fighting for a mightier self, a clearer self, a self of higher life.

The *Mind* of this world is not free from its body—and as long as the body is struggling for more life, the mind will go on struggling for more life, more mind. *There is no such thing as struggle for death.*

There is nothing on this planet but a struggle for Life.

Every physical or mental movement, every wave of the sea and every thought or dream is a struggle for more Life.

Love and love and love from
Kahlil

In October 1914, Micheline, the lovely young French teacher at Mary's school who had befriended Gibran and who had visited him many times in Paris, was married to Lamar Hardy, a New York City attorney. It is difficult to discuss with any certainty the relationship between Gibran and Micheline. He painted her several times, and one biographer claims that Gibran had had an affair with Micheline, but this has been impossible to verify.

Miss Haskell's School—Boston

Beloved Kahlil, 11/9/14

You are so many things to me these days, and my heart moves toward you in so many ways, that words are more than ever worse than silence—and yet silence is just pain until I remind myself of that wonderful thing within that makes silence not wholly silence, and absence not wholly absence.

And always, the moment I know I am going to see you, you begin to swarm in me, like bees in a hive—until I am filled and humming through and through with—with Kahlils, Kahlils, Kahlils.

I feel like a river—about to meet the sea.

Goodnight, goodnight, Kahlil—to the baby that is in you —and the planet—and the friend. I kiss your heart, that is the forge of Life—and the touch blesses me.

God bless you.—Love from Mary

[New York]
Sunday—Nov. 22, 1914

I feel much better today, beloved Mary, but I am not my real self yet. I am keeping very quiet so that tomorrow may find me fit for some work from a model whom I have engaged some days ago.

Mr. Montross' desire to open the exhibition on the 14th of next month is making things a little hard for me. I do not mind being ill once in a while—it rests one's soul a little—but when an exhibition is coming in three weeks, illness becomes bitter and ironical!

And all these good things to eat! And the wonderful instrument. How sweet you are Mary.

Love from Kahlil

[New York]
Beloved Mary,   Sunday—December 6, 1914

Everything must be ready by next Saturday morning! About seventy-five pictures, paintings and drawings must be *just so* in five days! And I shall have everything ready! I am already half dead. The thousand and one details that swim around my tired head are apt to drive one to the madhouse! Art is one thing and exhibiting is another!

Mr. Montross will send his men Saturday morning to take the pictures. They will be busy hanging them Saturday and Monday morning. Can you come on Saturday the 19th, or some day before?

Love from Kahlil

Miss Haskell's School
Beloved K.G.,   Boston   12/8/14

God will bless you and be with you—and the more tired
you are the more He is with you. You and your work have
had such wonderful things together—and this is for it a very
wonderful thing.—It will stand by you and help you through.

And for seventy-five of your things to be assembled in a
right setting—that is a New Day.—It puts a great trembling
in my heart. The wonder is, not that the labor is so great—
but that in three weeks you can have accomplished it. I
haven't ceased to feel, all the time, that you were *adding* to
your pictures, these past two weeks—I mean, painting addi-
tionally, even though the idea was staggering!

I wish I could do something for you, if it were only to
run an errand. I feel just as you felt when you knew I was
ill and you would have liked to bring me something to eat
or fetch me a handkerchief—I should so love to take some
details off your mind.

I will come later. It can be Thursday the 17th—for I've
no classes that day—or Saturday the 19th. Tell me which
it shall be—but don't think about that until next week. I do
not need more than a day's notice—and, indeed, I can do
without notice if it is for Saturday.

Mary

KG

[New York]
Beloved Mary,   Sunday, December 13, 1914

I have been addressing envelopes since early morning, and
the list before me is still long. Early tomorrow morning I
must help hang the pictures. In the afternoon there will be

a crowd. Everybody wants to know if I am to be there. Perhaps I shall have to be there for an hour or so. But I shall not go again! I have finished those pictures and I am finished with them. They belong to my past. My whole being is directed toward a fresh start. This exhibition is the end of a chapter.

I shall spend the coming week in sleep, deep sleep. I need it more than ever. And when you come next Saturday you will find me without the veil of sleeplessness and without burdens—save those of the future, for which you and I live. And shall we not spend next Sunday together as we always do?

Love from Kahlil

-◦≪ KG ≫◦-

[New York]
Wednesday, December 16, 1914

Listen, beloved Mary. The price I put on *Passion* or *The Great Solitude* is $2500. I thought that no one would pay such a high price for a picture painted by an artist who is unknown. But I have learned this morning that Mrs. Wilson wants the picture and is willing to pay the price.

Now, Mary, I have been thinking of this matter all day. We both like the picture and we both would like to keep it. For that reason, I asked Mr. Montross to give me a little time to think before he sends an answer to Mrs. Wilson.

Do you not feel that this picture is one of many other things which we must give up in order to move into larger fields? Do you not think that we should use whatever we have now as the means toward a greater and more lasting future? And do you not think that by saving the money which these pictures may bring I will be able in a few years to build a house in which we could show the larger and fuller expressions? These pictures are no longer a part of my life. Through them I have learned a good deal, and I shall learn more—I shall learn more by letting them go into the world, and by asking the world in return to help us in building that house which I love to see before I die.

Now, I must hear from you soon. It will be most convenient if you could send me a telegram as soon as you receive this. I know that you will tell just what you feel and think of this matter.

Love from Kahlil

--⟨ MH ⟩--

Miss Haskell's School

Beloved Kahlil,   Boston   Dec. 18, 1914

I too have thought much since your letter came yesterday morning—and always I conclude as I telegraphed—agreeing absolutely with you.

The uprising again and again of my life and desire for *The Great Solitude* made my greater love and desire for the thing growing in you clear and clearer—until at last my hanging on to the picture seems far away and long ago.

Of course, we must use it for the house and I'm glad we have the chance.

Mary

--⟨ MH ⟩--

[JOURNAL]

[Boston]
December 19, 1914

We talked about this master-passion for the great Reality. I told Kahlil how it had reached my consciousness and how

214

it seemed better than anything else, to follow it with him—even if following parted us by half a globe. He said it makes every specific thing a detail, as it is—and itself remains The Thing.

He asked me about Lesbianism. He says it is one thing he's never been able to understand. So I told him I thought it was based on the diffusion of sex in woman—through all her life—from dress to child-bearing and that a woman was determined into Lesbian oftenest probably by being sex-ripe and meeting no fit eligible man, but a congenial woman. I asked if he'd like to know my own experience with L. He said yes, and I told him. That with L. it was a very beautiful and illuminating experience for me, but I had never got repose out of being sexually caressed by her—though *she* got repose. I got only excitement—whereas simply *being* with Kahlil reposes me utterly. Now Lesbianism is so common as not to be strange.

Talking about work—"The one thing in work for me is to trust myself to be used—by Life, by Reality, by God.

We lay down with lights low, after dinner—my head on Kahlil's shoulder. Such a pulse! His heart beats *strongly*. He kept feeling, feeling the shoulder and back just past the arm —of my arm that was thrown across his breast.

I asked whether he'd get a fur coat. "They are too frightfully expensive. I can keep warm without," he said. But I think he needs one and ought to have it. I am warm for the first time, with mine.

"Do you find me dull?" he said. I said I felt as if great things had torn their way through him and carried off fragments of his flesh with their force and violence. "They have," he said.

Speaking of Lesbianism as a bit from the feast that a free sex life would be, he said he wonders whether *he* is a crumb instead of a feast.

[JOURNAL]

Sunday—December 20, 1914

Kahlil was telephoning when I got to 51 W. 10th this morning. He was animated from his phoning.

"All that I do I do because I can't help it. And all I can do is to trust to that and keep on. But, Mary, you mustn't worry about me."

"The real truth is," he said, "that I am chaotic inside. I have a notebook filled with things that came to me those days when I was doing the drawings—in these past weeks. My *Madman* is on my brain. The Syrian question is always with me. The exhibit is on—I have visions crowding in on me of new pictures. All these things are crowding and no one of them can get predominance yet. That is what wears on me and that is what wore during those three weeks—not overwork. I don't easily do more than one thing at a time. I asked you yesterday if you didn't find me dull." "I found you not emptied—but with things stirring round painfully," said I. "It was the confusion of too much," said Kahlil, "and it lasted until you started me off—on one definite line last night and I just turned to that."

This gave me a sidelight on the rest I've always seen him find in just being set talking, when he's tired!

I understood the truth of what he said. And I told him how the pathos of his possession by such floods had been with me yesterday in my lonely time at the exhibit and how I had hoped that if he exhibited again next season it would not be before March 1916. It should not be, he said—and it is his intention to get Montross to say definitely *now* that it shall be March. "Then I can go to Italy and work for the exhibit," he said.

"Well," said I, "I had three things to ask you and I'm ready to withdraw each of them if you don't agree. The first was not to plan for another exhibit before a year from March. That has settled itself. You have chosen March. The next was that you arrange for more comfort in living—either here or elsewhere. You ought not to have to look after bed or cleaning or bath or any such thing. Get a nice man, who can have things in shape and will keep your room and run your errands—and save your time." "And look after my laundry," put in Kahlil.

"But," said Kahlil, "you know I am not comfortable to have anybody in here. I had a woman come in twice a week to scrub the floor and make everything nice. But when the press came three weeks ago, I told her not to come anymore. I couldn't have anybody around. If I had a picture lying on the floor in a frame I couldn't have somebody moving it to clean up—things were in an awful mess.

"Then when it was all over I had a man come in and clean again. But I don't want him around either. I don't want anybody around."

But later in the day he said he was going to have a man come in to clean up. "And I may get another room," he said. "Perhaps I can even find one outside. I've always had to live where I worked, and vice versa and I'm used to it, and I have a peculiar sense that to do anything else would divide something in me."

He said, "I'm unwilling to spend money on luxury except for the mind and spirit. I don't like expensive food or expensive service or expensive clothes or expensive amusements. As I get older I may grow more particular. I may become a drinker, a *boulevardier*—who knows? But now I haven't time to bother about the taste and look of things. I take what is set before me."

"Money is to be spent for life—and for life only."

"I'd like to have two or three men nude around me here always and pay them well—twenty dollars a week apiece. For they'd help me in big canvases."

"I have got along ever since I came from Paris on twelve–fifteen hundred dollars a year, except for expenses for my work."

My second point then was agreed. He would be more comfortable—for the very sake of his work.

"My third request is," said I, "that you get a fur coat. I've been warm with mine for the first time in the north and I think the price of one is well saved in a day of a cold spared you—much less an attack of grippe."

"I *will* have a fur coat," he said. "Only it must be beautiful." "I didn't get a new overcoat this winter because I didn't have the money. Getting ready for this exhibit took money in a great many ways besides even the framing." "But apart from money, I haven't had time to buy an overcoat—now I shall. I can probably get one in Boston—there are two or three good fur places there." "You could probably make a better buy here," said I. "But it will be worth your while to pay twenty-five dollars more in Boston and save the time of the purchase when you get back to New York." "Yes."

He is coming to Boston for a vacation. It was a fine afternoon and Kahlil suggested we take a walk on the Avenue. We stepped out briskly—much as I walk alone, when walking, not especially looking—and kept right on, lock step—my elbow in his, though he never holds my arm except crossing the street. We often walk that way—just touching. We went up to the Park—to see the beautiful new fountain nearing completion by the Plaza Hotel. "That's one of the wonderful things about New York," said Kahlil. "Something is always springing up here—like this fountain for instance. The city's self is so real. I am always hearing and feeling it—that self."

"I haven't had such a walk for ten days," he said. And he kept warm, though I had to keep my collar up. By the Plaza it was cold in the wind—and his coat was open all the time. I felt his spring and vigor and saw his shining eyes and face.

We did not take the bus until we were back at the Library

and then at my suggestion—and inside, "We don't sit on the outside any more," he laughed.

From the bus we went to Gonfarone's and were at table by 5:30!

We saw a snake-looking tall man with small slender long hands serving his three comrades at a near table.

"Kahlil," said I, "will the Arabic papers copy the criticisms of your work from the American papers!" "Every word," he answered. "They are eager about this side of my work that they know nothing about. And they are eager to see what the Western mind thinks of me."

Then he laughed. "So far," he said, "I am an excellent draughtsman; I cannot draw at all; I am early Italian and modern French; I am obscure and childishly imitative; and I am a pupil of Rodin, of Davies, of Millet.—It is like saying, 'This is icy cold—it is a coal of fire; it feels woolly—it's hard as iron—it sings like wood when you hit it.' " "Is it thus about your writing, too?" said I. "Oh, yes!"

"Look at the sky, Mary," he said on the Avenue, "how beautiful it is there." He doesn't often comment on it. But this walk refreshed him and he enjoyed it with every sense, from the moment in the studio when he said suddenly, "Mary! It is a beautiful day! How should you like a walk?"—to our early arrival at Gonfarone's. "Do you see the moon there, with that star? That's what the Turks took their flag from. When they captured Constantinople the star was very near the moon. They took it as a good omen."

The exhibit is an immense stimulus to him. It closes all he has done and pushes him right on to another. He showed me his palette—thick crusted—"I didn't have time to clean it. It ought all to be like this (the smooth part next the thumb) —and it usually *is* so, every night. But those three weeks I stopped for nothing.

"I mended it (rivets at back) several times. And all these pictures have come out of it.—Yes, of course you may have it. I'll keep it here for you," and he put it behind the big curtain.

At the table I asked Kahlil whether he liked the ten pounds I'd put on—that he'd recommended in September. He said he didn't see them—I'd still do well for more. I said I didn't want more—more would be against my self-respect. I'd feel heavy.

In the studio again I showed him my calf and pressed my skirt against the upper leg so he'd see it. "Is that thin?" "I'm astonished," said Kahlil, "I never saw your leg and I judged it by your arm—as one naturally does."

"I'm just as well covered all over," said I. I asked if he'd look at me and see for himself. "If this room weren't cold," he said, "I'd ask you to let me." We warmed the room and I undressed. "But you are so much more developed from here down (about the thigh) than around the shoulders," said Kahlil. "You are so strongly made and beautifully proportioned. No, you are just exactly right." But it moved him to see me undressed. "Women of your type move men. Men are afraid to see you. They can't help being moved." So I dressed again. For we don't want the sex complication. But Kahlil put his arms round my neck and kissed me on the breasts, as we stood. I felt that touch all night and for three days after.

When I had seen Kahlil was moved—when he said it—I feared he would have such suffering as I've seen before. But we came through all right. We were both surprised at his being affected.

I had not realized before that Kahlil had never seen me. I've undressed to change my clothes in his room. And I've seen him. But I was so glad he did see me now. It was strange—to have stood for Davies, and remain unknown to the eyes of Kahlil.

I have ceased now to expect other than growing nearness, even though I can see no further nearness unattained. And this too brought us nearer. Every sex-stirring does. That is one thing that makes me so long for freedom for us both. Yet in our abstaining too we come nearer.

It seems to me that if I were ninety and he eighty, I should still long for the touch of his body. I should live just to have it next to mine.

At dinner we saw a woman with a bird of paradise in her hat and a meat axe in her look.

❧ MH ❧

[JOURNAL]

Sunday—December 27, 1914—Boston

Kahlil came in at 8. He arrived yesterday afternoon—went to dinner with Mary, and then to the room I had found for him at 9 Newbury Street, Miss de Wolfe's.

"How cold it is," he said. He was wearing my brown sweatercoat that I had left there for him last night—but he was contracted with cold.

"How good this is!" as he came into the room, to the fire and then, "Do you know, I haven't been here for years."

He looked pale still, and thin, and older.

He walked straight up to my desk and looked at *The Three Sisters* above it; shook his head and said, "Bad painting. Hard."

Noted my print of da Vinci's Christ-head. "Glorious. This is just the size of the original."

We sat on the couch. Part of the time he lay down, at my request, and I sat by him. I felt his mind working, working, but he said nothing.

[Boston]
December 28, 1914

I wrote K. that I would call him between 11 and 12 to see whether he would look for a fur coat that day.

In the afternoon we went to Copley Hall.

I had said when we parted in the morning that I might look at fur coats. "I want to get this exhibit matter off my mind before other things," said Kahlil. Again I felt how his mind must not be switched off by another, but dwells on the matter in hand in its own unique way and how peace lies for him only in being allowed to do it his own way.

As we walked from Art Club to Guild in the afternoon, he said, "Is there something on your mind, Mary? You seem as if there were something in the back of your head you were trying to solve." As a matter of fact, I had been heavily clouded ever since he left the night before—with sadness at the constant restraint in touch of him and demonstration. For I can't but avoid moving him, since I have known his suffering when it goes too far. And I felt chilled and barren and sad. I seemed to be missing so much! I didn't feel at peace or rest, as I usually do. But I had been absolutely unconscious that I was troubled. So for the moment I was put to it to find what could have made me seem preoccupied. Then I said, "Some days I find it harder than others, to live by what I know. And today I find it hard." I wanted to tell him the truth but I didn't want to intrude that old detail on his struggling mind. I didn't feel ready to discuss it by myself—and the very facing of the fact that I was blue made me inky-blue. Kahlil said nothing, nor I anything further about that.

[Boston]
Tuesday—December 29, 1914

K. came by tonight and through the ice slush of the mid-street for the sidewalks were ice—but no overshoes. Says he never bought a pair in his life—feet perfectly dry because shoes are sound.

"Now tell me about yesterday, will you?" he said. "You left it just as it was—and I thought about it a great deal after we parted."

So I told him how the lack of freedom kept raising protest in me; how the other night in New York every sex-stirring made me feel more what I missed; how I had thought of saying—let us be free and had finally settled it again in my mind.

"It's not settled," he said. "It never will be. Its nature is crooked. We are simply accepting a crooked thing because that is the best we can do. But nothing is settled that is not real and our lack of freedom is against reality. We've called it settled but to me it has never been." He went on, "You haven't faced this simply enough yet: We want intercourse." "We can't have it because the risk is too great," I finished his sentence. He said, "We've always been saying it in many more words."

"No," said I, "I've said it just that way ever so many times but it hurts so much to lack freedom. My temporary desire has obscured my solider knowledge—only I have to make my decision about it again and again. It doesn't stay put."

"You were going to say tonight, 'Let us have intercourse.'" said Kahlil.

"No," said I. "That wasn't what I finally said—or meant to say. I shall always end not saying it, but I may have to fight again and again. Didn't I stand solid the other night? I knew your permanent mind was not for intercourse and I stuck by it."

223

"Yes," he said, "I cried after you with everything in me that night. Mary, my sex feeling is stronger than it was a year ago. We miss something real. We are both sound and normal, you so vital to receive and I to give that the unnaturalness of all this is all the greater. But how can you speak or think lightly of accident? Think what it would be if anything happened to *you*. Think of any doctor you would go to. He might not speak insult, but his mind would put insult on you. The real thing that is between us would not be killed —it just Is, and just as it is not made by anything we know, so it can only end by its own law too, which we do not know. An accident would end so much for us. I tell you truly, I would leave this country and never come back again. The consequences are unthinkable if misfortune came. If I were merely in love, perhaps I could take it lightly and accept risk and forget it. But it isn't that way with us. Love—the greater love—is extremely careful about intercourse and is bodily shy. You know that.

"This thing tonight will stay with me ten days. I don't finish with things that way, when they are fundamental. And this is fundamental—as sex is in all life."

He was not blaming me. I had asked him earlier whether he realized I was not asking for intercourse. "Yes, yes," he cried, most earnestly, "don't think I misunderstand you."

The clouds were on him, and I was cold with chagrin for having plunged him again into that chaos.

"I simply decided," he said, somewhere in the course of saying the matter had never been settled, "that you and I wouldn't talk about it any more because we couldn't have freedom."

He kissed me. And many times in the course of our talking he kissed me or gave me a caress.

At the door he kissed me as if he were blessing me and touched me so with his hands. Then his eyes closed a moment and when he opened them he said, with a face that said even far more than his words, "Our difficulty is a little thing. We have a very great reality and this is only temporary." As he said this, he looked at me. I was gray and lined and old-looking.

[JOURNAL]

Thursday—December 31, 1914   Boston

At 8:30 K. came in half out of breath. Soon we were free just to sit down and I got him to take off his collar. He lay down and put out his arm for me to lie at his side with my head on his shoulder. I knew that he had been thinking about the night before last and I lay awhile silent, with my arm about him under his coat. He only asked me if I were warm and when I said, "Yes, I am sitting at the stove," laughed and said, "Am I your stove?"

I told Kahlil how a leak came in our hot water heating the other night—how the cast iron elbow that a train could not roll over nor injure was split by two tablespoonsful of water in it turning to ice. And how I wondered how many other changings had that invincibility and power; and whether it was analogous power in the death moment that makes the cheapest face majestic.

Kahlil said he had often wondered about that transfiguration. He thought perhaps it was the soul's perception at the moment of death, leaving a shadow of its consciousness.

"That is what I want to get into my pictures," he said, "that large quiet—that peace of Earth. You have stood on a mountain top, Mary, and seen the hills and distant valleys and you felt the majesty of them and of the whole. That is what the faces of the dead have.

"And I've seen beautiful gardens, large, well laid out, with not a spot unbeautiful, full of flowers and well arranged walks, with trees and lawns—and they are like many fine living faces."

I put my hand all over his beautiful face, as over flowers, and he stopped it on his lips, as he always does.

Kahlil must have decided to feed my hunger for his touch. Just in the ways youths put arms round one another's neck, his hand was always resting on me or moving up and down upon me—and sometimes he kissed me—on neck or hand or eyes. And then he kissed me on the mouth, with passion. And he was stirred and grew pale.

Beloved Mary,

These slippers are beautiful and I like them very much. I never thought that such light, delicate things were made for me. But they are too small. Size 7 is nearer to that of my foot than 5.

I would love to give $25.00 toward changing the colour of the Art Club Gallery. Mr. Page said that they are going to do it anyhow. Perhaps they may not like my offering the money. Could you find out. They have been so wonderful to us that we should take care not to hurt them. The offer may hurt their pride!

Yes, Mary, we shall have a fine exhibition in Boston.

Love from Kahlil

Saturday
Jan. 2, 1915
9 Newbury St., Boston

[New York]

Beloved Mary,   Monday, Jan. 11, 1915

I am sending you this poem to Ryder, to read and to correct its English. He is the one painter whom I honour with all my heart—and there is no other way by which I can show my love and respect. If you like the poem, I will publish it separately on Japanese paper and send it to him. It may warm his old and weary heart.

A strange thing happened last Sunday. Percy Grant* spoke of the pictures from the pulpit. I was told that he said many remarkable things about them and about me—though he knows me slightly.

The slippers are here. They are light and comfortable. I think they are too good for me.

Love from Kahlil

Miss Haskell's School
Boston   1/18/15

I was sorry, after I had answered your Ryder letter I had not copied the poem for myself—for I love it and I miss it. You will send me those two sheets again, won't you—whether you change the poem or whether you do not.

They came so like a wider, more beautiful air to breathe—to me—a reminder from my greatness to my smallness.

And now I want to know how things are with you.

When I come back again to New York, I want to bring

---

* Grant, an American Protestant Episcopal clergyman, was pastor of the Church of the Ascension in New York City.

something back with me—and perhaps *Rose Sleeves* to stay
here instead of there, if it is not shown to people—because
it is very lovely for here.

Love to you from,
Mary

—❦{ KG }❦—

Beloved Mary,

   I have been asleep during the past three weeks. I have
thought of a thousand things which I must do this year. I fear,
Mary, that I shall never be able to realize my dreams fully.
I always fall short. I always get a shadow of a shadow of the
thing I want.

   It used to give me pleasure to hear people praising my work
—but now I am strangely saddened by praise, because praise
reminds me of things not yet done—and somehow I want to
be loved for what I have not done yet. I know that this sounds
rather childish, but how can one help wanting what one
wants? Last night I said to myself, "The physical consciousness of a plant in midwinter is not directed towards the past
summer but toward the coming spring. The physical memory
of a plant is not that of days that are *no more* but of days that
will be. If plants are certain of a coming spring, through which
they will come out of themselves, why cannot I, a human
plant, be certain of a spring to come, in which I will be able
to fulfill myself?"

   Perhaps our spring is not in this life, Mary. This life may
be nothing but a winter.

K

Miss Haskell's School
Boston   2/2/15

I had been wondering about you for three weeks—for when the air turns silent, I don't speculate about what is happening. I just know big things are at work—and I wait.

I am always with your coming self, Kahlil. To what you say of loving what is not yet realized, my whole being says Yes. The future of each thing is like the plan of a building; the part built so far is the past—and the present is the bricks now being laid. Is it chiefly the bricks that we love when we say we love the building? Life is a never-finished building.

What-To-Love is a fundamental human problem. And if we have this solution—Love what may Be—we see that this is the way Reality loves—and that there is no other loving that lasts or understands.

It is the Future I love in these things of yours hanging here.

But you know, Kahlil, it is the Future, that unlimited something—in a picture of anything, that makes it beautiful. There is nothing static in loving what one has done that is beautiful.

And it is only for just now that the pictures lose meaning for yourself. Years will restore their meaning to you.

As of pictures, so of you—and of each of us.

I think so often about bulbs: how they must suffer, so long thrusting their white flesh through the snow hard-packed crystals of the soil, in the dark—and what it must be to them, what they become at last.

And as I find most things that are in me also in the structure of life, I believe all Dreams are in that structure too. Not only shall you fulfill yourself as you now dream—but the fulfillment shall be dream far past your dream. God has dreams for you; you shall fulfill those.

But they are so far beyond any pictures you shall paint,

Kahlil! The pictures—and all your work—are food your soul eats. They are for you—not you for them.

High in the mountains summer goes mad: she takes but a few weeks and she brings forth and ripens, all in those few weeks.

You have mountain-summers—you bring forth winters between your summers. The pause is just as precious as the active time. Indeed, I cannot like the word "pause": what has happened is but a transfer of activity to a more inner field. The greater Kahlil has you perhaps more to himself then: at least it is no unhappy period for the whole you.

You used to care much for praise, K.G., because it was reassuring about your yet unproved self. I did not understand, in those days, that real worth is praise for one who must read himself in a thousand eyes besides his own. I knew nothing about the light that comes from other people's reaction to us.

Have you noticed how long a little child lingers with its food—and how youth contemplates and recontemplates all detail? When my girls go to the play, they tell afterwards every least thing He did and said and how He looked and laughed. You used to contemplate your work as fondly as that.

You no longer recontemplate your work done—and when people press you with it, it is somewhat like emphasis of old on your hair and eyelashes. It leaves you lonely, undiscovered. It is You that needs to be echoed and reflected from the others.

And so big a Future is within you, that towards it again in you, as in earlier years, is vagueness and question about yourself. The bulb is in the dark because it is making a New Self. Again you crave reassurance, light. It is a bitter time. And I do not know what its flower will be—or whether in this life or another. But I know its greatness. If it is not picture or poem, it will be a new creation beyond these.

I know *You* are preparing now—in this very interruption

to all that is wanted and wished for. That is the dearness and the glory of this baffled time. The stars are defeated because the sun is coming. And I find myself always on the horizon towards your sun.

Mary

----- ⸱⸱⸡*KG*⸲⸱⸱ -----

Beloved Mary,

[New York]
Tuesday—Feb. 9, 1915

You not only understand my silences and my formless days but you also become one with them in spirit. My silent days are your silent days. How utterly impossible it is for me to do anything without you—and how absolutely necessary your spirit is to my daily life.

The other cold day, I found Ryder in a half heated room in one of the most poor houses on 16th Street. He lives the life of Diogenes, a life so wretched and unclean that it is hard for me to describe. But it is the only life he wants. He has all the money he needs, but he does not think of that. He is no longer on this planet. He is beyond his own dreams.

And he read the poem. There were tears in his old eyes. Then he said, "It is a great poem. It is too much for me. I am not worthy of it. No, No, I am not worthy of it."

Then, after a long silence, he said, "I did not know that you are a poet as well as a painter. They did not tell me that you are a poet when I went to see your exhibition. I have been wanting to write a letter to the lady who wrote to me about your work. I wrote many letters to her but I burned them. One must wait for the spirit to move before one can write a letter."

He promised to sit for a drawing.

His head is wonderful—very much like that of Rodin—only it is unkempt.

Love from Kahlil

Miss Haskell's School

Beloved K.G., Boston 2/23/15

I have sat here hours and hours through the night, living a life with you that I could not translate into words or consciousness.

I could not write. Letters to you are periods in my life. I have never been able to write at will to you. Every word that reaches you has had a thousand impulses toward you ahead of it.

K.G., will you let me have a drawing—just to keep by my desk—now? I want one very much. Can't you send a drawing by mail safely and at not a great cost of time? You know, if I tell you with every voice in me—what that presence means to me even in thought. Even as I ask for it, and forms come before my eyes, my head swims. But with the real thing I shall be warmed and freed and companioned.

Love from
Mary

[New York]
Sunday 3/14/15

Spring is here, beloved Mary, and it is hard to stay in this studio. Every day I walk in the Park. I wander in lonely places

233

until night falls—and when the lights begin to peep through the naked branches, I return home.

Walking alone with a notebook is the greatest joy I can find in this city. I think my thoughts and I talk to you.

Life is *not* "a tale told by an idiot, full of sound and fury, signifying nothing" as Macbeth thought. Life is one long thought. But somehow I do not wish to think *it* together with other human beings. They pull one way with their minds and I pull the other way—and one can only stand *so much* mental pulling. Mary, one of the things that brought us so close to each other is that we both pull toward one point. And we do not fear so-called loneliness.

I have made two drawings of Ryder. One of them is not finished yet and I must go to him again. But, oh, Mary, how tired and weary he is. He told me the last time I saw him that he is painting pictures in his mind. He can use his hands no more.

Two of the long poems in *The Madman* were read at the Poetry Society of America. A long discussion followed. Some said they were "wonderful" and some said they were strange and incomprehensible. Mrs. Robinson, Theodore Roosevelt's sister, stood up and said, after "My Soul and I Went to the Great Sea to Bathe" was read, "This is destructive and diabolical stuff. We must not encourage such a spirit in our literature. It is contrary to all our forms of morality and true beauty."

Now, beloved Mary, I am going out to walk in the sunshine. The day is warm and clear. I shall take my notebook with me and I shall talk to you about things which I cannot very well write.

May God keep you, dearest.

Love from
Kahlil

234

[New York]
Beloved Mary,   Tuesday (3/16/15)

Did you transfer this money to me because it is more convenient—to have it in my name or did you wish to add to the large sums which you have already given me?

You know, Mary, that I have all the money I can use for years. You have freed me absolutely from any worldly care, and I feel quite sure that my future will be also free. I know that I need not fear want. So I would rather have this money in my name only for the sake of convenience. It must remain yours.

Here comes my model and I shall work on a large picture. It is one of the seven pictures which I have in mind. It may take me months to finish the series. Perhaps we shall call it "Toward the Gods."

Love and Love from
Kahlil

[J O U R N A L]

Saturday, April 10, 1915   New York

K. looked dark and pale—badly. He has had a pain lately about the heart.

We rode in the bus to the Museum. Every moment was joy.

We walked out and sat where the riders went by on the track above us, silhouettes vs. the sky—riding all so vilely! Presently I said I wondered sometimes if it were a lack in me that I get so little out of individuals—find them so uninteresting personally—keep on saying, "Nothing I want in him." "Nothing I want in her," over and over again—whether there was what I could not perceive or appreciate—since every human mechanism is in itself so marvelous. Kahlil said, "I've often thought, Mary, you look too little into yourself." "Why," he said, "with your vision of the days and nights, do you spend so much time and thought and interest on the vision of people so infinitely less than yourself? Why not study Mary Haskell's inner being—that is so much more than these people you've been with these few days?"

Kahlil had hit my sick spot—the tastelessness I so often feel in life because I'm away from him. And I've always felt he wanted me independent and not interested in things for his sake. But it dawned on me by degrees that we were now opening up, and all the unspoken, unfaced indifference I've felt at life unshared by him, and the pain of it—and the spasmodic efforts I've made to be more warm to Life for its own sake—filled me suddenly, and I couldn't talk—though I wanted to cry. I didn't want to have Kahlil think I grieved because we aren't married, or that I want to live with him—for I don't—because he doesn't want it. Yet I didn't know how to connect him at all with the matter and not give him exaggerated notions about my feelings. So I simply said he was right—he had touched an old wound in me. I knew it; and I told him I tried sometimes to care more and often succeeded —oftener now than before. He feared he had hurt me—I assured him No. And I let it wait until after dinner—lest I cry.

After supper we went through the typewritten *Madman* for retouching punctuation. And then I told Kahlil I was glad he had spoken to me in the afternoon about myself and that it helped me. And that he *couldn't* hurt me by anything he could say—since 1913 when I knew he loved me.

Then—perhaps through my saying I could have avoided all my pangs from 1910–1913 had I looked within in 1910 as I did at last in 1913—we got back into our old experiences of 1910–1913. And for three hours we each told at last what the other had not known, of things that had given pain.

Kahlil has always been gentle to me. I had only his difference from other men who'd loved me to explain all my torments—that he did not talk or write about love—or, indeed, write much at all. But he had to tell me my attitude, my words, my deeds, that had lacerated him.

And he had to tell me of himself. "When I came back from Paris, I gave my heart simply, frankly, wholly. I was just a boy putting all I was and all I had into your hands. And you met me coldly, quizzically." He told me things I had said—that I had done. And I saw myself as never before. I had flatly disbelieved him and handled his heart as if it were a brick. I understood at last what I had *been*—and how Kahlil had perceived it and how he had yet stood fast by me. Never but twice a protest—once when he told me I thrust him 7000 miles away—and again when he asked me on what terms I wanted our money matters to be between us. He did not speak now in detail of these—he simply said—"I was helpless. I wasn't brutal to you. I didn't know how to meet it when you were brutal. I kept on saying, 'Why? Why?' You were interested in my work—but I was bringing you my heart all the time. I'd work in that little room and then hurry to you with whatever I had—whether it was wet or dry—those two evenings a week—and you know I just waited the days between for those evenings to come." He told me how often he'd been physically sick with the anguish of his situation—and I had seen nothing, felt nothing.

I said to myself while he talked, "And you thought *you* were the loving and the unloved one, Mary!"—I felt, and feel, that I reaped then—and still reap—a full harvest of all the sloth and insensitiveness of spirit I ever indulged in myself, in being able to put Kahlil through such unjust suffering.

But it took me some time to reach this light! Kahlil and I together just reached the knowledge—he of me as well as I of him—that I had at least believed I loved him—and that he had really loved me. So much unguessed longing showed itself to each in the heart of the other—so much of what each had been aching to know *was* in the heart of the other—and so much weight and smart vanished in the very telling. We

237

stopped at 2 a.m. infinitely glad for having spoken. We opened the can of pineapple still left from my package of December to him and ate from it in a whirl of laughing—and I knew our talk had helped us.

But in me not yet an end. I lay that morning in confusion of being. Only at 10 did I see how I had buffeted Love, and taken Love's name in vain—and feel the real Boy who had come so frankly and lovingly, and what I had been to him.

I had hesitated about talking the night before because every time I've seen K.G. now for eighteen months, we have had some heartshaking talk or experience, and I've dreaded making our meetings too costly for us to have them.

In the following account Gibran once again speaks to Mary about his family. It is touching to see how he continued to lead Mary to think that he was well-born, that his father was a wealthy man, that his early years were completely different from what they actually were. And is sad because he and Mary were close in so many ways, yet Gibran either felt he could not trust her with the truth about his background or, perhaps, did not have the faith in himself necessary to acknowledge it as it had been and not as he wished it had been.

─────────────── MH ───────────────

[JOURNAL]

[New York]
4/11/15
(Sunday)

Kahlil had slept wonderfully, and looked better. The pain in his side had gone.

238

The little yellow settee was still before the window where we had sat through the storm until 2 last night and now we sat there again. "Last night," said I, "we both learned things about our early relationship that we had never known and found more misunderstanding on both sides than we had realized. It took each of us a long time to find the heart of the other." "Yes," said Kahlil. "Well," said I, "the origin of it all goes back to me. Instead of questioning your love, I ought to have seen that your very offering it was the sweetest, most loving thing possible from one human being to another. And when we found out the mistake about marriage, I ought to have realized at once that the mistake could have sprung only from love and was itself just love and tenderness, instead of feeling hurt as I did and making up my mind not to believe you again lest I be hurt again. And I realize now how hard and unloving I was."

"What hurt me so," said Kahlil, "was that you couldn't see *me*. You couldn't believe in me. You were interested in my work but a man's work isn't the man. There's a peculiar essence in any real person that is his reality. You stood off from the real me like an indifferent spectator. I had no core, to you."

"No," said I, "I thought I believed in all of you except as regarded myself—but I realize now I never conceived you as a whole at all. I just thought of you piecemeal."

"You couldn't believe in *me* and disbelieve in me toward yourself," said Kahlil. "You just didn't know me. I couldn't reconcile the things you said sometimes with what you usually were.

"You are tender. And you are generous and kind. I couldn't see how the hand that gave the gift could make it weigh so heavily. It was almost like a Dr. Jekyll and Mr. Hyde in you."

We talked through lunch, about those old misunderstandings. Kahlil said he thought our friends had made things harder for us, by the way they talked to each of us. Charlotte had told him she was trying to have Harry Lorber and me marry, and he had gathered that I knew her scheme and shared it; whereas I was now hearing it for the first time. And how Charlotte had kept saying to him, the night when we painted up, "Isn't she beautiful?" and Charlotte, coupling remarks with men's names in a way that implied, "See what a fine woman! I haven't quite decided who I shall give her to."

He made me see how he had thought I did not care for him and how he had withheld expressions of affection after he came to New York because he thought I didn't want them, and how he had been deeply unhappy and baffled.

We went to the Natural History Museum on 8th Avenue after lunch and had a wonderful afternoon—meterorites.— "Visitors from other worlds—nothing thrills me more," said Kahlil. "I'd rather have the tiniest piece of one than anything else I know."

"It is so wonderful to see things together," said I. "And that's what I mean when I speak of loneliness. It is seeing and hearing things, without you. I want you so much to be seeing them too. When I get a pretty dress I want you to see it. It is hard for it to seem worthwhile, just because you can't see it. I know I oughtn't to feel this way, and I try not to. But that is the sick spot in me you touched yesterday. And that's why I said it would disgust you." "It doesn't disgust me," said Kahlil, "but you must love all these beautiful things for themselves, Mary."

While we sat watching the ducks, Kahlil outlined the life of his family since their leaving Syria.

I asked whether his father and mother were still husband and wife in spirit when she was living and dying here and he was staying in Syria. "I don't know," said Kahlil. "One soul's knowledge of another soul is limited." "It seems so strange an end to their life," said I. "It was a tragedy," said Kahlil. "When we left Syria we waited for my father in Egypt. Then we went on to France and waited there, and then we were going to Belgium to wait. My father was delayed at first, because there came a chance to save a good deal of the property.

And then, he was held by the Turkish government. They did not imprison him but he had to remain at the seat of government.

"And then my brother thought he could succeed in this country and we came over. And he did succeed. Everybody loved him—he was courteous and sweet and upright and gentle. He established a fine business. Then came my mother's illness—cancer. Then my youngest sister, Sultana, died. I heard of her death in Paris—from the Turkish consul-general who was a friend. My brother got tuberculosis. When he died we found the business $24,000 in debt. I took as a partner the man we owed most to. We cleared the debts and closed up the business debt-free at last. Meantime my mother died, too. The three died all within nine months. When my sister Mary and I had settled everything, we had nothing. About $2000 owing to us—but it was in small sums—$50 here, $100 there—and we let it go. We took one or two rooms. I wrote a little for pay, and sold a few pictures $100, $150, $200 apiece. My sister was working and so we lived. Our father could probably have sent us money but we didn't like to ask. I wasn't on good terms with him.

"Our relatives would have given us money. Mihail Gibran came to see me in Paris. Mihail is big and free in mind and loves fine things and books and art. But I didn't want to accept any money from him. My father died while I was in Paris.

"While we had been poor in America, my father had been living with horses and servants. It was hard for him to break his habits. He just did as he had been accustomed to do. He was pretty discouraged and I'm glad he had that much to the end. The debts on the property were enormous. And all my things—my own, from my mother's father—not my father's —are there thrown into the general lump for the payment of my father's debts.

"On our mother's illness we spent $4000—on my sister Sultana we spent as much. My brother went to Cuba for three

...pent more than $7000. It was from doctor to ...d doctors brought from anywhere. There was $15,- ...n illness, you see—and my brother's absence lost the business $15,000.

"We were advised to bankrupt, but preferred to pay everything back. Many simple people had brought their money to my mother and begged her to put it into the business for them. These were paid first, in full and with interest. The richer ones—merchants—would gladly have taken 50 per cent. They had liked Peter and had made much through him. But we paid them all.

"I could have saved money while I was in college—but I could hardly blame myself for not having done it, unless I had been a prophet. I had money enough, for my mother and brother sent me money—and my father gave me money, too. I simply spent as any well-born boy naturally spends."

Kahlil thinks marriage is usually a failure.

"Why are unmarried women more interesting than married women? You see a woman glowing with life and growth at twenty-five and she marries a man who is alive and interesting, too. When you meet them five years later she is faded and dull—not physically, but as a being, as a life. Why is she less a life?"

We sat almost silent in the studio—on the little yellow seat by the window until it grew cold—and then on the couch. I even slept a little, with my head on his breast. He almost slept, too. But the silence was full of living things and words. I went at 11:30 and Kahlil said, "These have been two glorious days for me and this one has been the most wonderful." He followed me at an interval of three minutes—at my request, for my suitcase was so heavy I was unwilling for him, with his game arm, to carry it. I took the wrong turning for the car and, retracing my steps, saw him coming along. He did not see me, so I made the softest little call. But even the softest— it reached him. His head flashing round—such a lovely look and smile—and farewell when I said no to his offer again to carry my suitcase. I turned once more and saw him.

He is finding letters hard, as I do. So we are writing even less frequently. Yet we both want letters and need them.

Kahlil told about Ryder. He is 60–63 or 64, and seems 80–90. Kahlil says Ryder used to be a beautiful creature and rather a dandy; used to wear white a great deal, and was a conspicuous figure on Fifth Avenue. But he loved a woman whom his friends thought not worthy of him, and they planned to part him from her. They got him to go abroad and when he came back she had disappeared. Ryder was never himself again. "Probably he hasn't bathed since," said Kahlil. He has two rooms, one on 14th and one on 16th Street—but he received Kahlil in the room of an old English lady of 80— because his own room was too cold. He sleeps at 16th Street on three chairs with old clothes on them. Of money he has quite enough, but seems lost to comforts. "He made me ashamed of being clean." He is so gentle, so courteous—"May I take it for you?" he said, when he saw my portfolio, though he uses his hands with such difficulty. He has no will of his own."

When Kahlil had finished drawing him, he looked at the picture carefully. "It was a great revelation to me—such looking—as if he were looking—as he was—to see what life was in it. Then he said, 'Wonderful work. You've drawn what's inside me—the bones and the brain.' "

Kahlil told me how he got one of his sittings from Ryder. "I don't try to make appointments with him because an appointment keeps him anxious for days beforehand. I just start when I am ready to try for him and take my chances. This day I put my portfolio under my arm and started for Ryder's —near 16th Street. I saw him walking along very slowly— he takes steps about two inches long. He went into a restaurant and ordered lunch. I waited outside for him. He ordered corned beef and cabbage, and ate very slowly. It took him till quarter past four to eat, his hands are so feeble. I waited until he was through; then he came out. And he said, 'O, Mr. Gibran, I saw you through the window. Have you been waiting all this time for me?' I said I had and I walked along with him. In a step or two we passed by a saloon and he said, 'Will you have a drink?' I said No, but that I'd be glad to wait for him in his studio. He went in and took one. He went into two on his way home. When we passed a bar on the street, he said, 'Will you have a drink?' And usually has taken one while I waited. He probably feels the need of the stimulant."

----- ❦ *KG* ❦ -----

Beloved Mary,   Sunday, (April 18, 1915)

Yes, Mary, those two days, Saturday and Sunday, were very wonderful. In speaking about the past, we always make the present and the future more clear and solid. For a long time I had a black fear of unveiling the past; a fear caused by my lack of directness and frankness. How infinitely better it would have been if I had had the courage to speak of pain. I suffered in silence—and silence sometimes is apt to make suffering deeper—because silence itself is deep. It is more comfortable for most people not to speak; as a rule they make a mess of things when they think aloud. But with us it is just the other way. Talking brings us nearer and nearer by brushing away the dusty corners of our beings. The only silence which we both love is that which understanding creates. Other silences are cruel.

May God bless you, beloved Mary, May God keep you and me.

Love from Kahlil

244

Miss Haskell's School
Boston
Beloved Kahlil,   Sunday, April 18, 1915

All week the past has been opening before me and I have remembered more of what I did and said—the outrages and the unkindnesses.

And I so feel that I did not believe the few loving things you said, or hear the many you did not say; and how far from simply and tenderly I loved you. And I know somewhat how I hurt you and what I threw away from myself and kept away from both of us.

Seeing these things, I feared I had harmed that which is between us, and had made it forever less than it might have been. That would be the hardest punishment I could have, for all eternity.

I asked our Greater Selves if it were so—for a while I heard nothing. Then I saw with my eyes a mountain through the mists and I knew my fault had been not from the heart but because I was not yet at the heart.

Our Life, yours and mine together, is the life of our Greater Hearts; and I do not affect it; but it by degrees affects me and will confirm me in time to itself, as it has already confirmed you.

But I am sorry for all I spoiled, and for every pain I gave you—and sorry that sorrow cannot undo what I did.

Beloved Kahlil—it seems not as if I had been writing to you —but writing with you. And the days are so swift—because they do not seem away from you. Do you know how I've often told you that in the Sierras we are never out of the sound of rushing water? So I am never out of the feeling of you in me. Bless you.

And God bless you—and bless us both. Love to you, my beloved Kahlil.—Love and love from

Mary

245

Beloved Kahlil,   May 21, 1915

You do not seem "absent" to me. On Sunday night, deep in the small hours, it seemed hardly possible that it was not the actual You I felt and spoke to, and not the studio about us.

If you cannot come now, I can still see you. For I take the Sunday midnight train to New York and my Savannah train leaves New York at 3:30 p.m. on Monday.

These days are full of individuals. I feel sore from the aches and darkness of mind that have been confessed to me within a week; and faces have made me shut my eyes—there is too much to look at. This is new to me. It has come, I think, through three years of you, God bless you—God bless you always, My dear One.

Love—Mary

[New York]
Sunday   5/23/15

I can tell you, beloved Mary, how much it gladdens my heart to hear you speak of your work as you did in your last letters. I have often wanted to speak of your work as a form of Life creating Life; but somehow I did not allow myself. I thought you do not wish me to. And now that it came from you I feel that a great thing is accomplished. When we meet we shall surely speak fully of it—not as something new, but as an old thing newly realized. I have always thought, Mary, that a Revelation is simply the discovery of an element in us, in our larger self, the self that knows what we do not know, and feels that which it does not feel. And what we call growth is nothing but knowledge of that larger self.

God bless you, beloved Mary,

Love from Kahlil

[JOURNAL]

Wednesday, June 30, 1915   New York

"Well," he said with his flashing smile when he opened the door—that smile is like the bursting of a flame. It leaps from his eyes and lifts his forehead and plays like summer lightning all about his head and even in his body.

"I have a little more done on the Prologue of *The Earth Gods.*"

We set right to work—and ended the new paragraph of the Prologue at 4:15. "Isn't it always so?" said Kahlil. "The time flies from us so fast."

A boy came with the black chairs. Kahlil has had them re-covered with the gray velvet like his curtains and he sent off the yellow sofa now for like treatment and mending. The woman keeps his brasses clean and all very nice—his floor is redone at intervals—he is a most cleanly housekeeper. A little mahogany chest he has bought—"You know I don't like mahogany. But it's about the only nice thing one can get cheap" —and the purple piece he has nailed above it makes it all right. And he got for $1.00 in Boston, three lovely little plain red lacquer bowls—out on a red strip on his table. *Pretty!*

When we went out of the studio, Kahlil kissed me on the mouth and I kissed him on temples and neck. His neck is so strong—feels powerful under my lips and today I said so. "Yes," said Kahlil, "my neck is strong, and my hands, my shoulders aren't because of the accident I had.

"When I was ten or eleven years old, I was in a monastery one day with another boy—a cousin, a little older. We were walking along a high place that fell off more than a thousand feet. The path had a hand rail, but it had weakened and path and rail and all fell with us, and we rolled probably one hundred fifty yards in the landslide. My cousin fractured his leg, and I got several wounds and cuts in the head down to the skull; and injured my shoulder. The shoulder healed crooked —too high, and too far forward. So they pulled it apart again and strapped me to a cross with thirty yards of strap [he showed five or six inches wide] and I stayed strapped to that cross forty days. I slept and all, sitting up. I was not strong enough to take ether when they broke the shoulder again. If it had hurt less, I should probably have cried out. But it hurt too much for me to cry. My father and my mother were with me."

"I wish we could wear white," he said on the street. "All I'd need would be two suits—for I live so much in old things in my studio and I could wear a white suit when I dressed for more than a week. But it is so conspicuous. Everybody would look at one—and I want above all not to be looked at."

I was commending the parlor car to Kahlil from New York to Boston—for its solitude—to make six worthwhile hours.

"They could be such creative hours for me," he said. "But I can't escape people. Last time, a minister and his wife talked all the way. And it doesn't end there. Almost always they ask my address. I try now not to give my address. This minister and his wife, as soon as they heard I painted, said, 'O, you are the Syrian artist!' Because the exhibition was a great deal talked about. I've never found any way not to be talked to. Everywhere I go people begin and I don't know how to avoid it."

We took the surface car to the Mortens' street and then parted. Kahlil took my hand and said again, "Mary, I hope you are going to have a glorious summer and I know you will." His smile was so loving—but all the forecast of pain as before was in his face—like a vision of *his* summer—and his face was *white*. Though he looks better today, all that suffering is underneath his face and every now and then it comes through like a searing iron, and withers skin and features. His hand, when I came in today, was not warm—that is always warm. I turned back afterward and saw him. I waved.

--------------------------------- ⋅⊰ *MH* ⊱⋅ ---------------------------------

[California]
Wednesday—July 7, 1915

Beloved Kahlil—sweetest friend, Blessed One—

Morning began in the sky, all crowded and shining with scattering storm. I looked out and saw you—"Kahlil's day," I said—and it was yours into black night. The time between dawn and dark could not be counted—yet it seemed not a few moments. Each moment a saying of God, "Thus I am," and again, "Thus I am."

Sometimes far across an endless earth I saw snowy mountain tops entering the tender skies as tenderly as a breath—and then we mounted to the dark plateaus with their level horizons and the chasms carved unfathomably below them. Then heaven and earth were swept away, and a shadow was scooped beneath us, and we ran with the clouds like stars through the blue void; and when heaven and earth came back, they were deep and sparkling like God's eye—the heavens were the hollow of His eye and the earth His eyeball.

Sometimes we saw just simple wilderness, cloud-banked—sometimes it was fierce and pinnacled, and big eagles flew about the tops. Once a great plain, filmy like mist, spread round us to the mountain on the edge of the world—and asleep upon it, like a dream-flower, lay a single purple hill. Sometimes the emptiness and silence was like a mighty grave and the grave of many pasts terribly ended—and you felt that

God had emptied these places and that the full ones he had filled.

The sun sowed light like seed, and the earth drank it like rain. Stem and seed, plume, and leaf-blade, and flower were myriads on a vessel of light. The whole surface of the globe flashed and roughened and smoothed again.

The air came into you like pure space. I envied my lungs for your dear lungs' sake—my eyes for your dear eyes' sake—my heart for your refreshing. For your dearest things would have come flying into your windows like doves—given, just given—you need not bleed for them. Yourself need but simply receive not only from the Invisible—but with every cell of your body from every cell of the body of earth and heaven. There is nothing to fly from to yourself or to God—for only God and yourself are there. There is no seeking—God puts His hand on your face, and while your soul melts at His touch He turns your face to His face.

I was so full this morning of the sense of how clear God is when there are no trees—or clothes to hide earth and sky—and how much more delicately glorious earth is than anything that grows upon her. And I was thinking of what psycho-analysts call a "complex," meaning a hidden influence that colors all a life (unknown to that life they say). About four days ago I realized that perhaps God had a complex, His hidden love, too, that He fuses all His life with, but tells us nothing of, and that glorifies Him as none glorifies me. And I thought of earth, free out here to the sun—and suddenly earth became living like flesh to me—real—divine—beloved—free in deserts only, where she is but with the sun and brings nothing forth; elsewhere, a mother, perforce, because that is the way things are; and we, her children, as horses and birds and weeds are her children, biting her breasts and marring her fairness, and wearying her—and dear to her. But the terrible, glorious, ravishing reality was not her motherhood—I don't even know that so clearly—but her self—and something else—that she loves.—Then the lines came to me from your

Prologue—of when the Gods gave the earth in marriage to the sun—I felt as if I knew the marriage now—and that maybe earth keeps man out of the deserts on purpose.

God bless you—Beloved—great soul—precious Kahlil.— God bless you and keep you.—Love from

Mary

K.G. dear—get a blue serge suit if you see a nice one; I love dark blue for you. And it wouldn't be much trouble, yet it might save your dear hair for you to put kerosene oil (save the mark!) on your scalp overnight. It evaporates, and it kills any hostile germ—and even feeds a bit at the same time. Five cents worth at a grocers and just put it on with a single motion— 1 minute!

⸙ KG ⸙

[New York]

Beloved Mary,   July 17, 1915

You and I and all those who are born with a hunger for Life, are not trying to touch the outer edges of other worlds by deep thinking and deeper feeling—our sole desire is to discover *this* world and to become one with *its* spirit. And the Spirit of this world, though ever changing and ever growing, is the Absolute.

The saints and the sages of the past ages were seldom in the presence of the God of this world, because they never gave themselves to life but simply gazed at it. The great poets of the past were always one with Life. They did not seek a point in it nor did they wish to find its secrets. They simply allowed their souls to be governed, moved, played upon by it. The wise man and the good man are always seeking safety— sometimes they find it—but safety is an end and Life is endless. The past seeks nothing. His Kingdom of heaven is not

251

a Nirvana. His one desire is to become a flute or an arrow or a cup. And by becoming one of these he suddenly finds himself standing in presence of God. He becomes one of the discoverers of this world. And he discovers it not only for himself but also for those who possess a natural willingness to listen to him.

Your last letter, Mary, is the most wonderful I have received. It is an expression of that sacred desire to find this world and to behold it naked; and that is the soul of the poetry of Life. Poets are not merely those who write poetry, but those whose hearts are full of the spirit of life.

These are warm days in this city. I go out every day to the park or to the woods. But I am not working much. Somehow one's dreams are not so active during summer, yet dreams and thoughts grow fast and well.

Love from Kahlil

--❦ *MH* ❧--

[mid- or late July 1915]
Wenatchee, Wash.

Beloved Kahlil,

I have heard for the first time things you have been saying to me for nearly five years. Kahlil, I have done you all the wrong I could do. You took me to the tenderest centre of your heart and it was from there that I gave you every blow and every wound.

Never have I let you be yourself. I said I wanted you to be free with me. But if ever you were, I hit you. With you I was like one in a room in the dark, who knocks everything down. But this room *was* You, and the things were the most sensitive things of the soul.

You could save yourself only by shutting the door. But you did not save yourself; the blind stumbler himself falls at last upon the door also, and himself shuts it.

I have hurt you and crippled you at the very core; in health, in work, in relations with other people—in the spring of life, the core itself.

I said to you, Kahlil, how precious it was to be near you—and so, that I should never have to look back and feel, "when I had it, I did not know how beautiful it was," and that I had been conscious, both how beautiful it was, and that I knew its beauty. This I believed. But it was not true. I did not know I was near you—nor what it was to be near you—nor You. What matters most to know, I did not know.

You were always ready to be rested and refreshed and born anew, with me—and I never let you be. My soul treated you like an inferior—and did not even rise, to do you honor.

I have been in one long, continued sin against you, Kahlil. What I want, is to confess to you with my Soul the utmost wrong, through all these nearly five years—wrong which you have known and suffered all this time.

Mary

[New York]
August 2, 1915

All is well now, beloved Mary, all is well, and though it is hard to divorce ourselves absolutely from the past, we should not dwell in it. You and I are able to look upon yesterday as one might look upon the sad face of his mother who bore him in pain and in pain gave him birth.

Indeed we have had five long years of great pain. But those years are extremely creative. We grew through them and though we came out covered with deep wounds, we came out with stronger and simpler souls. Yes, simpler souls, and that to me is a great thing. All the tragic processes in human life, and this war is one of them, are working towards the

253

simplification of the human soul. I feel that God is the simplest of all powers.

And you know, Mary, that each and every human relation is divided into seasons of thoughts and feelings and conduct. The past five years were a season in our friendship. Now we are at the beginning of a new season, a season less cloudy and perhaps more creative and more eager to simplify us.

And who can say, "This season is good and that season is bad?" All seasons are natural to life. Death itself is part of life. Though I have died many times during the past five years, the marks of death are not upon me and my heart is without bitterness.

Kahlil

❦ KG ❧

[New York]
Friday—Aug. 6, 1915

Beloved Mary,

I am going to Boston next week. I shall stay there until you come.

These days with me are quite silent. I have not written a word of English since you left and the little Arabic I have written is strange and painful.

Ryder is very ill in a hospital. He is feeble, both physically and mentally. But I love to sit near him, and I enjoy talking to him.

A thousand thanks for the picture-book. Let us talk about it when we meet.

May God bless you.

Love from Kahlil

Little Yosemite Canyon, Cal.

Beloved Kahlil, August 6, 1915

Your letter of July 17 holds a whole life. It is a door to me by day and by night.

This year I am high in our canyon—for when I began again in my old rock-heap, all night creatures in the dry leaves worked about my head, and on the third day as I came into my bed place, a young rattlesnake was coming in too through the rocks opposite. He ran softly back—but I realized suddenly that I was in a snake-paradise—and I abandoned it.

Then I come up to meet the evening and the sky—to this great ledge, where all day the heat has been too fierce. Here is my new little bed of cedar boughs. On it I seem far up towards the rim of our mighty mountains. Their naked tops are golden now with the setting sun—and away across the Canyon the upper forests are shining in the gilded haze. Below, all is shadow.

Soon this shadow will turn utterest blue. Slowly it will rise, till forests and mountains and the edges of heaven are enveloped and floating dim in the trembling azure.

Then comes Night—long night. The stars and the Milky Way rise high and close behind my head—and set high and far beyond my feet. I see them many hours.

The hours, the days, the nights, are full of you. You are always leading me where alone I cannot come or enter. May God be with you, blessed and beloved Kahlil and Master—and fill you and bless you.

Mary

HOTEL DEL PORTAL

EL PORTAL

CALIFORNIA

Beloved Kahlil,   August 9, 1915

My desire, beloved Kahlil, is to discover you and to become one with your spirit. It is for this I am alone in the mountains and alone everywhere. Life is the Great Spirit, in your spirit, in my spirit, is still Life. There is one Life, with many doors. And it is Life itself that leads me through you as my door. All division from you has been for me division from Life— and all oneness with you, oneness with Life.

In the morning I sit with you under a great pine and great cedar that grow above the forest and a little below my bed— there the air moves lightly all the day. In the afternoon after my bath, when it is fresh down by the river, and the few struggling trees along its granite sides begin to cast scattering shadows, I stay down there with you beside the rushing waters. Sometimes a trout tries to leap up the long rapids, and falls back—a water ousel dips along the rocks on the opposite bank —and little dark lizards dart by, or stop on their hands to look —that is all.

Night and morning I see from my bed an eagle come home and fly forth, half way to the sky on the western mountain; and he makes my heart ache with you. And there are the same three bird-pairs we watched last summer—jays, flickers, hawks. Mice and squirrels are more, and fiercer—and I still hate their habits.

I must go down for food. And I'm hoping for a letter from you, beloved K.G., unless, and I pray God every day not, I have made you ill as I have before, adding to all the weights already on your heart.

Love from
Mary

Your letter is here. I have it. Bless you.

256

Cohasset, Mass.
Aug. 20, 1915

This place is very beautiful. It is between the deep woods and the deep sea. I take long walks among the green shadows of the trees. The clean air, the open spaces and the refreshing silences have renewed my spirit. After a few days in Boston I would like to come back here.

May God bless you always.

Love from Kahlil

[J O U R N A L]

Wednesday, August 25, 1915   Boston

Kahlil got to talking about his childhood. His father made many plans for him—unlike his mother, who "respected me. She left me to plan for myself. Her attitude was that if there were teaching between us, I would teach her, not she me. She believed in me. We were not just a mother and son. Father opposed my writing and painting. He wanted me to go to the Polytechnique in Paris."

After his father's death, relatives settled everything—and everything went except the actual house. That, heavily mortgaged and eating itself away with interest and taxes, stands. Several people have wanted to get it for Kahlil.

K. could not live at home because he was dependent on his father and father was absolutely out of sympathy with his work. "In Paris I learned from our consul, on whom I called, because he was our friend, of Sultana's death."

He came straight to Boston and was here while Peter and his mother died. Then he and Marianna were penniless—and from the father came nothing.

The Gibrans are a fair race, slight and tall. Six hundred years ago, two Gibran princes were crucified in Antioch. In the thirteenth or fourteenth century a Gibran went to France and Italy and tried to start another Crusade. Kahlil's father had gray-blue eyes and light hair. The mother's people were churchmen in large numbers and all the children looked like them.

Kahlil honors the Arabs, too, because their peninsula has produced three great births: the Chaldeans and Assyrians, the Hebrews, and Islam—and it remains unchanged—full still of that unconquered ripeness of life as simple as it was ages ago —as direct—between earth and the stars—and Kahlil believes another birth is coming from it.

"Shut your eyes," said K., "and imagine the nebulous first mist—see at last somewhere in the beginning." Then he went through its getting larger, hardening—heat developing, the bursting, the world and other planets coming off—the gradual evolution of inorganic, organic, soul and God.

I did shut my eyes most of the time. I had never done that before, listening to Kahlil—his face has always so held me. He was sitting in the low, straight arm-chair, and I at my desk. Sometimes I'd open my eyes, and see that beautiful face and meet his deepening eyes. It was his last evening here. Next day, I felt as if Christ had been sitting in that place as well as Kahlil —the two friends.

"I talk to you about my inner self," said Kahlil, "and always with the knowledge, that you will hear not what I say, but what I don't say."

To my delight, Kahlil liked the fur slippers I got him in San Francisco, and the wee basket the Philippine children made from Seattle and the little travelling double basket like mine.

[JOURNAL]

[Boston]
August 27, 1915

I learned still more about the wounds I've given Kahlil. It was the talking after the time Nattie and Adam* were here that hurt most. And it seems I used to speak of his personal appearance—I remember telling him his small size would keep him from being appreciated by a certain type of American woman (!!!)—so I know I must have said all he remembers and perhaps more. I even said something critical about his table manners. I don't know what. And his table manners—like all his manners—are the most beautiful I've ever known.

Miss Haskell's School
314 Marlborough Street, Boston
Beloved Kahlil,   Saturday, Sept. 11, 1915

I knew you were planning an evening with me—and freedom perhaps for another.

I had thought you would stay in Cohasset through next week, and the sight of your letter made me fearful at once about Ryder. It was a relief to read it was the Syrians who recalled you. But I'm so sorry you've had to go back already. Yesterday, in the terrible heat, I was glad all day that you were still among quiet woods.

And shall we not see each other after all, beloved K.G.? If you will let me, I will come to New York next Saturday, arriving at the Grand Central at 6:06 or 6:10—and go straight

* Mary's sister-in-law and brother.

259

to you—and we can have Saturday evening and Sunday. Say Yes, dear Heart—and all this week we shall be having so much together, too.

There is a whole little notebook filled, in my desk—that I must bring.

Love to you,
Mary

Last night on the Esplanade a tiny lovely child kept running here and there in circles all his lonely own, and singing—loud—with mouth and arms and hands wide open like a flower—strange intervals from his own heart. I heard him first from far off. I heard him far off again, when I was half way home. I listened for you too, who would have so loved it with me—the little sky-child.

——— ❧ *KG* ☙ ———

[New York]

Beloved Mary,   Wednesday—October 6, 1915

Yes, talking by wireless over long distances is indeed mighty. It is an enlargement of the soul of man.

But man had always talked by wireless—a different wireless which transferred all the *real* messages from one part of the Earth to another. And the subconsciousness of man always acted according to these messages. A world-deed that happened in India became known to the soul of Egyptians. And what the soul knows is often unknown to the man who has a soul. We are *infinitely more* than we think.

Ruskin, Carlyle, and Browning are mere children in the kingdom of the Spirit. They all *talk* too much. Blake is the God-man. His drawings are so far the profoundest things done in English—and his vision, putting aside his drawings and his poems, is the most godly.

I am sending you a drawing. Put it under glass if you can. The paper on which it is drawn is not strong enough to stand many things. I have tried, Mary, more than once to make a copy of that head which you liked but without success. But I shall try again.

Love from Kahlil

---------------◦◦◦❦{ KG }❧◦◦--------------

[New York]
Dear Mary,   Sunday, October 31, 1915

I have not been able to do much work. So much is going on inside that I find my hands motionless and silent. Life is deep and high and rich—and I am so busy drinking Life that I cannot do much of anything else. But when drinking Time is over, and the days become too cold for walking, I shall work and work and work.

Love from Kahlil

---------------◦◦◦❦{ KG }❧◦◦--------------

[New York]
Beloved Mary,   Sunday—11/21/15

I have kept in my heart all the things you said during your last visit. That which is between us is like the absolute in Life —everchanging, evergrowing. You and I, Mary, understand each other's larger self: and that to me is the most wonderful thing in life.

Love from Kahlil

Thank you a thousand times for these wonderful books. They are just what I want. I have never been so interested in a subject as I am now in Astronomy. It is *the* proper study of man. Human beings are local and their vision is so limited that they all need Astronomy to raise them beyond their tribe, race and country. When the collective minds (I do not mean God) of this planet become conscious of other worlds and other spheres, their local interests, which are behind all wars and all human difficulties, would be no more.

I work every day. Much will come out of my heart during this winter. O, Mary, I wish I could break my heart to get things out as I want to. Human hands are stupid, shy, unknowing. Our hearts are better than their images and between them and our hands there are a thousand veils. When one works from the inside out, one is in an eternal childbirth. It is a daily reconstruction of the self—and, as you say, yesterday is a thousand years away.

And your letters, your sweet and dear letters—when I read them, and sometimes I read them as if they were written to someone else, I feel like a plant growing in light. And I forget my own shadows. Do you think, Mary, that someday I shall be like the man to whom these letters are written? I want to, with all my heart and soul.

Love from Kahlil

This letter, dear Effendi, is really to confess that I've mailed you a little woolen scarf. I got one, too, just like yours. It ought to be longer—but it is the only woolen scarf I've thought pretty—and they are so warm around your neck.

I've looked at you and fed on you and listened to you, while I write, until I'm all tied-up bubbles, like a blackberry skin. But it is early morning—and school will open soon. So goodnight and goodnight.

Love from
Mary

❦ *1916* ❧

[New York]

Beloved Mary,   Thursday—Jan. 6, 1916

The wonderful robe and scarf are here and are comforting and warm. But Mary, you should not have given me the robe. I have many warm things for the house, and you have none.

I have been thinking of writing, of giving forms, to the one thought that changed my inner-life—God and the Earth and the soul of man. A voice is shaping itself in my soul and I am waiting for words. My one desire now is to find the right form, the right garment that would cling to the human ears. The world is hungry, Mary; and if this *thing* is bread it will find a place in the heart of the world, and if it is not bread, it will at least make the hunger of the world deeper and higher. It is beautiful to speak of God to man. We cannot fully understand the nature of God because we are *not* God, but we can make ready our consciousness to understand, and grow through, the visible expressions of God.

Now, Mary, I come to you for a word. Will you write me a letter, a simple letter, about your most sincere conception of this perception, this burning thing that is taking hold of me?

Love from Kahlil

Monday night

Beloved K.G.,   Jan. 10, 1916

I have tried to answer you simply but I can't. I'm *sorry*.

I have always believed what you said to me of God, even when I might not understand—because you love God. And so I never questioned this new perception of yours. I thought simply of grasping it and living it. But when you asked for my "sincerest conception" of it, I asked myself, "Do *I* believe it?"

I do believe it. I cannot help believing it. And it is the largest and most creative perception I too have ever known.

You have found the simple, universal reality of Growth— true from the nebula up through God; and its simple method —through creative consciousness.

Darwin perceived Evolution—in organic life. There has been evolution in the conception of Evolution. That conception is completed now, in your perception that *Reality is Transmutation of Matter:*

Everything is matter
All matter is seeking further form
Soul is the highest form of matter

You know the perceiver is an element in every perception. Our truths of today may not have been truths for us aeons ago—are perhaps now not truths for God. But for the selves we now know this perception of yours is a reality of transfiguring power. It makes us conscious that we were latent in the nebula—and that we can rise to God.

And it clears us of so many mists, so many dead bits and details, so many tangling things. It sets us so free. It simplifies our consciousness, enlarges us. It makes us a flame of desire.

Love—and love—and love

from Mary

[New York]
Sunday—Jan. 30, 1916

This perception, beloved Mary, this new knowledge of God is with me night and day. I cannot think of anything else. I can do nothing but be with it and be moved by it. When I sleep something in me keeps awake to follow it and to receive more from it and through it. My very eyes seem to retain that slowly developing picture of the birth of God. I see Him rising like the mist from the seas and the mountains and plains. Half-born, half-conscious, He rose. He himself did not know Himself *fully* then. Millions of years passed before He moved with His own will, and sought more of Himself with his own power and through His own desire. And man came. He sought man even as man and the soul of man were seeking Him. Man sought Him first without consciousness and without knowledge. Then man sought Him with consciousness but without knowledge. And *now* man will seek Him with consciousness and with knowledge.

God is not the creator of man. God is not the creator of the earth. God is not the ruler of man nor of earth. God desires man and earth to become like Him, and a part of Him. God is growing through His desire, and man and earth, and all there is upon the earth, rise towards God by the power of desire. And desire is the inherent power that changes all things. It is the law of all matter and all life.

With love from Kahlil

[New York]
Thursday—Feb. 10, 1916

Did you know, beloved Mary, that I still have enough in the bank to last me a year? You give, and you give without measure.

I live, Mary, in deep ecstasy. The days and nights are enveloped with burning rapture. The one thing my heart always longed for is with me now. I love Life and all things in Life—and you know, Mary, I never loved Life much. For twenty years, I had nothing but that urgent hunger, that thirst for what I did not know.

It is different now. Wherever I go, and whatever I am doing, I see the same mighty power, the same mighty law, that makes the elements flower into souls and turns the souls into God.

The soul is a newly developed element in Nature—and like other elements it has its own inherent properties. Consciousness, desire for more of itself, hunger for that which is beyond itself; these, and others, are the properties of the soul, the highest form of matter.

The soul seeks God even as heat seeks height, or water seeks the sea. The power to seek and the desire to seek are the inherent properties of the soul.

And the soul never loses its path, anymore than water runs upward.

All souls will be in God.

The soul never loses its inherent properties when it reaches God. Salt does not lose its saltness in the sea; its properties are inherent and eternal. The soul will retain consciousness, the hunger for more of itself and the desire for that which is beyond itself. The soul will retain those properties through all eternity, and like other elements in nature it will remain absolute. The absolute seeks more absoluteness, more crystallization.

When the soul reaches God it will be conscious that it is in God, and that it is seeking more of itself in being in God, and that God too is growing and seeking and crystallizing.

Love from Kahlil

[New York]

Beloved Mary,   Wednesday, March 1, 1916

I cannot say much now about that which fills my heart
and soul. I feel like a seeded field in midwinter, and I know
that spring is coming. My brooks will run and the little life
that sleeps in me will rise to the surface when called.

Silence is painful; but in silence things take form, and we
must wait and watch. In us, in our secret depth, lies the knowing element which sees and hears that which we do not see
nor hear. All our perceptions, all the things we have done, all
that we are Today, dwelt once in that knowing, silent depth,
that treasure chamber in the soul. And we are more than we
think. We are more than we know. That which is more than
we think and know is always seeking and adding to itself
while we are doing nothing—or think we are doing nothing.
But to be conscious of what is going on in our depth is to
help it along. When subconsciousness becomes consciousness,
the seeds in our winter-clad-selves turn to flowers, and the
silent life in us sings with all its might.

This Life reveals much of that which we do not know—but
it is Life after death that reveals all.

John Masefield is coming to see me next week. I would
like to make a drawing of him. He is a good and a kind man.

May God bless you, beloved Mary,

Love from Kahlil

[New York]

Beloved Mary,   Sunday—April 9, 1916

When one's soul is dwelling in that region of moving
thoughts one loses the power of words. But I have been talking to you all the time, and I always know that you know that

we are walking and talking together. One must have a *friend* to talk to in the silent hours of the night and during the long walks in the parks. And you are that friend, beloved Mary.

I have been working all the time—and seeing as little of people as possible. The great gulf between people and myself grows ever wider. Sometimes I say to myself, "The gulf is caused by something wrong in me. When that wrong is made right, I shall be very near to all people and shall perhaps love them with a new love."

Love from Kahlil

--~⊰ *MH* ⊱~--

[JOURNAL]

314 Marlborough
Boston
Friday—4/21/16

K. came for the evening; had arrived last night, for Easter with Mary.

"I've not seen Ryder recently. He's in the clutches of a woman who is afraid if anybody goes there, I'm told, that they are trying to take him from her. Several people have told me that she takes his pictures out and sells them and is taking care of the money for him. It is the same house that he went to after his illness, and he is very well taken care of. I've seen him once there, when she was away."

The Ruby Ring—The Poets' Ring

He showed it to me—worn on his forefinger—the most beautiful pigeon-blood that I've ever seen—in a gold setting, Syrian design. "It was given to me—by many people—from New York and other countries. About two months ago, six or seven people came with it to the studio one evening—that was all—there was no speech—no paper. These people know that if there were anything public I—" he hesitated for the friendly expression for "No!" and I said, "that it would be distasteful to you." "Yes." They had chosen the stone, and taken it to Louis Tiffany for suggestions for a Syrian design. And an Armenian on the Avenue had set the ring. Kahlil felt the gift, with his heart—"They put so much money into it, for me, when they ought to have sent that money to Syria. "It is too much to be worn anywhere else" (about his forefinger). "They knew I wouldn't wear a diamond." The stone is a ruby.

Kahlil has been writing a great deal. Several bits added to the three *Giants*, and for *The Madman*. Two more Grave-Digger poems—one, that the Grave-Digger buries nothing that is alive; the other on Incense Burners; a poem in which "I" walk to the sea and there see three great ones. One of them speaks wisdom, another sings a song—and they all sing together. "Oh! I'm in a world of them," said Kahlil and laughed: "Grave-diggers, Giants, Madman, Mustafa!"

"You know I'm called the Grave-Digger now, very often. Some think I'm bitter and destructive—but you can't build without tearing down. And we are like nuts, we have to be cracked open. Sandpaper would do the work, but it would take so long! The gentle touch does not wake people."

--◆{ *KG* }◆--

Beloved Mary,   [New York]
Wednesday—May 10, 1916

Yesterday I wrote these two little parables and I am sending them to you for correction—and also for suggestions. I have been writing quite a little lately—all in Arabic. I must add to my *Madman* as much as possible. Perhaps I might submit it to a publisher sometime this summer.

These are the two parables:

In my father's garden there are two cages. In one there is a lion which my father's slaves brought from the desert of Nineveh; in the other cage is a songless sparrow.

Every day at dawn the sparrow calls to the lion, "Good morrow to thee, brother-prisoner."

In the shadow of the temple my friend and I saw a blind man sitting alone.

My friend said to me, "Behold the wisest man of our land."

I left my friend and approached the wise man and greeted him. Then we conversed.

And after a while I said, "Forgive my question; but since when hast thou been blind?"

"From my birth," he answered.

Said I, "I am an astronomer." Then he placed his hand upon his breast saying, "I watch these suns and moons and stars."

Do tell me if there is anything wrong with these parables, beloved Mary.

Love from Kahlil

--◦◦{ *MH* }◦◦--

MISS HASKELL'S SCHOOL
314 MARLBOROUGH STREET, BOSTON

Beloved K.G.,   May 14, 1916

Your two parables are beautiful. The sparrow-one is a living seed—the astronomer the seed's fulfillment. I love them both.

I have just a tiny change, for rhythm, to suggest in each:

"In my father's garden there are two cages. In one is a lion, which my father's slaves brought from the desert of Nineveh; in the other is a songless sparrow." The original way sounded a little burdened, to me, with its extra "there" and "cage"—and I like better a comma between "lion" and its descriptive clause.

"And [added] my friend said [omit *to me*], 'Behold the wisest man of our land.' Then [added] I left my friend and approached the blind man and greeted him. And [instead of *then*] we conversed.....Then he placed his hand upon his breast, [add comma] saying, "etc.

While I was saying the "Lion & Sparrow" over and over to find what the extra words were, at first, I objected to the beginning of all the first three clauses, one of them a main topic and the others its sub-topics—with an in-phrase. Trying every change I could think of, that should not spoil the "value," I got one that I liked. "Two cages stand in my father's garden, in the one is a lion" —— & —— the rest unchanged.

I realize, however, that you didn't want to begin with "Two cages"—and that "In my father's garden" gives a quality of more vagueness and incidentalness—more atmosphere. "Two cages" is harder. I don't mind the in-phrases, now—and I like the gentler, smoother quality, and the remoteness of the slower start.

I read a book, recently—long, intimate communications to his father by a dead Harvard student. It was a shock. Himself, his before-death self, is going right on, now. (If the communications are real.) Death has not changed him.—I have taken for granted that death does great things for us.

"Myself is eternally up to myself" is what I felt after this book.

I've been coming to that realization ever since, in the year of "The Absolute." You said, speaking of boyhood, that every human life is too good to waste.

Now, I see everybody a little *maker*—making Himself. We

never make anything but ourselves or accomplish anything else, do we?

And our self-expressions—tell of moments of ourselves that were real and vital enough to take forms. They are embodiments of memories.

Isn't memory the source of our conception of permanence and of time? Existence—movement—and time are wholly relative. I wonder whether all life does not measure time by events, as we do (save conventionally)—whether the life-cycle to us—and Earth's life-cycle to Earth, no longer than ours to us or the cell's to the cell?

No doubt memory will grow with consciousness, as long as consciousness continues to be our growth-form. Is that how it is, that some day, as you have said, all the ages of our life will lie open to us like a book, from first to last? Memory will have grown gradually complete. And may not "scientific discovery" be one of the ways in which subconscious memory becomes knowledge?

Good-night. And Good-morrow to thee, brother-prisoner: —and God bless you.

Love from
Sunday night   Mary

--- ⋅⋅⋅❦ *KG* ❦⋅⋅⋅ ---

[New York]
Beloved Mary,   Tuesday (May 16, 1916)

I am so glad you liked the two little parables, and thank you for the corrections. The words you took off were not needed. I have other parables in my head, but I don't seem to know just how to put them in words. English is not the language for parables. But one is apt to find faults with his tools when he cannot use them well. The fault lies within me. But I *will* learn how to write English. Since the Idea of God came to me I almost lost the little knowledge I had of English. I find myself hunting for words which I have always used. What I really need is a long mental rest—and Shakespeare.

No, Mary, death does not change us. It only frees that which is real in us—our consciousness—and the *social* memories that lie in our consciousness. A man in an airplane sees the earth differently, but not with new eyes. Human consciousness is the fruit of the infinite past. The infinite future will make it ripe but it will never change its properties.

May God keep you, beloved Mary, and may God bless you always.

Love from Kahlil

--------------------- ⚜KG⚜ ---------------------

[New York]

Beloved Mary,   Sunday (June 11, 1916)

A Syrian relief committee has been formed. As secretary of the committee, I shall have no personal life during this summer. It is a great responsibility but I must shoulder it. Great tragedies enlarge the heart. I have never been given the chance to serve my people in a work of this sort. I am glad I can serve a little and I feel that God will help me.

And I do not know what is going to happen to me. I shall simply trust myself to life.

Kitchener's* death is like a great reward. But it seems to take the English people a very long time to understand the soul of things; and I fear that they will not look upon his death as his final gift to the cause. England's national conceit

* Horatio Herbert Kitchener (1850–1916), a popular English hero, was killed when his ship was struck by a German torpedo during World War I.

must die before she can do anything really great in this war. The only people in England who ever understood anything in a large way were the poets: and they never were given the chance to serve their country, as poets of countries served theirs.

England must die before England can live outside the shell.

Love from Kahlil

--◄{ *MH* }►--

MISS HASKELL'S SCHOOL

314 MARLBOROUGH STREET, BOSTON

Beloved Kahlil,   June 12, 1916

Since your letter came, one thought has been with me all the time: can I help you? Can you use me? If you can, it will be so great a joy to me. I have all July free—I told my aunt long ago that I would spend only August with her. And though until July I must be here from Monday through Friday noon, I could come to New York for the week-ends remaining in June—if it would be of use. You know I am not fastidious about work—I'd run errands or write notices or do any jobs that came up and were within my scope—if you could use an American who does not know Arabic.

Lovingly,
Mary

--◄{ *KG* }►--

[New York]
Wednesday (June 14, 1916)

Thank you, beloved Mary, thank you. But there is nothing for you to do, Mary. The work of the committee is going

275

well now, and we have a large number of men and women doing all sorts of things.

The hardest work before us now is to get all the Syrians to cooperate with the people of Mount Lebanon, and then to have the Turkish government permit foodstuff to get into the country. We can manage that through the American government.

I wish I could write more, beloved Mary. But, as you know, my life now is not my own.

Love from Kahlil

[New York]

Beloved Mary,   Thursday (June 29, 1916)

It will take patience to make all the Syrians of North America work together. The most difficult thing before us is getting food stuffs into Mount Lebanon. We are quite certain now that the Turkish government wishes to starve our people because some of our leaders there are with the Allies in thought and spirit. The American government is the only power in the world that could help us. The State Department in Washington assured me that this government is really using its good offices to alleviate the conditions in Syria. But you know how things are in Washington just now. Too many world problems and too many difficulties are being solved.

I have given, in your name, $150 to the Relief Committee. It is the largest contribution from an American so far.

The Arabian revolt is indeed a wonderful thing. No one outside of Arabia knows how successful it is and how far it will go. But the fact that there was a movement is a thing which I have dreamt of and worked for during the past ten years. If the Arabs receive help from the Allies, they would not only create a kingdom but they would give something to the world. *I know*, Mary, the reality that lies in the Arabic soul. The Arabs cannot organize without the help of Europe, but the Arabs have a vision of Life which no other race possesses.

Love from Kahlil

In 1916 Mary spent the summer in Savannah, Georgia, at the home of J. Florance Minis. Minis was married to Mary's first cousin, Louisa Porter Gilmer, a daughter of General Jeremy F. Gilmer of the Confederate Army. They lived in a large house on West Gaston Street.

President of the South Western Railroad Company of Macon, Minis, who was born in Philadelphia in 1852, had been for many years one of Savannah's outstanding citizens. An alderman from 1883 to 1885, he served as chairman of the Finance Committee of the City Council and at one time was president of the Savannah Cotton Exchange.

The summer of 1916 was a happy time, and Mary fell in love with the countryside and the graceful Southern city. Florance was generous to her, and genuinely welcomed having her with them. This was an important summer for Mary: she became reacquainted with the South, met friends from her childhood days, and saw family for the first time in many years.

⋯⊰ KG ⊱⋯

[New York]

Beloved Mary, Tuesday, Aug. 22, 1916

It has been extremely hot here. Somehow I cannot make myself go away, but I shall have to, and soon, too. I need the change badly. When you are working on a relief committee you become drunk with something sweeter than comfort.

Every dollar you receive brings with it a little breath of life, and you feel strangely soft and tender in your inside. I am sure you know what it is.

Yes, Turkey refused to allow Relief in Syria. But we can send money to be distributed amongst the needy. *It is* true that harvests are good this year, thanks be to God, but there is a bitter need for money. The Americans in Syria are able to distribute whatever we send them. The American government can do much if it chooses. But to choose the hardest way (and the hardest way is usually the right way) is to be superhuman in this age of local interests, local desires and local righteousness.

Love from Kahlil

MISS HASKELL'S SCHOOL

314 MARLBOROUGH STREET, BOSTON

Beloved Kahlil,   September 20, 1916

Each beautiful day and night makes me glad you are in Cohasset and makes me pray that you may have a good long stay. Earth and sky speak in the heart, and sustain it. And in great spaces the distant are always with us. Life is not explained, but we are molded to consent with Life.

Shall I send you Jung's book now—and Freud's *Interpretation of Dreams*? They are ready, whenever you'd like them.

They lead to interesting thoughts and illuminations. But so far, psychoanalysis reminds me of a powerful engine, doing excellent work—in tunnels only. One would think the Universe was *inside*—and the world. That is the psychoanalyst's limitation. But its work *is* excellent and vital.

I kiss your hand, beloved Kahlil. God bless you, bless you always.

Love from
Mary

Beloved Kahlil,   November 2, 1916

I want to see you, to talk with you, but not to write. My hours are immersed in personalities, in my trade—I am asking the worm to let me be her sister, and my heart to bring forth things dear to children and to parents—and the *threshold* of my neighbor's tomorrow to hold my *feet*—in order that this little school may grow.

And I'm wondering whether the President of the United States isn't the one I must try to approach in behalf of realities in schools.

The war bites harder and harder into me. Does it not into you? It seems to live its own life and perform its own work in me like another personality, and to do this in many other people also.

I'm doing some very simple psychology with some very simple girls; my oldest class—beginning by being very thorough *just now* on the fundamentals of heredity and the nervous system. It is the solidest, most fruitful feeling thing I ever got them into—and it is a perfect magazine of anti-parochial ammunition. It makes us hear within us the voice of the Beginning, and beyond us Unendingness. And it gives me something that I can offer to Head Mistresses with sensibleness to them. *Hope* is in me, to get a new idea to grip them, if it seems the thing to do when the moment comes.

Lovingly—Mary

[New York]

Beloved Mary, Sunday, November 5, 1916

The United States Navy has granted The Committee a steamer which we, in cooperation with American Red Cross Society, are trying to fill with foodstuffs. I think that no less than $750,000.00 worth of things will be shipped. All this, Mary, means work, work, work night and day. But it is by far the best work I have done.

And I have been in a *hurry*, always in a hurry, since I came back from Cohasset. Never have I been so conscious of Time, and the desire of not losing a minute. To lose a minute in a relief work is to lose a chance, and one cannot lose a chance of any sort when the cries of thousands of sufferers are filling your soul.

With love from
Kahlil

MISS HASKELL'S SCHOOL

3 1 4 MARLBOROUGH STREET, BOSTON

Beloved Kahlil, Sunday—Dec. 17, 1916

I love today very much, because the *Caesar** gets off; and because I can write to you. I have waited for this each day and each night, with thoughts of you.

The weeks have seemed long. And you will laugh when I tell you they seemed especially long because I've had a real, complete little ⅔-inch meteorite to send you. It will come now as soon as I can get to the post-office to register and insure it. I shan't let it go without both.

* A relief boat to Syria.

This is its story. In Arizona—but on no map of Arizona accessible to me—is a great crater-like hole more than a mile square, I believe—with vertical walls and no apparent cause. Certain Indians say that a star fell from heaven and buried itself there; others, that a god came from heaven and there entered the earth. Many believe a meteor made the hole and the crater has been bought, and diggings begun here and there, for the iron-bearing meteor mass that may be unknown depths below the surface. Not many miles north of this great crater is a little canyon, Diablo Canyon, in the bed of which are numerous tiny meteorites, like a shower fallen in the wake of the big meteor. Their meteoric nature appears in their metallic properties and peculiar to meteorites—full, for instance of microscopic diamonds—and in the lack of other possible origin for them. Ours is a little Diablo—and someday I will find out more about it from Harvey Davis, who got it for me from a friend out there after nine months waiting. You will love it, as I do. It is crowded with Infinities, and as *grim* and as heavy as Birth and Loneliness.

I often look your way to find God, dear Kahlil, and yet so constantly I am praying Him for you (about you, I mean), for your body, for your mind, for your heart, for strength, revelation, love and joy. And then I stop choosing, and just say your name and sing it. And I think God sings you to me too, and reads you to me and shows you—so full of the planet and its souls and of things yet unfelt by other men. I wish I could tell you how I thank Him for you.

And writing that, I say to myself, "If you will *be* what you want Kahlil to hear, he will hear it"—and I know this. The more I hear, too, K.G., and the wider consciousness I get (and there has come something more to me this fall) the more I hear you—as it has always been. It is only our absolute that feels near to us or gets near to anyone else, isn't it?

Love from Mary

[New York]

Beloved Mary   Tuesday—Dec. 19, 1916

May God bless you for your blessed letter—for every word
in it and for the heavenly spirit that runs amongst the words.
And may God make me worthy of it all.

When the hand of Life is heavy and night songless, it is the
time for love and trust. And how light the hand of life becomes and how songful the night, when one is loving and
trusting all.

I, too, have been through a period of childbirth, painful and
creative and full of questionings. There were times when the
hand of Life seemed like a mountain on my breasts. But I know
now that there are wings fastened to every heavy thing. And
I know also that it is the greater hunger that makes the wings
motionless.

I have been preparing the exhibition, redrawing some of the
drawings and even making some of the mats myself. And we
have changed the date of the opening from the 15th to the
29th of January. The change is a good thing in many ways.
The 29th is not so near the holidays. It is the very heart of the
season (as they say). And if I can get everything ready by the
10th, I might come to Boston for a little visit. But if I find
myself in a working mood I shall stay here and work. I must
make up for those lost months during which I did nothing. I
go only once a week to the office of the Committee now, but
I am still the secretary.

I met Tagore. He is beautiful to look at and to be with,
but I was disappointed with his voice. It is bodyless, and it
made his poems less real to me.

And a real, complete little inch-by-⅔-inch meteorite.—O,
Mary, I would rather have it than anything else in the world.
When it comes I shall hold it knowing I am holding something
many millions of miles away. Thank you, Mary, thank you.

Love from Kahlil

❧ *1917* ❧

[New York]

Beloved Mary,   Wednesday (Jan. 3, 1917)

The meteorite, the precious meteorite, is the most wonderful thing I have ever had. It feeds my imagination and it sends my thoughts into space and makes the infinite nearer and less strange to my soul. I hold it every day and each time I bless you with all my heart.

Tagore speaks against nationalism while his work does *not* show or express a world-consciousness. He is an Indian with all the beauty and charms of India. And though he is sensitive to the blessedness of life, he does not see life as an ever-growing-power. God is, to Tagore, a perfect Being. All sophists dwell on the perfection of God. To me, Mary, perfection is a limitation and I cannot conceive perfection anymore than I can conceive the end of space or time.

Love from Kahlil

[New York]
Beloved Mary,   Friday (Jan. 12, 1917)

I am sending you another little parable—to read and correct
its English—when you have the time. You see, Mary, I go to
your school, too, and I could not have written a word in English if it were not for you.

The poem on God is the key to all my feeling and thinking.
And if need be I will change its present form, because I want
it to be simple and clear. But I will wait till I know just what
you think of it.

This little parable, too, belongs to what I have been going
through the past year. But these short glimpses are not enough.
Large thoughts must be expressed in a large way. My English is still very limited. But I can learn.

I am full of work, Mary, and with God's help and your
blessings, I will fulfill the little spark in me.

Love from
Kahlil

[Boston]
Jan. 15, 1917

Thank you, thank you, K.G., for "The Three Arts." It
laughs at its own tears so deliciously and strangely. It is big,
and I love it. You won't be publishing it this month, so I am
keeping it too, to bring—with its little word-changes—not
many changes; Life, whatever language it uses, expresses Life.
Your English is creative. And you learn it from the English
Genius.

I am trying to hear things I never listened for before. I
want a new ear and a new tongue for the poem on God. I

can't write about this poem, beloved Kahlil. My self that needs no tongue is speaking with your self that needs no ears. If we have a creative speech, you and I, it is that.

God bless you.

Love,
Mary

MISS HASKELL'S SCHOOL
314 MARLBOROUGH STREET, BOSTON

Beloved Kahlil,   Jan. 29, 1917

Your beautiful hand met me this morning—and now at night. It is very strange, and full of a trembling, half-warm, half-cold—this sense of those forty pictures all in presence together: to be seen and heard and felt in public. You must be very tired, bless you.

And I am wishing—as I have been wishing for more than a month—that those pictures could be shown in Boston too. I do wish it very much if it could well be.

If I don't hear from you on Wednesday, K.G., I'm coming this Friday—Friday, not Saturday, because I want to have two looks at the pictures.

I have a little honor-roll on vellum that I'm going to beg you to design for me when I come. Blake is the only man whose lines I love enough to use.

Goodnight. God send you sweet sleep, beloved K.G., and God bless you always.

Love from
Mary

[New York]

Beloved Mary,   Wednesday—Jan. 31, 1917

I want you to come and see the drawings. I could not have made them if your blessings and your loving thoughts were not with me.

I have a dinner engagement for this Friday evening. We can dine on Saturday and spend Sunday together, too, as we always do.

"The Seven Arts" and this exhibition are making my daily life full and rapid. It is all so wonderful—even when I am not working; and it is even wonderful when I am so physically tired. Life is sweetly rich—not less rich when it is painful.

Will you not telephone me on Friday or Saturday? I have my own telephone now and I do not have to run up and down those stairs all day long! The number of the telephone is 9549 Chelsea.

Love from
Kahlil

―❧ *MH* ❧―

[JOURNAL]

7/28/17   Boston

Back of the little powerhouse under the willows in deep shade—steep above the water, we sat on a gray cement vat top.

I had been saying that I always felt the thinking was shallow, when a man or a woman was "disappointed" in—or "knew" the other sex—lumping a whole sex. Somehow it led to Kahlil's saying, "I can't get along with women." "Women are better than men. They are kinder, more sensitive, more stable, and have a finer sense about much of life. But I have always found them too personal."

I said it was because his gentle manner and voice, his understanding, his interest—don't convey that he is a fighter and most impersonal.

"That is just it," said Kahlil, "I'll sit by a person at a dinner. There is a great loneliness in almost everybody—and a great unspoken hunger to express oneself. A woman responds to being talked to and finds herself telling things she never told—says to herself, 'At last! I have found somebody who understands.' If she would let it go at that, all well and good. She wants comfort, help, and discussion. So she gives a dinner and asks me to it. And then she asks me to come again. I refuse the first time and second. The third time I usually go because I don't want to be rude. And she wants to add me to her life—see me, talk more about herself, her life, her problems. If she is married, she is not happy. 'Her husband is good, but he does not understand me. It is like living with a stranger after all these years,' etc. Whatever her circumstances, her talk is about herself.

"And I really don't want that. I have just got to stop 'understanding.' I am interested in people—in their structure and in human life.—But I want to see them in their large aspects. I want to be loved. But not in a personal way. I want people to love me—but I *don't* want them to *have* me. I don't want a me and thee relation.

"I have been told that they say of me, 'Mr. Gibran lifts you way up and shows you what you never conceived and then he lets you drop down to nothing.'

"The essence of what is between you and me," said Kahlil, "is most wonderful and beautiful. I have used this phrase before to express it—'You are here also.' It is a kinship.

"There is also a language. It is not a matter merely of words. Sometimes you have not even begun to speak—and I am at the end of what you are saying. And I don't think this is dependent on time—on the years we have known each other. The root between us is ten years old, or more—it has been the same thing all the time—though it has developed and grown."

My heart was overflowing with peace and the silent singing of all our visit.

Nothing speaks more of the terrific tenderness of Kahlil than the response that reveals itself to any love or understanding of his real soul. I was speaking of our never having had physical intercourse—and saying that I simply could not judge its value for the soul. I said that Kahlil had probably never been as near to any other woman as to me. More like a flash than he ever speaks Kahlil put in, "I have never been one hundredth part as near to any human being, man or woman, as to you."

After supper he put his feet up, stretched out, and rested my head on his breast. "And now," he said, "while we lie, let us do a parable." And he half-told "The Blessed City." We worked it out on the spot. Kahlil gave me his copy and dictated another to me for himself to take. We never worked better together.

"Think," I said, "of the people who love your work. If they could come into these rooms, don't you suppose they would envy me?" And, "Think how rich I am, K.G., how *rich I live*—with these things. They are as practically mine as if I'd bargained for each of them by contract." And, "Do you suppose there is any sum that could get *Rose Sleeves* away from me?"

Kahlil said, "Did you know that I was trying very hard to get your likeness in *Rose Sleeves* and in the central one of the *Three Women*. Your face was fuller then—much. The eye is yours." I told him then that one of the children had asked me once whether *Rose Sleeves* were my portrait. And one of them told me they all thought the central woman in *The Three Women* was my portrait.

I hung *Rose Sleeves* over my desk to show Kahlil how lovely she looks there and *Consolation* above the bookcase. He liked *Rose Sleeves* so much here that I left her overnight, and now I cannot give her up again to the other room. Here she stays.

Beloved Kahlil,   October 12, 1917

School opened on September 26.

When I've signed my name to this, I'm going back to *Neurology* and *Child-Training As An Exact Science* and *Greek History for Young Readers*, and *Golden Treasury of American Lyrics*, and *The Shorter Poems of William Wordsworth* and the *Complete Atlas of the World* and a pamphlet chuck full of Massachusetts' churches, and *Elementary Science*, and forty books at ten cents per that I got last Saturday at a second-hand counter as a library of allure to the two or three weaklings in school whose infra-mentality gives me anxiety. That list represents my classes—for one of my teachers is in the mountains still, and I'm taking on the half-work that would be hers. I thank heaven that whatever happens, parents always purr when I take a class.

The first period of intense pressure is about over and now things speed up again only for about ten days each month. But somehow even a strain itself seems but part of what goes to create a beautiful something that I am aware of this year for the first time. With a certain pitch of life there comes a look, a bearing, almost like an exhalation, in teachers and girls. Almost a slender being, like a *youth* made of light, seems to float about the mid-air of school. The others make him, and I see him. His presence is our success—work turned to ecstasy, to life.

Of course school was never so happy and different. The girls all say it is much larger—though by actual count it has not changed! Certainly it is much nicer—with unforeseeable improvements and simplifications. It's just like a rush of life let loose—creating a delightful order of its own.

I'm glad to get a minute to write to you in, but I really talk to you *off* on the rim of great wheels that reach from me to the stars—and to Other Stars—and when I come back to speech the reallest things seem gone.

Lovingly
Mary

--------- ✦ *KG* ✦ ---------

Beloved Mary,   Saturday—October 14, 1917

God bless you for your dear letter.

What you told me about "Haskell" is beautiful and wonderful. That Spirit, that half visible Being that speaks in silences, is the greatest reality in a school or in a house or in a nation or in the world. Living up to that super-being is the only living worthwhile. A House-God is the living, growing godly desires of those who dwell in the house. The "Haskell" "youth made of light" is really the light of your larger self and the larger selves of your teachers and girls.

May that loving and loveable youth grow stronger and mightier. I am sending you, Mary, these two parables. I wrote them in a hurry because I wanted them to go with this. Will you not change that which you do not like? And will you not make their limping English less limping? Thank you, Mary.

Love from Kahlil

MISS HASKELL'S SCHOOL
314 MARLBOROUGH STREET, BOSTON

Beloved Kahlil,   [ab. Oct. 20, 1917*]

The parables, you'll see I've changed rather freely. I'm not sure of them yet—for after all, in English too, when you say a thing idiomatically, it is something I could not have said. I always trust my tiny revisions of your mere phrasing much more than larger changes I may make. But surely you won't be publishing either of these before I see you—and we can make the final form together.

I like the "Sleep-Walkers" very much—and the idea of the other. But I hesitate a little at the use of the atheist to express it—because in some form or other every learned man now, as well as the unlearned, believes in God—and atheism is no longer a reality of common thinking. But I suspect I don't catch the parable.

Lovingly,
Mary

[New York]
Wednesday—October 31, 1917

Yes, beloved Mary, we know without knowing that we know, and we unconsciously live according to something in our depth which our surfaces do not understand. The real thing in us is in the presence of all that is real outside of us. Even when we doubt we are not doubting. Even when we are saying "No" to Life, something in us cries "Yes." The *No* is heard only by man, the *Yes* by God.

* Finding this letter undated, Mary penciled in this approximate dating after Gibran's death.

You have given the two little parables the one thing they needed—unaffected simplicity. Perhaps I will be able to tell you just what I mean by "The Two Learned Men," and then we might give it another form. I have other parables in mind —we might write them together.

Love from Kahlil

                     KG

[New York]

Beloved Mary,   Thursday—Nov. 15, 1917

Thank you for the sugar and the books. I shall consume both with much care!

Somehow I have never been able to enjoy fully reading a book on sex. Perhaps I have not been curious enough, or perhaps I have been mentally timid. But I now want to know all things under the sun, and the moon, too. For all things are beautiful in themselves, and become more beautiful when known to man. Knowledge is Life with wings.

Love from Kahlil

                     KG

[New York]

Beloved Mary,   Sunday—November 25, 1917

Will you not read, correct, change and make whole this prose-poem to Rodin? I would like to have it back soon— Tuesday morning, if possible—so that I may publish it together with my drawing of the great man.

I wrote it this morning so that the event may not pass without a word from me.

Love from Kahlil

292

❧· *1918* ·☙

[JOURNAL]

Boston
Sunday afternoon—January 6, 1918

Kahlil came after lunch—until 6:30—bright and relieved at the beautiful day. Someone had been with him, almost to the door and had told him a story called true, from an English magazine. Of how one of two aviator-friends went higher one day, on purpose, than machines had yet been, fell and, dying, pointed upward, with the single word "Monsters"; how the friend remembering always, climbed to the same far height, and found the monsters—dim, large creatures, through the eye of one of which he and his machine passed. "One never knows anything about the truthfulness of such a story," said Kahlil, "but I've never seen why the air should not have inhabitants of its own."

"I wonder," he said, talking of the mother of Christ, "how much she knew about her son? She probably knew he was a source of trouble and that he was a good man. Probably after his death, and largely because of his death and the devotion of his followers, he seemed much sweeter to her than while he lived. While he lived, perhaps his miracles and hearing people talk of them impressed her. He spoke Chaldo-Syriac—the vernacular—while the cultivated spoke Hebrew. There was great mixture of blood in that upcountry where Christ came from, too. Chaldean and Greek and other strains. I don't doubt that all these mixed elements in the life about him had a tremendous influence on him; in the inner spirit, they affected nothing.

"Christ's death, as well as his life, had a wonderful effect on his followers. The day will come when we shall think but just of the Flame—of the fullness of Life that burned in him. Socrates and his followers' relation was more mental, but Christ's followers felt him more than they felt any of his ideas. And look what he did to them. See John—what a poet he became. Paul was a splendid advertising agent and his work worked against as well as for the real Christ. A supreme spirit is born with a vision. He thinks that all other people have the same vision. It takes him years, usually, to find that no one else has it. Perhaps eighty times out of a hundred, the discovery makes him bitter and cynical. Another one of these lovely spirits will simply be supremely lonely. His inner self becomes a hermit. He learns the language of the others and speaks it. He throws a little of his real self into what he says and does, but there are a few—perhaps five percent—who just live their inner life all the time, despite the world about them.

"Christ changed the human mind and for men found a new path. Michelangelo had been led by all the painters and sculptors before him. His path was one already known."

--------- ·· *{ KG }* ·· ---------

\,

Beloved Mary,

[New York]
Monday—Jan. 21, 1918

Never before have I known a week such as the past week. It was hard and eventful and beautiful. I found, on my return,

294

a mountain of letters, and another mountain of things that I must do.

The poetry evening was earnest and eager and full of real animation. The War is changing people's souls. It is turning their carelessness into hunger, and it is making them want that which they never wanted before.

Many wanted me to read at this society or that club. I even received an invitation to go to Chicago and read before the poetry society. They said they will give me fifty dollars and my railroad expenses.

I had to dine last night with Mrs. Robinson and read to a group. Mrs. Robinson is the sister of Colonel Roosevelt, and she told me that she wants me (very much) to meet the Colonel at her house. After that, I thought, I will ask him to sit for a drawing.

It is cold, Mary, and it seems that another freezing spell is coming. But I manage to keep warm and well. God is kind to me in many, many ways. I do not deserve so much Heavenly Kindness.

I am sending two wash drawings. I am sending them just for the colour in them—your walls need a touch of colour here and there. They are not nude enough to offend any person in Boston—I mean the two drawings, not your walls!

Love from Kahlil

Thursday night (Jan. 24, 1918)

O, dear K.G.—Your dear letter came, and later, the two wash drawings—and I thank you! You were so sweet both to write and to send me the lovely drawings. Already I see them on the walls, though they are not yet framed. They make me smile every time I look at them. I shall add them to those now around my desk—for they all make too spacious a world for me to spare any.

Love from
Mary

MH

[Boston]
Jan. 25, 1918

Blake is mighty. The voice of God and the finger of God are in what he does. And how strangely remote he seems from even the very things he does! What he writes seems so often done in a foreign language—as if he were used to another speech, and were employing this one simply because it belongs to the land he finds himself in. It is like one drawing or playing with heavy gloves on, or with very cold fingers.

He really feels closer to you, Kahlil, than all the rest, to me —and he feels more beyond and apart than all the rest, as if he moved in a larger consciousness.

The new wash drawings are with Mr. Wright now, being framed. I'm to have them tomorrow. You ask me if I'd like to have more. The question makes me feel like a sea beach lying in the sun. On the beach are pebbles, only the beach and the pebbles and the sun—and the pebbles are your pictures. Is there room for more?!

In course of time, I want the *God and Man* that you were doing when I was last in New York, the painting that is among your pictures what the *Spirit of Light* is among the wash drawings. That picture dropped three veils away from before God in my consciousness—my heart, my soul, my more-than-self, themselves like a frame of blessing, whenever I think of it. I've known what I never knew before, ever since that five

The Spirit of Light

minutes. And the *Spirit of Light*, with which I doubly and trebly live, means as much to me. It lifts me up a thousand times a day, and all through the night while I sit here with the earth.

I think I've always sought the earth, and inwardly shunned man. Now I find myself seeing man with new eyes—finding him the marvel of marvels. It's like being just-born.

If ever you have anything, or do anything, K.G.—that you would like to send me—send it!! You know how I shall love it. If it is as big as a postage stamp, I can have it set in a brooch—and if it's bigger, I can hang it on the wall. For now that I group things, each can find its place.

Love from
Mary

--⟨ *KG* ⟩--

[New York]
Tuesday—Feb. 5, 1918

Beloved Mary,

How glad I am that you liked the two wash drawings. I am sending two more with this. The large painting, *God and Man*, will be yours when it is finished. No one else should, or could, have a picture which you like so much.

I am sending a new parable. It is rough and badly written. Will you recreate its English and send it back to me before the week is over? I am getting all the parables and some of the prose-poems together. I might succeed with some publisher.

The Poetry Society gave me the most wonderful reception I have ever had. Never before have I met with so much kindness, generosity, and real interest. Before the winter is over I am to read again—they will give me an entire evening, they said!

On Sunday I read again at Mrs. Robinson's to a wonderful crowd. And I was to meet T.R. today at tea, but a bad cold

299

keeps him in bed—and the ten-below-zero keeps me in this corner!

Talking to people about poetry and reading to them give me a great deal of real pleasure. Human beings have changed remarkably during the past three years. They are hungry for beauty, for truth, and for that other thing which lies beneath and beyond beauty and truth.

Love from Kahlil

-----◆{ *MH* }◆----- ————————

[Boston]

Beloved K.G., Feb. 10, 1918

This enchanting parable is like a dawn-breeze out of a new horizon—fresh, delicious—and juicy. Its English is full of a profound vitality that makes it free and beautiful. I've underscored in pencil every place I've changed in my suggested copy—and you'll see how slight the changes are. And of course you know they are offered but tentatively. I never feel so sure, when you are two hundred miles away.

And what shall I say for the two dear wash drawings, Kahlil? I took them right down to Mr. Wright, because I was going for the earlier two—and I hate to wait ten more days to get them back.

I think of you all through the bitter days and such part of the bitter nights as I'm awake in—and wonder how it feels in the studio.

The music of everything beats faster—and when you read and talk to people, K.G., doubtless there are countless vibrations caught now that wouldn't have been caught even a very few years ago.

Mary

[New York]
Beloved Mary,   Tuesday—Feb. 26, 1918

These are hard days indeed. When better days come what we have learned will be of great value. Life, Mary, is altogether too kind to me. I only pray that it may be as kind to others. I am often unhappy because I am treated so tenderly. While others—millions and millions—are handled so roughly.

On Thursday I am to address the Poetry Society of America. I have not the slightest idea of what I shall say before I read. I never do until I face an audience. Plans and designs always fail with me. I can only trust myself to the Spirit, and that Spirit is always generous and ocean-handed.

Love from Kahlil

[New York]
Beloved Mary,   Sunday—March 10, 1918

The reading at the Poetry Society went well. It was a large and gracious audience. Too much appreciation is apt to make one feel strangely small—and I really felt small. They liked the poem "God" more than anything else.

I have bought a winter suit—another shade of brown. And I have bought some shirts and gloves and a few other practical things.

Love from Kahlil

[Boston]
May 6, 1918

Kahlil in the evening—up from visiting Mrs. Garland at
her farm on the Cape—looking marvelously well—solid,
browned, bright-eyed and unnervous, unworn.

"I have had a glorious time. I felt like work and was able
to do it. It was a wonderful place and Mrs. Garland is a
remarkable being—so full of energy and sense, and with a
splendid sense of justice. A worker—helps wash the dishes
if help is needed; helps to cook if that is needed; is a tailoress
and seamstress and writes, too—has written two books. Her
three boys were back from college for their vacation—
splendid beings. They worked on the farm—everybody
worked. There were a lot of boys on the farm last summer
besides the Garlands, making money and eating well and
having a fine time with eight hours work a day and the rest
of the time for all sorts of things.

"The daughter, Hope, fourteen years old, has a great gift
with her hands—for drawing, and even more for modelling,
and especially modelling animals. She has an eagle there, for instance, and the head of a bull, that are real *beings*. One of
the things I admire most in Mrs. Garland is the freedom
she gives others. With the boys, for instance, she tries to
learn from them instead of teaching them. She means everything in that community of two thousand, and everything
that can be saved for the government is saved—every grain of
wheat or rice or other food—every plate at table is cleaned.
She eats all that is on her own and in the nicest way has
everybody else doing the same way. And money is not wasted
—nothing is wasted—though there is so much. It is all put
to *use*. In the morning Mrs. Garland and I might have breakfast together because the others had gone off a little earlier

—we might be at 8 and they have been off at 7. Coffee and a few little things would be brought in and when breakfast was over she might begin to write and I'd begin to write. And if after a while I wanted to go up to my room, I could do it without even saying anything.

"Yes, the big piece of English work I wrote you about has been brooding in me for eighteen months or more. In the past few months it has been growing and I began it. It is to have twenty-one parts; I have written sixteen of them."

Kahlil told first the prologue—not yet written. In a city between the plains and the sea, where ships come in and where flocks graze in the fields behind the city, there wanders about the fields and somewhat among the people, a man—poet, seer, prophet—who loves them and whom they love —but there is an aloneness after all, about him. They are glad to hear him talk; they feel in him a beauty and a sweetness; but in their love of him they never come close. Even the young women who are attracted by his gentleness do not quite venture to fall in love with him. And while the people count him as a part of the city, and like it that he is there and that he talks with their children in the fields, there is a consciousness that this is all temporary—that someday he will go. And one day out of the blue horizon a ship comes toward the city and somehow everyone knows, though nothing is told, that the ship is for the hermit poet. And now that they are going to lose him, the feeling of what he is in their life comes to them and they all crowd down to the shore, and he stands and talks with them. And one says, "Speak to us of Friendship—and so on. And he speaks of these things. It is what he says about them that I have been writing. And when he has ended, he enters into the ship and the ship sails into the mist."

And at the end one says to the poet, "Tell us about God," and he says, "Of Him I have been speaking in everything."

"I am not trying to write poetry. I am trying to express thoughts. I want the rhythm and the words right so that they shan't be noticed but shall just sink in like water into cloth;

and the thought be the thing that registers. But we must always remember too the man who is speaking. It is what that special personality says to the people he knows, and he has to speak in his own way."

He didn't read the one on Love at first. We read and reread those we had worked on. And after he had gone through those that were still in half-draught and had therefore to be read slowly, with pauses—he read Love also—none more beautiful. It reminded me of the Face he showed me last in New York, and called *The Breath* and it said all that Love itself shows the heart.

"Do you notice how full these things are of what we have said in talking together—sometimes years ago?" said Kahlil. "There's nothing in them that hasn't come from our talks. Talking about them with you has made them clear to me.

"I am keeping my mind from working on this," he said while we were trying a phrase or two in the "Counsels" *— "because yours comes to it fresher than mine. English still fetters me. I don't think without looking for words. In Arabic I can always say what I want to say. I have coined words and phrases in the Arabic—to say what I wanted in the way I wanted—in my way. When I was a boy it was my desire to write in Arabic as well as anybody ever wrote in Arabic. And in all these years, even from the time I first began at sixteen to publish or to be known—with all that has been said and written against my ideas—no one has ever criticized the way I said it or called it poorly said."

When he described the Hermit poet of the "Counsels" and the relation of the people of the City to him, it was a description to the very heart of the way people are toward himself. And he expressed it with an accuracy, a mastery, complete. The words fitted as close as light. It is a solemn thing, and incredible to look into his eyes and have him say as a poem

* The words of The Prophet, in what was to become Gibran's book by that name.

304

what is in his deepest heart. The words seem like little waves on a sea of solitariness under great skies.

We talked hardly at all for the "Counsel" took all our time.

He liked the framing of the pictures. "They are all framed beautifully." As it was raining, he wore my black rubber coat—much closer over his vigorous thick chest than over mine. He is splendidly solid in heart and lungs—"Hit there with your fist—hard," he said, speaking of his chest—"and see."

MISS HASKELL'S SCHOOL

314 MARLBOROUGH STREET, BOSTON

Dear K.G.,   May 8, 1918

If you will talk to the school—it will be on Friday at 11:30. I'd dearly love to have you do it and really it is more for my own sake and the teachers' than for the girls'.

You needn't decide ahead, and you need not let me know ahead, either way. We have that thirty-five minutes to do as we like in, anyhow, at school; and if you are not here, we will sing and read and talk; and I shall know that the Lord is using you somewhere else. And with me, anyhow, you will be, in consciousness—for you are always present with me when I meet the school as a whole and am asking that both speech and silence shall be given me.

Love and blessing to you,

Mary

[Boston]
Saturday night, May 11, 1918

Kahlil was in his new summer suit of Irish homespun—one of the prettiest he has ever had—"That is the reason I wore it!" he said, when I said I had not seen it before.

He has "missed" a real opportunity—"I missed a lunch with Mister Roosevelt and his sister, all alone." He showed me Mrs. Robinson's letter—forwarded—with real disappointment. "I've met Roosevelt, of course, but never in such an intimate way as that. Mrs. Robinson is a remarkable person—full of interest in everything—and with *so* much energy. She can have a dinner of twenty people and knows how to keep them all going at once. She and her brother are alive and sweet and strong. And Mr. Robinson is just like a big elephant. He is a big man in real estate."

I asked him about the girls' design work in school and drawing. "I think they ought to have it, Mary, because it makes them visualize and what they visualize they will never forget. We are creatures of form and color and learn so much by means of form and its color. But why limit it to Design? Why take such a little piece of Art? It would be a small being that would just dwell on the designs for wall paper and cloth and book covers. Why not take it all?"

We took up the "Counsels." Kahlil had copied those we worked on the other night and they were complete. But when we came now to "Talking," I felt something he had not meant in it and we talked long getting at it.

"I'm continually tortured by people's talking; I can't stop listening to what they say. A stream of words, words, words— just the workings of an active mind and a bubbling heart said without realization in the saying, gives me actual pain.

"For six years now you and I have been thinking, talking,

working together. A great many ideas have become part of ourselves so that we don't recognize any longer how we got them. By concrete I mean practical. And to me a concrete life, a real life, a practical life, is to think larger thoughts, to feel more deeply, to imagine strange things, and to go further away. That is what I care about. And anything that makes for this is practical to me. A bed I want warm and hard enough for my body. That's all there is to a bed. Food I want delicious and clean. That finishes food. Anything beyond for bed or food is impractical. The vision is the most practical thing on earth."

The "Counsels" had to be simple, apropos to my comment on "Talking." "It isn't bad to have some parts that are not soft or sweet. This man *cares* and he is telling the truth— and he need not always tell it in the gentlest way. The ideas I don't pretend are new. Many things that one has outgrown, another has not. For people at large one cannot write just as one would write for you and me. A thing cannot be only said. It has to be said again and again—in different ways. A symphony says in each movement usually one big thing— sometimes two or three big things—and then it repeats that one thing or two or three over and over—each time differently. But all the time it is the same music. And it is *that thing* which *is* the symphony to them."

⸱⸱❦{ KG }❧⸱⸱

[New York]
Beloved Mary,   Wednesday—May 29, 1918

I am sending you the twelfth "Counsel" on Buying and Selling. I just wanted you to read it. I am sending you also a little poem. It will speak for itself, yet it may not speak at all!

Last Sunday, at Mrs. Douglas Robinson's, I dined with

Senator Lodge,* General Leonard Wood,† and Dr. Lambert, the head Surgeon of the Red Cross. We talked about the war. There is something about General Wood that moves one's very depth. He is a force, much needed now, yet not used. I have read, since Sunday, that he is not to serve in France. The whole affair hurts me so much that I have been tempted to write him a long letter. Dr. Lambert's experiences in France are *thrilling*, and he knows just how to disclose his experiences. He has the gift of words. Senator Lodge is writing a paper on the *Tempest* of Shakespeare!

Alfred Knopf, the publisher, wishes to bring out my "Parables." I have not talked with Mr. Knopf. I shall surely tell you all about it after I see the man.

With love from
Kahlil

Sunday night
Last of May, 1918

Beloved Kahlil,

I bless your dear heart for sending me "Defeat." Yes indeed, I do love it.

And there are no mistakes in the English. A few little suggestions I would make, sometime, if you would like me to.

The plan for the "Counsels" is so fine and *elastic*—their lines are the lines of *Life*. They are beautiful at every stage, and grateful to the heart and lifting to the spirit.

Mary

* Henry Cabot Lodge (1850–1924), U.S. statesman and author.
† Leonard Wood (1860–1927), chief of staff of the U.S. Army before World War I, and later governor general of the Philippines.

[New York]
Beloved Mary,   Saturday (June 1, 1918)

And will you not read this also, when you have the time?
I am sending these things to you because I cannot keep anything from you and because I always need your help.

Love from Kahlil

------- ·-·◄{ *KG* }►·-·· -------

[New York]
Beloved Mary,   Wednesday—June 5, 1918

I feel that there is something in this "Counsel" which you
will like, though I know that it is not so well written as it
might be. Perhaps there are too many words in it! Perhaps it
is not simple enough in form. But I feel sure that after passing
through your knowing hands it will be.

I hope that you do not mind my sending you these things,
now that you are so busy. Please do not give them a thought
until you have nothing else to do.

With love from
Kahlil

------- ·-·◄{ *MH* }►·-·· -------

[Boston]
Sunday
June 9, 1918

Here are the "Counsels" annotated. But I really don't want
to send them, K.G. I want to keep them. Will you send them
back to me sometime? They grow lovelier and lovelier. It

seems as if each "Counsel" is lovelier than the others and then the others, reread, seem not less lovely; and so they spread far out into the light of my heart just as the wind blows out into the evening.

I'm not sending the "Poem to Love." You didn't tell me to, and it is faultless. It is so much better to me in your hand than copies by me. Just tell me if you want it. God has given you the words to sing and to speak for many who are dumb.

I long to tell you how full of sweetness these "Counsels" are. I wish I had all the other "Counsels" to get familiar with. I draw them up like breath, and am, in the very act of the breathing, in a larger world with the skies and the horizons of every day.

In the daytime and the nighttime, Love from,

Mary

⊷❦ KG ❦⊷

[New York]

Beloved Mary,   Tuesday—June 11, 1918

Bless your eyes that see both the spirit and the body of the "Counsels," and bless your hands that give so abundantly.

I am sending back the three "Counsels" in the shape with which they left your hand. I know you want them just like that. In the "Counsel" on houses the verb "breed" was left out in copying. Of course it should read "the unholy spirit breed (or hide) in cells unvisited by sun and air." And in that same "Counsel"—how do you like "and bees build not their hives on mountain peaks" in the place of "butterflies flutter....."?

I did not know that "grove of enchantment" meant "delusion of delights" or "deceptive pleasures." I only thought of a grove full of real enchantment for the heart. Do you think, Mary, the popular idea should be in the way?

I am glad you like the poem on Love. Three or four of my poet friends think it is the best thing (as a poem) that I have written in English. There is a line in it which reads in your copy, "And let me die and perish." Do make the little change. And, of course, you can keep the poem. I have a copy.

The Poetry Society of America asked me to talk on Walt Whitman and his influence. I said I shall next winter. I am trying my best not to be a *talker* about things. There are so many who can do that much better than I can. I would rather brood in my studio.

With love from Kahlil

KG

Beloved Mary,

[New York]
Friday—June 21, 1918

Mr. Knopf and I have gone over almost everything concerning my little book *The Madman—His Parables and Poems*. The contract was signed yesterday and the frontispiece was given to the engraver while I was there. The book will come out sometime in Mid-October. There will be three drawings in it—the frontispiece and two others.

I have been doing many things during the past two weeks. The gulf between the Syrian work and my own work has to be crossed every day, and that is the thing that tires me. But tomorrow I am going to give myself a wonderful rest! First, I shall go to Rye for a few days. Then I shall go to Long Island. I might be able to work on my "Counsels" while resting. And, of course, I shall send them to you as soon as they take form.

With love from
Kahlil

311

In 1918 the Cambridge School for Girls merged with Mary's school. Mary took with her most of her pupils and teachers. The two schools, now joined, became known as the Cambridge-Haskell School, with Mary as headmistress. According to the school's historian, Persis M. Lane: "Miss Haskell's vitality and enthusiasm brought new vigor to the school. She was a tall, slender woman with large deep-set eyes that radiated warmth and understanding. Her flowing dresses and long strings of beads gave her an almost classic appearance. She seldom walked; she flew. She made her students feel that they were important, and inspired them to make their best efforts."

Mary initiated an Open Air School for Children in the second and third grades. In winter they were bundled up in layers of sweaters, covered by sleeping bags. The windows were opened wide; the children bounced about like rabbits and wrote with mittened fingers.

Beloved Mary,

[New York]
Thursday—July 11, 1918

The last letter from 314 and the first from Cambridge tells me so many wonderfully sweet things about the past fifteen years, and tells me so much of this *now* and of the future. 314 was the stream from which I drank the water of life, and I shall always think of that large room as the birthplace of all that is worthwhile in me and in my life. But, Mary, wherever you are is 314.

May the blessings of God be on 36 Concord Avenue and on all those who come to give or to take in it. And may God make your work a part of His sacred work.

I am sending you, together with this, six prints of the

frontispiece of *The Madman.* They are less clear than what will appear in the book. These are just proofs. The other two drawings you have seen but before they were finished. They are two of the ten drawings which I made for my long Arabic poem. The first is for the poem on God and the second is for the Madman when "the sun kissed his own naked face for the first time."

I shall send you proofs of both these drawings as soon as I receive them from the engraver.

In the country I was not able to write. The sea and the green things took me out of myself—or rather took the words out of my mouth. *But* I made some wash drawings, about fifteen, which, I think, are by far the best I have done as a group.

May God bless you and keep you always.

Love from Kahlil

⸺❧ *MH* ❧⸺

3 6 CONCORD AVENUE

CAMBRIDGE

Beloved Kahlil, July 24, 1918

Mary [Gibran] has been helped by the osteopath—really helped—and the knowledge that she is better is cheering her and lifting away her apprehension, and that will help her too. She is encouraged by her improvement to trust the doctor, also, and that promises well for the future. I think she will consent to keep being treated as long as she needs to be—and I have much hope that she may be beginning a term of real health presently. Her heart is splendid and her lungs absolutely sound.

I can run an automobile now, K.G. It's simple and I like it better than being driven. I got a car from the School—perforce —to bring girls out from Boston. But we've no garage yet, and various details are keeping me from using the car. I'm hoping to take Mary to Cohasset in it.

Fifteen wash drawings! Oh, Kahlil! It seems too good to be true! Are they big ones like the *Gloria* you showed me last time?

Love from
Mary

---- ----

Beloved Mary,

I am leaving for New York tomorrow noon. I telephoned you this morning just to tell you that I shall keep next Saturday and Sunday free so that we may have a visit and good, long talks.

My days here have been rather fruitful. I have added seven new processions to the original Arabic poem. But each new procession calls for a new drawing. So you see, Mary, that I am not only hard pressed by things outside of myself but also by things inside. But all is well with me and God is most generous and kind.

Telephone me Saturday morning if you like. It is *Chelsea* 9549.

Love from Kahlil

---- *MH* ----

[JOURNAL]

[New York]
August 31–September 1, 1918

We walked a little up the Avenue after dinner and in a doorway a white cat was lying, so softly asleep with her paws on the two sides of her head, that we turned back to look at her again. "Dead!" said a man who had just touched her with his cane. And she *was* dead. "I thought it was a little too beautiful to be alive," said Kahlil. And we talked on about the look that comes, as divinely, when people die. Kahlil spoke of his mother's face—"She died of cancer of the stomach, with the most frightful suffering. Yet her face gave never a sign that she suffered. Her mind was clear; her soul commanded her body, and she lived her real life to the very end. The day before she died she was talking with me about the mysticism of Thomas Aquinas and of Ste. Thérèse. She was for a while in the Massachusetts General Hospital and the head physician there used to come and sit a while with her to talk. Her talking was always so delightful. When I was in Paris, there came to see me the French officer who had been in the French Expedition of 1886(?) in Syria. He was a great friend of my father and had stayed at our house. He came to see me because he wanted to tell me my mother was the most wonderful person he had ever met. In Bsherri many people say today, 'I swear by the grave of Kamilah Gibran.' To me they say still, 'By the memory of your mother.' I never saw her when to the least being she was less than a sister or to the greatest less than master. She gave me to understand, even when I was three years old, that the tie between us was as between any two other people, a tie of liking each other—and that we were two separate beings brought together by life and by shame. She was the most wonderful being I have known—I can see her face now, so thin; and yet it grew only more beautiful. The bony structure was so fine—the nose seemed even more fine. Her enormous eyes grew even larger. When she died, the face filled out again. The color came back and I have never seen anything so divine as the glorious expression that was there.

".....Yes, I have felt her near me in many other things besides the time when I was painting her picture." .... We talked about her while we sat in the square at 23rd Street looking up at the night clouds and the light on the Metropolitan Tower. It was a big, brooding sort of night.

Kahlil read some of his *Procession* in the Arabic and told me the idea. The processions are aspects of life as seen by man in two selves—the self of civilization—we called him "civile"—and the spontaneous simple self like certain shepherd lads of the Near East—a man as he accepts and chimes in with life, not analyzing, doubting, debating, or defining. The two meet where their two worlds also meet—on a ridge of land just outside the city and at the edge of the forest and they talk of many things.

An old German brought magazines to the door to sell and Kahlil bought a couple. "I make it a point to buy every other time. He really needs it." The magazines were old German ones.

He had a new "Counsel"—on Love—almost the most beautiful thing he has written in English. We made a tiny change or two then and there. He then read some older notes on Love from one of his notebooks—and they followed beautifully upon the new passages and made all one.

I got Kahlil to read all the "Counsels" again. I love them with all my heart and he loves them, too. "They came out of my own heart, and they are all real to me. I thought of many different structures to use, and when it came to me to have the poet-prophet and the crowd with different ones crying 'Speak of this' and 'Speak of this also!' I knew that would do.

"Have I told you about the man I saw sitting" (outside Jerusalem) "on the same rock every day—just gazing upon the fields? I said to my guide, 'Who is that man?' and he said, 'Oh, he is a little off *here*' (touching his forehead). People called 'touched' are very significant to me; so I went up to him and spoke to him. He returned my salutations most graciously. And I said, 'I have seen you here four or five days.' 'Yes.' 'What do you do?' 'I look upon the fields.' 'And is that sufficient?'—'Isn't that enough?' he said, as if he meant, 'Wouldn't 1/1000 part of all that wonder and glow, more than fill you up?' .... I have never forgotten it.

"I saw a sparrow feed a blind sparrow in Boston—in the Public Gardens about twelve years ago. I used to go there often. I'd buy a quarter pound or a half pound of enriched wheat that the Syrians prepare to feed the doves and the sparrows. One day they were feeding all around me and I noticed that one sparrow was flying off with his grain every time, instead of swallowing it down and waiting for more, as all the others did. So I watched him. He flew off about thirty feet into the grass to another sparrow who was sitting there. The waiting sparrow would lift his head—with un-seeing eyes and my sparrow would put the grain into his mouth and fly back for more. Carefully I moved by degrees over until I was within four or five feet of the sitting bird. He was as large as my sparrow—and my sparrow was a good fat one. And he was adult—with full wings. I waited until they all flew away. The seeing sparrow went close to the blind one and shoved against his shoulder, or, as if he were nudging him, and then they rose with the rest. They kept extremely close together. It was the most moving thing I have seen among animals."

❧ *KG* ☙

Cohasset, Mass.

Beloved Mary,   Wednesday—Oct. 2, 1918

I tried to get you on the phone this evening but you were not there. I wanted to say that I am leaving this place tomorrow afternoon and that I want so much to spend an evening with you before going back to New York. Are you free tomorrow evening and may I come if you are free? I shall call you to-

morrow afternoon just as soon as I arrive at the station, and
then you can give me an answer.

The month which I have spent here has changed me wonderfully. I feel now like a different man.

May God bless you always.

Kahlil

MH

40 Concord Ave.
Cambridge, Mass.
Oct. 27, 1918

Beloved Kahlil,

Thank you for *The Madman*—the dear living treasure,
the valley full of springs by day and of stars by night, the
mountains that speak, and the silent mountains—and, most
of all, dearest of all, the soul and The Soul that we dwell with
these. We hunger most of all for our soul. And in *The
Madman*'s presence many veils dissolve between my soul and
me. That is why I love it, and why I love with unspeakable
blessing to you for it, the drawing on the cover.

Love from
Mary

KG

[New York]
Thursday, the seventh day of
November, One Thousand Nineteen
Hundred and Eighteen

Mary,

Out of the dark mist a new world is born. It is indeed a holy
day. The most holy since the birth of Jesus.

The air is crowded with the sound of rushing waters and
the beating of Mighty Wings. The voice of God is in the wind.

Kahlil

[New York]
Beloved Mary,   Sunday, Nov. 17, 1918

One is filled with the sense of living many lives at once. One's heart is everywhere in these mighty days. Our thirsty spirits stand now on the bank of the Great River. We drink deeply, and we are full of gladness, yet the sweet water itself is thirsty. It drinks us while we drink it.

Long ago, Mary, I said to myself, "God dwells within a thousand veils of light," and now I am saying, "The world has passed through one of the thousand veils of light and is nearer to God." Everything is different. The faces on the streets and in shops and on cars and trains are different. There is a new look in people's eyes and a new ring in their voices. And it is not just the victory of one part of the world over the other that brought this heavenly change. It is the victory of the spirit over that which is less spirit; the victory of the highest in man over that which is less high. The drop of holy oil, placed four years ago in the depth of the deep sea, has risen to the surface. It is the inevitable triumph of the strongest in man; strongest because it is the most blessed.

But why do I write these things to you, Mary? You have always known them; and you, more than anyone in the world have strengthened my faith and knowledge of them.

Love from
Kahlil

December 30, 1918
January 7, 1919
Cambridge

Three visits with Kahlil, on his Christmas visit to Mary in Boston. He was pale and tired when he arrived but the warmth and comparative rest outwardly did him good. On the tenth Kahlil read to the school from his *Madman* and from his unpublished "Counsels." "That was the sweetest audience I ever had," he said. "They were so responsive, they knew when to be silent, and they laughed at just the right time." He read charmingly—just exactly as he reads when in his studio.

Before we went in, four of the tiny girls were in the hall and I let them shake his hand. "Hello!" he said, quite delightedly to them. Even Barbara's face broke into a beaming smile, and she shook hands eagerly. He began directly when he was before his audience: at the close he simply vanished—no chance to speak with him—and waited in the office while I went for the machine.

--- *MH* ---

Beloved K.G.,

40 Concord Avenue
Cambridge   1919

I've a great favor to ask.

The girls want a school ring—just something beautiful—not of necessity symbolic—and they want it now because they've only a month left and they want the design from you. Will you draw us one? Do it if you can.

They haven't decided yet between silver and gold, but the ring they will wear all their lives. I like the idea, but I declare to you I don't want any ring in any school of mine except what you make (design) for us.

O, K.G., I fell from grace the other day—saw three ties I liked at sixty-five cents only per—and yielded. Yes, I knew when I did it that you have enough to make a mummy's wrappings, yet I added these and I'm sending them. If you were like any of the men you know, you wouldn't call your ties many anyhow!

51 West Tenth Street Tuesday
Beloved Mary,   March 25, 1919

Tell me, Mary, do you want me to invent a design for the school seal or have you something in mind which you want me to draw? I have never made a seal, but I would love to make one for the Cambridge School. Will you not tell me just what would be most appropriate for a girls' school? If you are not in a hurry for it, I would like to make it at the school when I come to Boston sometime next month. But if you must have it soon, just send me a sketch of what you want and I will execute it.

Love from
Kahlil

51 West Tenth Street
Beloved Mary,   Thursday—May 1, 1919

Here is a design for the school ring. *It is an open hand holding a rose:* or rather a flower growing in an open hand. I like the idea, and if the design is well executed it should make a beautiful ring. I hope you and the dear girls will like it.

And I feel also, Mary, that this design can be used as a seal for the school. I do not remember seeing anything like it, do you? An open hand is a beautiful symbol, and when you place a flower upon an open hand it adds much to its beauty.

Thank you, Mary, for the beautiful ties.

Bless your hand upon which roses grow.

Love from
Kahlil

322

[New York]
Saturday—Nov. 8, 1919

The evening with Kahlil, after the Head Mistress Association. He looked well, though he has never taken on again the weight he had last fall and winter.

He showed me the printers' proofs for the book of *Twenty Drawings* and two originals that I'd not seen—*Struggle* and *Compassion* (the Centaur). More and more beautiful his things become; more and more infinitely expressive.

"I shall publish two things in English next year—another book of Poems and Parables, and another book of Drawings. After those I'll publish *The Prophet.* I have the Arabic original of it, in elementary form, that I did when I was sixteen years old. It is full of the sacredness of my inner life. It's been always in me; but I couldn't hurry it. I couldn't do it earlier."

❄ *1920* ❄

[J O U R N A L]

April 17, 1920
New York

An evening past all wonder—with Kahlil. The studio building bought by the artists living in it—*The Forerunner* ready
for press, and five new drawings—two other great drawings,
the first of thirty under way.

"I've a great, glorious piece of news for you! A group came
along to buy the building and our rent was to be put up
300 per cent; so, we bought it ourselves, the twelve artists who
live here. The Jacobses, who live below me, and I will put in
bathrooms and share the expense of the piping.

"I've accepted Pond's* offer to make a lecture tour next
winter, but on the condition that I do what is within my
physical limit. I've given five readings here recently. Three
of them I was paid for, but I gave the money back for one—
my reading in the Public Library—for them to buy more

---

* Established by James Burton Pond (1838–1903), this lecturers'
agency managed Henry Ward Beecher, Matthew Arnold, Mark
Twain, and Sir Arthur Conan Doyle, among others.

Arabic books with. They have a very fine Arabic collection. I read also in a theatre and that was perhaps the most thrilling audience I ever had—mostly Jews—such fine young men and women. So full of flame! So ardent! And so keen! They just devour you with their minds. You feel that they not only love what you read, but they understand it—they know what you mean. A remarkable people! What they have read! —There's nothing they don't read!

"I have only ten days before all of *The Forerunner*, with five pictures for it, must be in the hands of the printer. I have just written the epilogue and I was going to send it to you. I've changed the first piece, which you've heard. We'll go over them and finish everything. You won't mind that! You're the only human being who likes work as much as I do!"

A new picture was only half concealed on the easel and so before supper he showed it to me. Oh! so beautiful; so full of that planetary completeness that is blazing out in all of his present work.

Dinner at eight; so we went to the Athens Restaurant, new, on Sixth Avenue nearby—goulash and stewed corn. "I often take this here"—and tea. He smoked hardly at all our whole visit through, and he's thin.

The pictures!

1. *The Forerunner*—like an arrow and the Greater Arrow.

2. *The Slave and the Old Queen*—(for the story of the slaves fanning her).

3. *The Dying Man and the Vulture*—"See, God Himself is another vulture—plucking this (the soul) to Himself to eat," said Kahlil. And the Vulture!—the bird of God—the hunger whose soul has knives for a beak and wings on which to search the universe for food.

4. *The Earth*—Mother of the Heaven Mother—and the Heaven.—Mother is the smile of God—like all the constellations gathered into wreaths of radiance and children—around the Sun that bears them.

5. *"And the Lamb Prayed in His Heart"*—the Baby so

like the Star of Tomorrow—that lives in your heart when he dawns upon your eyes—that henceforth you can never be without him. It is a new Baby for the world.—

Then a water color—

The River of Silence—that is all rivers, and all rocks, and all silences.—

"But there are two big ones—both unfinished—to show you." And when I had seen those two—all the aeons of Life were completed, to me—and had borne their destined fruit.

1. *Three Women*—that reminded me of the three in his old early painting which I have, the baby in their laps—and man before them lifting up man who is smaller, on his hands to them. Divine consciousness has filled their flesh and uses it to shine through.

2. A face—a woman's—a mother's and within her breast two babies—"This is the face I've been trying for twenty years —and I've drawn it at last. This picture has already done more good than anything else I ever drew. All the time of Man is in it—from his least beginnings in protoplasm upon infant earth—to faraway Tomorrow. And so it is in the faces of the *Three Women*, also."

And another face hung in the studio—white on a blue background—terrible, with prisoned flames, and a look as if drenched with flowing tears—though never weeping. "That's a face I saw in the subway; she was between two women who were taking her, I suppose, to a sanitarium. It was so full of things and all bottled up tight!" Kahlil set his jaw and his fists to show the tension.

I showed him the framing of the wee Christ he had drawn me in ink—the little red enamel frame—"Oh, Mary! you've done this so beautifully! How it carries, even at a distance!"

"You know wherever I am I carry pencil and paper. I never throw anything away. So I've a lot of these little things, and I put them all in one place—to save them for you. And someday I'll paste them in a book for you."

The Brazilian edition of *Tears and Smiles*—in the quaint style of the Spanish people there—with a pug-nose cut of Kahlil in front and a photograph of the translator. "He's from my own town—but brought up in Brazil—and he learned Arabic in order to read my work. I know him well from my letters. I'm told the translation is in the most beautiful Brazilian."

At last, he read me the Epilogue for *The Forerunner*.

Never have I heard him so read. All of it had gone through my heart and my whole understanding, so that I was changed by it. He read it all—how he had loved men—all that were in human form—loved them absolutely and none heard his love or saw it or felt it or understood it and he had loved alone.

Only this I had not known, that when he upbraided and denounced men, then they had begun to love him. I knew they loved him but thought they had always loved him as much as now; only that their love was so feeble, so straight, beside his, that it still left him alone and lonely.

That he loved them now even more lovingly than ever, this I knew. But, oh! I knew it better from the ending of the Epilogue.—"Do you like it, Mary?" "I did it about ten days ago." Then we read it all over for corrections—it needed having no word changed, so wonderfully sound is it.

"I heard *The Procession* sung all through a while ago. A Syrian friend was celebrating the birth of a son with a party, like the Arabian nights, with all the beauty but none of the lust. And at midnight, there appeared an old man with flowing beard and a beautiful youth and they took the two parts and sang them through to old Arabic themes that they had found. I was so moved, I wept."

[J O U R N A L]

April 18, 1920
New York

Today we copied Tyranny, and the Epilogue to *The Fore-runner*.

"My whole being is now going into *The Prophet* In *The Prophet*, I have imprisoned certain ideals, and it is my desire to live those ideals. I have sought *The Prophet* ever since I was fourteen or sixteen years old, and only now am I becoming conscious of his truths. He is the ripening of all my life.

"I love people more than ever. But I don't come near to them. I'm always pursuing. I have to do this alone and so I am not a real companion to people.

"When we aren't loving, or when we are not beautiful, we are merely busy with something else. Although we all want to grow in circles, we actually grow in straight lines, and we are learning one thing at a time, while other things wait. That is why we seem slow sometimes in certain growths. We can't say, 'Now I'll grow in this direction,' or 'now I'll grow in that direction.' We have to take growth as it comes."

When I was dictating from Kahlil's manuscript of *The Last Watch*, I cried. Kahlil said, "Mary, I don't mind your crying. Probably nobody in the world has cried more than I. I cry a great deal, here alone."

"I have to learn each thing for myself, my own way. You probably think I'm finicky because I make this stenographer's copy so fussily. But you don't know what I go through later if I don't put in every comma and make every letter and mark unmistakable. The stenographers have no imagination. They simply copy words, *as they see* the words."

We looked up "fledglings," in the dictionary, and in the dictionary we found a little drawing Kahlil did in the fall of

1896 at Beirut—a little girl in marble effigy, or else just asleep, with flowers growing around her—very, very lovely.

Kahlil's English is the finest I know; it is creative and marvellously simple. And now he rarely misspells a word, though he still uses the dictionary as aide, and rarely misses an idiom.

"One of the saddest things is the irony of life. You express something and you are misunderstood. You try another way, and you are misunderstood far worse." (Apropos to *The Last Watch*, where Kahlil tells that love was rejected but that Hate, assumed as a mask, won men's hearts.)

"If I say to a man, 'I understand why you think as you do. It is simply because you are in a certain stage of development. I don't agree with you, but I don't think you could have been different under the circumstances'—he'll turn his back on me and go away. But if I say to him, 'That's a damned bad argument and your point of view is rotten'—he'll want to spend as much time as he can with me to hear himself abused.

"I love light. It is painful to sit in a dim room. I love the light resting on things. I feel it all the time. There's a light in this face, the right-hand face, at *our* left hand (pointing to the *Three Women* picture). And in that face I see something you've spoken of often—that look that is in the faces of the dead.

"Oh! to think how *much* we are! To be consciousness conscious of itself, contemplating itself!

"Some believe God made the world. To me it seems more likely that God has grown from the world because He is the furthest form of Life. Of course, the possibility of God was present before God himself.

"Those new pictures mean a great deal of work. I spent four or five days on that one face (the left-hand one, to our eyes), and the whole picture is to be finished as carefully as that face. It's a technique just the opposite of the tendency of today, but I'm always opposing the tendency of the day." (laughing)

"I'm tending toward much larger canvases. But *The Prophet* is my real work. I write *The Prophet* and make those pictures so that while I'm writing and drawing, I shall *live* these things. The ideas and the ideals are the Self I must realize. It is to realize myself that I live.

"People are always longing for someone to help them realize their best selves, to understand their hidden self, to believe in them and demand their best. When we can do this for people, we ought not to withhold it. We ought not to be just an ear to them."

If Kahlil has omitted a dot, or a final *s*, or a period, and I say, "a dot here," or "an *s*, K.G.," or "a period"—he says, "Oh!"—and puts it. And it is that "Oh!" that I wish could go forth to the world, as his pictures go and his writings. It is as if he were summoned back from a far journey, and were instantly, willingly here, acknowledging the call—but all that he is called away from is in the little sound. Its sweetness is the sweetness of the worlds he has to himself, has to himself because others don't perceive them, even when he tells them of them. And something in it betrays how willingly he would share his worlds and himself—how utterly loving he is—and how utterly lonely.

Tuesday—April 20, 1920
New York

When I came at 7:15 the head of Rodin was on the easel. "I've finished *The Heavenly Mother* today—all except one arm—worked four or five hours on it.....see. All the earth mother and child are complete, and the circle of figures. I think I've made her kinder and sweeter. But that raised arm and hand I don't like at all, and I'm going to do it over.

The Heavenly Mother

"I'm working on other 'Counsels' for *The Prophet*, one on Crime and Punishment, one on Good and Evil, one on Freedom, one on Government."

"K.G., you are so *solid*," I said, as often before, of his torso, which is as firm as if he were oak-ribbed. "Why, Mary, I've a good lung box. Probably what kept me from being strong and large was my shoulder. You know how that was hurt, I've told you? Well, the actual fall, before I reached the soft slope, was about the height of an eight story building and then I rolled with the powdery soil for perhaps two hundred yards more. The other boy broke his leg. I broke my shoulder blade. I healed up, and could move my arm perfectly; but I was crooked. So they broke the bone again. I was not strong enough to take ether, so they had to break it with me all there. Yes, with their hands. Our cousin, a splendid surgeon, was wonderfully powerful in his hands. And then they stretched me out on a cross and I was like one crucified for forty or fifty days. And that was a wonderful thing in my life. It was the beginning for me of consciousness of people. I felt how wonderful they were. They used to take me out and when they did everybody used to come up to me. It was like a procession. After that shoulder, I never grew an inch more, in my life. Probably the shock simply stopped me. And the next year came the leaving home for Egypt and then Paris. And at last we came to Boston. For me, personally, it was great good fortune. If we had not come, my parents would have sent me abroad to study, but not to study what I wanted! Then I'd have gone back and stayed in Syria. My mother's desire was to be a nun. Her father was a monseigneur and she had four brothers and two sisters. They were people of wealth and all the others came to nothing special. The sons were spendthrift and they went through the family means. But my mother was the youngest, and the Bishop used to say, 'I have one child,' she was so near to him. There is an ancient convent near Bsherri, a heavenly place, and my mother loved it. By the time she was eighteen or nineteen she had planned to go into the convent. She had arranged to give a lot of money to it, and all was fixed. Then her people said, 'Of course this can't be,' and her first husband proposed to her and many influences were brought to bear. She married and later she married my father. But when I was eighteen or nineteen we were talking in Boston one day and she said, 'I've sometimes thought I may have made a mistake after all, not to have gone into that life.' 'But,' said I, 'if you had gone into that life I should not have come.' She said, 'My son, you were inevitable,' and then she said, 'You'd be one of the angels.' I said, 'But I'm an angel, anyhow!' And she said, 'Let me feel your wings!' She put her hands on my shoulder-blades, and felt them, and then she said, 'Broken wings!' "

Of Ryder's face, when I said it had the look of a deserted house when even the glass is broken out of all the windows, "But empty is not what you'd call it. Rather the life is remote, withdrawn. He had a real magnetism, a great delicacy and gentleness. He lived in a room with all his possessions piled up around him. But there was, in his work, a magic that was unique. He used to be the best dressed artist in New York. He loved a married woman whose husband treated her badly. Ryder went away on a trip and when he came back he couldn't find her.

"I'm working, you know, on the 'Counsel' Crime and Punishment. I never can divorce myself from the criminal. When I read of a forgery, I feel that I am the forger, and of a murder that I, too, have committed murder. If one of us does a thing, we all do it. What collective humanity does is done by each of us. What is in one of us is in all of us. What is in the poet is in everyone."

We prepared *The Forerunner* for the typist and the printer. It took us from about 10 to 1. Kahlil says he writes faster in English from dictation than alone, and I love working with him. It is repose itself to work with someone who considers only perfection and never stops short of it while there is hope.

"I love to see people but I want to know when to expect them. Some very lovely people used to like to drop in on me, people I'm very fond of. They just wanted to come in for half an hour, but that half hour might cost me my day, because I have to pull my mind away from what it is working at and often it can't get going so well again in that particular way for hours. So I had to put a stop to it. I make it plain always that I love to see people but that they must write or telephone first."

Wednesday—April 21, 1920
New York

"Sometimes I sleep eight hours, sometimes ten, sometimes four, and several times I have gone two or three nights together without any sleep at all. I just lie in bed and read. Presently the dawn comes, and the day, and I make coffee. I go to work as usual and night comes again and the same thing happens. When I've been very hard at it and have had to see many people, I'm apt to sleep ten hours—just deep, quiet sleep."

"This country needs hundreds of soul-doctors. But they mustn't be theorists or nationalists or internationalists. They must have a universal consciousness and be able to help people look in a different direction. An idea that hurts or enchants us acts like a magnet. Presently it becomes our fixed way of thinking and feeling. Then we need something to make us turn a little and see another part of reality. When we find that one thing has aspects we hadn't thought of, it occurs to us sometimes that other things too may have more aspects than we see.

"To me all reality is movement. Repose is the harmony of motion. But Nirvana is motionless.

335

"Love is conscious. It is a creative impulse. It has no object except to fulfill itself.

"The sense of season and of day and night was quickened in me by my mountain trips on horseback during the summers I was at college in Lebanon. The nights in the meadows high up in the mountains, so full of flowers. We'd make camp by the spring and sleep under the stars. How the heavens are there, with the stars so brilliant and the sky so full of many depths! We'd wake early in the morning and Venus would come up—she casts a shadow there. The brook and every flower, the birds and even the rocks seemed to sing.

"My mother did not cook and wash and scrub for me. But it is her mothering *me* I remember—the inner me.

"Man is the best design of all those the earth life has yet produced. I'm thinking, when I say that, of everything on earth as a design—plants, crystals, animals, etc.

"When anyone seems slow, he is slow in a certain direction; that is not because he lacks life but because he is doing something else. And what he is doing is what he needs to do. It may be something he is unconscious of. But we are unconscious of much that is real in our lives. The same life is in him that is in everything."

April 1920 saw the formation of Ar-Rabitah. This was a group of Syrian writers in New York who wanted to serve the Arabic language and its literature. Members included: Kahlil Gibran, Nasseebarida, William Catzeflis, Rasheed Ayoub, Abdul-Masseeh Haddad, Madra Haddad, and Mikhail Naimy.

It appears that until this year Mary was still sending Gibran the money she had begun to send in 1908.

CAMBRIDGE SCHOOL

36 AND 40 CONCORD AVENUE

CAMBRIDGE, MASSACHUSETTS

Beloved Kahlil,   Sunday—4/25/20

The great wash drawing is hanging now on the big wall in my office. It makes me pray. The man who kneels in it is my own heart. It is a great, beautiful, loving reality and I hear its voice in the whole building.

We hung it on Friday night so the School has not seen it yet. *Rose Sleeves* is in the hall, and when *The Crucified* comes, the *Beholder* will be in the hall also. But perhaps *The Crucified* will do well to stay a month more in New York while people are apt to be coming through who will want to see your work. I think that is best if it has not already started.

We forgot to wrap up the little eiderdown robe for me to send to storage the evening I left. It won't be much trouble, will it K.G., to put a paper round it and send it to me? And you might put your fur collar in with it. I'll send them to cold storage and that will be better for them than just keeping them moth-proof.

Mary

CAMBRIDGE SCHOOL

36 AND 40 CONCORD AVENUE

CAMBRIDGE, MASSACHUSETTS

Beloved Kahlil,   Wednesday night—April 29, 1920

The Crucified is here and I think I never half saw this beautiful, beautiful picture before—its form, its feeling, or its

337

color. Surely it was my inner light that was lacking; the outer light in the studio cannot have been so different from the light here. It is an infinity in each of its selves, in strangeness, in splendor, in tenderness, in pain and longing and silence.

It is so terrible in its pain that talking about it seems like talking about a soul in torture. It's the most beautiful, the most appealing, the most rebuking, wonderful, and dearest thing I ever had. It is the Heart unveiled.

And what can I say to you, Kahlil, for letting me have this! I wish I could say to you what it says to me. That would be real speech. But, you understand, you understand better than I myself.

God bless you, beloved Kahlil.

Love from
Mary

[JOURNAL]

Cambridge—May 20, 1920

—Kahlil for the afternoon, looking well, though he's tired.

"I had a fine evening at The Society of Arts and Sciences. William Butler Yeats was there, and he read too and talked. I spent an evening with him and his wife. A strange being. When he is there, absolutely dumb, but at the dinner I sat by her and she was very much alive, interested and well read. No doubt she helps him a great deal. She understands so much and can ask so many questions. And he needs to be helped so much. For instance, he was sitting talking, deeply in earnest and very eager and just here, say, was his tea. He kept feeling here and there for something. She said, 'You want some sugar, don't you? Here it is,' and then he was all right."

About democracy—"The very core of democracy is love."

"Woman as woman has one great purpose. It uses her, and through her it uses man. In the deepest wells of her being it is springing up, the creation of life. She loves a man and loves him sincerely. She loves his dreams or his vision or his art or his learning or his business. But through it all, he is her means to her great end.

-------------------------------- ⊰{ *MH* }⊱ --------------------------------

[JOURNAL]

Monday—May 22, 1920
Cambridge

"We see a thing first in fancy, then in imagination; then we know it, then it becomes matter of fact to our perception and then we forget it. But when we forget it, it lives on in our subconscious and it has made us a little different by becoming part of us.

"Man is the most crystallized thing on the planet. When I paint a picture, I try to give the picture a presence. It is the coming together of certain elements in a certain way, as if they made a sort of path along which God can come through to our consciousness. Sometimes it suddenly appears in a group and everybody wants to say the most important things he knows about the things that are most important. God and the universe are two universes occupying the same space. They are but one universe."

"I can't think of the *end* of anything. Well, then, what is the reason for thinking of anything as having a beginning?"

"*The Procession* has been sung in Cairo, with thousands of people."

[New York]

Beloved Mary,   Monday—July 19, 1920

I have just returned from a refreshing visit to the country and found your still more refreshing letter. Of course, I wanted you to like the *Breath on a Window Pane* but what you said of the Christ Head means infinitely more to me. I *did* feel, after making that drawing of the beloved Jesus, that it was nearer to my heart, as an expression, than anything else you have. But I was not sure whether it was the face I *saw* or the face I *drew*. Oftentimes when one is drunk with an idea, one is apt to think that the expression of it is the wine. We have two pairs of eyes, Mary, and we are always mistaking what one pair sees for what the other pair sees.

My sister and I cannot get the rooms at Cohasset this summer. But it does not matter. I shall come to Boston. I can always do more work in the city than in the country. And I *must* do a great deal of work this summer or else be snowed under.

I am so delighted to hear all the good things about the school. There is nothing more wonderful than building up things. *Building up* outside of us really means *building up* inside of us. The outside is but a replica of the inside.

With love from
Kahlil

[J O U R N A L]

Cambridge—August 20, 1920—Tuesday

Kahlil for the afternoon. He walked straight up to the Mother picture. "That frame is fine and just right. It enlarges the picture. The way the frame repeats the color that is in the arm is a great thing." Then he went to the Christ Head. "Yes. It's far ahead of anything else you have. I'm so glad to see it." I said that the woman's head with the baby's head was the only thing I could hang near it. "Yes. But she has just a hunger for something which He has found," said Kahlil.—Later, "Wouldn't that Face be a good thing to use as the frontispiece to my *Prophet*? It would have to be redrawn, for I wouldn't touch this one, for the reproducer."

"People say such complicated things about my drawings. An English critic has written about my book of drawings, and oh! such meanings and such significances as he finds intended! —things I never meant at all! For when I draw, if it happens that I do something a little nice or with some worth, I'm unconscious. Three or four hours after it's done I can't tell you anything about what it looks like. I'm not that way when I write. I do know what I'm writing, but I don't know what I'm drawing or painting. And actually when I read all these things that are sometimes said, I feel almost as if I were cheating. For I worked as simply as a child and I don't recognize at all much of what I'm given credit for.

"The only way to work is to do everything with the best that is in you. With the deepest heart of the heart and with the Eyes that are the fountain of the tears. I know living poets who never write from their inmost selves. They fear to be alone. And it hurts to be alone with themselves. They will not face that pain. If there is anything in my work that draws people, it is probably that something that speaks to the aloneness in each one of us. I *love* to be alone. And it is when I am alone and far away, whether I'm in the physical company of people or not, that I love them best. Then they are dear to me. But just let even a thumb's pressure be put upon me to tame the wild something in me, and I feel it like a fetter. It rouses something bitter in me."

He has done the "Counsel" on Crime and Punishment for *The Prophet*, very profound and new and beautiful.

We went over the whole "Counsel" and at the figure of the weaver with threads black and white, we stopped, for I questioned the metaphor, and Kahlil had to explain it to me. "But," he said, "the fact that I have to explain it shows that there's something wrong in my expression."

He brought *The Tempests*—just received, in Arabic—a very lovely format, in grayish paper, beautifully printed, just the form he likes, and wrote in it for me.

"*The Forerunner* is in press now. *The Prophet* must be finished in two or three months for the reading tour. I am to read in New York first at the best time of the winter, probably early February, then in Boston."

--◆{ *MH* }◆--

[JOURNAL]

Cambridge—August 27, 1920

We took down one more picture, and Kahlil said he would send me three.

We changed one word more in "Crime and Punishment."

"I'm a one-track person. While I draw here, I love to talk, but when I am really working, I do absolutely nothing. I think about nothing else. When I was doing *Tempests*, for two or three weeks nothing else was in my thoughts. It was the same way when I was getting the drawings ready for *The Forerunner*. I work a long day, eight hours or more.

"I'm probably one of the surest of people, and stubborn when I'm sure. If all the other inhabitants of the earth, for instance, believed that the individual soul perishes with death it would move me not an atom to agree with them, because I know my soul won't perish.

"Several of the 'Counsels' will be loved and accepted at once, because of a beauty in them; the 'Counsel' on Crime and Punishment will take hold and make people reverse their consciousness. The one on Marriage says, of the man and the woman, 'Let them fill one another's cup, but let them not drink of the same cup.' What do I mean by that? I mean, let them not try to live the same life! They start doing just that and they end by hating one another and living apart, even if under the same roof.

"We are creative, when we make over the impressions that come to us into something of our own and give them a being of our own."

[JOURNAL]

Cambridge—August 31, 1920—Tuesday

"I've brought a new 'Counsel,' " said he, when he came. It was on Freedom. "I want to say only those things that are at the source of things. I want the root out of which the fruits will grow. I want to use figures and symbols that are planetary. I use the footprint as a figure, because the footprint will be here as long as there is a planet."

A big storm broke, with torrents of rain and with thunder. Kahlil was elated. "Mary, a storm does something for me that nothing else on earth does. In a storm like this one I rode on a white horse at a run, galloped fifteen or sixteen miles. The horse was probably a little bit maddened. I was exceedingly happy. My first memory is of a storm. I tore my clothes to run out into it. They ran after me, and brought me back. I was soaked and they rubbed me with alcohol. But I ran out into many another. Everything I've done that is biggest has come from a storm. My latest book is named *Storms* (*The Tempests*)." There came a great thunder roll.

"That went through me like Christ speaking to me," said Kahlil.

"This is the twenty-first 'Counsel.' You know twenty-one

was the number I originally planned, and now I shall set to work on the story at the beginning of it and on the Farewell. But if in the meantime other 'Counsels' come to me, there's no reason why they shouldn't be added. The number can be twenty-three, twenty-seven, or twenty-nine."

"But not twenty-four, twenty-five, twenty-two," said M.E.H. "No," said Kahlil. "I never think of those numbers. They aren't for me. 3, 7, 9. You know 7 is probably from the five planets the ancients knew, and the sun and the moon. And 12 was sacred too, from the months of the year, and 4 from the four seasons and the four points of the compass. And 3 we can never get away from."

We wrote down a number of his short sayings, from the English ones in his notebook and from the Arabic ones on sheets, to collect for copying; and spent most of the visit on them. The time flew and, as usual, we missed the right car.

"There are almost no people whose English I kneel before. I have a sense of English and I know many words, for I've an ear for words. It is the shaping of my English expression that comes slowly to me. English is a fine language. There's nothing that can't be said in it, but one has to use many words. If a thing could be said in ten words, I've tried to say it in three. What was long said, by everyone and in several ways, I've tried to say in a way so perfect that hereafter people would remember only my way. I want to take a common stone, and carve upon it a face that no one can forget."

[JOURNAL]

Cambridge—September 3, 1920

"You know some of those sayings we've been talking about are bitter and distant from me now. But if I throw away everything I outgrow, I'll throw away a great deal. And they were real for me when I wrote them. Well, I've thought of a form and a setting that will hold them just as they are. I am on a journey to the Holy City. In the morning I overtake a stranger. He is sad and bitter. The next day he is a little less bitter, and we are nearer the Holy City. The third day he is still less bitter; and so he changes on through the fourth and fifth and sixth, and on the seventh he is saying the planetary things. And we arrive at the Holy City. I lose sight of him. In the evening I see him near the wall of the temple."

"Praising God is singing hymns to one's self."

"There are painters who would call this dish of grapes beautiful, and they would paint the grapes, trying to get just their very bloom and color and light and roundness. But when you look at the grapes, think of the vines, and how they grow, and the harvest. Think of the store where the wine is sold, and the mouths it goes into: one from this part of the city, another from over here. And think of the bowl they are in, made in China, and think about the Chinese and all you know of the life of the Chinese. Seeing things that way enriches the imagination. And children can be taught to do this. Take the corner of this desk: think of the wood it's made of, how the trees grew, and then how they were cut down in the forest. And of the men who cut them down, and what each man's life is in his own home. This simple exercise opens everything.

"My mother was always doing little things that put me in the way to love others besides herself, always pushing me away or out a little. She freed me from herself. And she said things to me when I was twelve years old that I'm just realizing now. When I was sixteen, she said, 'Yes, you'll write like this until you are thirty-five. Then, you will write.' I didn't like that and she said, 'No, I didn't mean what you are thinking I meant. People will always love what you write. And I like those things, too. You've found yourself. But you'll have to live a great deal before you find that other man. And you'll have to write what he has to say.' 'But I can write these things now,' I said. 'No,' she said. 'When you're thirty-five.'

———— ❧ *MH* ☙ ————

[J O U R N A L]

Cambridge—September 7, 1920—Tuesday

Today Kahlil brought the beginning of *The Prophet*. How Almustafa had waited twelve years for the ship of purple sails, and when he saw it come, how he spoke to himself of the dearness with which his pain had clothed the city in his heart, so that he sorrowed to depart.

"Almustafa, the chosen and beloved, he who was a dawn unto his own day, had waited twelve years in the city of Orphalese, for the ship of purple sails to return and bear him back again to the isle of his birth.

"Every day, upon the high hills without the city walls, he stood searching the distances for his ship. But the ship came not; and his heart grew heavy within him, for deep was his longing for the land of his memories and the dwelling-place of his greater desires." Then, in the twelfth year, on the seventh day of which is the month of awakening, came the ship of purple sails, and he descended the hills to go. But he could not go without pain, for all the self that he left in the city, and for his heart made sweet there with hunger and thirst. "Fain would I take with me all that is here." Yet, "A voice cannot carry with it the tongue and the life that gave it wings. Alone must it seek the ——— and alone and without his nest shall the eagle fly across the sun.

"Now when he had descended from the hill, he turned again towards the sea and he saw his ship approaching the harbor. And he beheld her mariners, the men of his own land, upon her bow." Forgot the wording here, but he hails them, "riders of the tides," and says, "How often have you sailed in my dreams, and now you are come at this awakening, which is my deeper dream. Ready am I to go, and my eagerness, with sails full set, awaits the time." (I forgot again, until) "But another breath will I breathe in this air then shall I go with you, a seafarer among seafarers.

"And you, vast sea, sleepless mother, who alone are peace and freedom to the river and the stream, only another winding will this stream make, only another murmur in this glade, and then shall I come to you, a boundless drop to a boundless ocean.

"These things he said in words. But in his heart more remained unsaid. For he himself could not speak his deeper silence."

That much, Kahlil has written, and planned the rest, How Almustafa when he comes down from the hill whence he saw the ship, will find all the city meeting him, for now they know, and they know they love him; and they follow him, and ask him to counsel them, one after another questioning him; and to all of them he delivers his counsel; and then they go with him to the ship; and he speaks his farewell; and it is ended. A little of the farewell, too, is written.

"I thought," said Kahlil, "that I would use the name Almustafa only in the book, at the very beginning. And through the rest of it, say 'he.' 'Almustafa' in Arabic means something special, the Chosen and the Beloved, too, really between them both." And he debated whether to use the phrase "the Chosen and Beloved" after the name. When I asked about omitting the "land of his memories," Kahlil said, "All that is written here is written with many things in mind. Each thing is a symbol of man's life as a whole, and the 'land of his memories' is all our historic past. Life bears us from our great past toward our greater future. I may find something better than the 'purple sails' for the vessel. But of old, vessels with purple sails were actually used for certain sacred errands, so I used this image.

The Forerunner is a small book also. "Ideally a book should be small. I want you to be able to read a book at a sitting, before you go to sleep at night, or to put in your pocket and take it out on an afternoon walk."

We need to learn to be our own critics. A poet has a vision, when he is in another world. He comes back from that world and he tries to tell his vision. He may not get the actual thing into his poem at all, or, if he is an artist, into his picture. But when he reads his poem, every line in it reminds him of something in his vision, and he lives the vision over again as he reads.

Saying: "When I stood, a clear mirror before you, you gazed into my depths and beheld your own image. Then you said you loved me. But in truth it was yourself you loved. I am content." (I remember it imperfectly.)

Saying: (imperfectly quoted) "When I stand before that beautiful great presence which is invisible, I am held and still, with awe. Then you pass by, and see me, and say to yourself, 'How meek he is! And how humble! Of what is he afraid?'"

Saying: "You say to me, 'We shall not know your worth until you are dead.' In truth you shall not know until then. How shall the heart of a seed be known, except the seed die? And if indeed you would know my worth, it is that I had more in my heart than on my tongue, and more in my desire than in my hand."

Saying: "I am sick of your small selfishnesses. Give me a great selfishness, and I will call you a god."

Saying: (imperfectly quoted) "Your heart is your temple. When you enter therein to pray, take with you all men. For in your prayer you cannot rise higher than their dream, nor humble yourself lower than their desire."

About Christianity. "Christianity has been very far from the teaching of Christ. In the second or third century, people were not vigorous enough to take the strong food that Christ gave; they ate only the weak food in the Gospels, or what they thought they found there and in the teaching of the men that came after Christ. They could not face the gigantic self that Christ taught. They could not conceive the real life where you lie on the earth and look up at the stars.

"The greatest teaching of Christ was the Kingdom of Heaven, and that is within you. Is a man that has the Kingdom of Heaven within him poor? If I am nothing, and you are nothing, here are two nothings together. And what have you? What has the whole world if everybody considers himself nothing? But if the Kingdom of Heaven is within you, if you have that calm in yourself, that quiet in your centre, if you are in love with life, you love your enemy because you love everybody."

— ⋅⋅⋅❧ *MH* ❧⋅⋅⋅ —

[JOURNAL]

[Cambridge]
Friday—September 10, 1920

"In *The Prophet,* the subjects are simple and belong to everyday life. There are many things we talk about, you and I, which I would not take up in the 'Counsels,' because they are metaphysical. Well, in the Land of his birth, the prophet can speak of all those subjects and a thousand others. He is free.—That other book will be a book of the *other life* within ourselves. The philosophy will be put so simply that a child can understand it. The framework will be easy.

"The most significant thing Christ said was just four words: 'I say unto you'—'*I* say'—'All the rest of the world teaches you so and so, *but,* I say unto you.' It was his own projection upon the world and upon life that he gave them, what he was living out from within himself.

"To think about oneself is terrifying. But it is the only *honest* thing: to think about myself as I am, my ugly features, my beautiful features, and wonder at them. What other *solid* beginning can I have, what to make progress from except myself?

"Invention is the only thing, with me—the pushing out through one's own skin, projecting one's own self. A seed that has not sprouted, and a seed that is bursting its shell, may have equal power, but for me the one that is bursting its shell is the one that registers. To be conscious is to see the newcomer with my own eyes, and feel with my own hands, not to borrow Mrs. Smith's eyes to see with and her hands to feel with and her words to tell about the newcomer with. Whatever I have, let me open my heart and pour it out. Let me not hesitate to put my arm lest someone cut it off; or lest my movement be foolish and someone hit me. Let it be foolish, if foolishness is my best today, and let someone hit me hard. Then I may be a little less foolish next time. When two people meet, they ought to be like two water lilies opening side by side, each showing its golden heart, not closed up tight, and reflecting the pond, the trees, and the sky. And there is too much of the closed heart. When I come to you, we talk for four or six hours. If I'm going to take six hours of your time, I ought to unfold for you, and to be sure that it is myself I give."

Cambridge—Tuesday—September 14, 1920

I showed Kahlil J.M.'s letter, written in the emptiness of the loss of her baby and her sense of futility and her questioning about God. "Oh!" said Kahlil, his face drawn. "That's the world I work with! The life made all of surfaces, and out of it, a cry. You can't leave her to find God in herself. You have to help her. The fact that she says, 'You don't believe in God, do you?' shows she wants to believe in Him.

"There is an aloneness in every man. He can be helped to look at the invisible. It may take a long time to reach a consciousness of God. God can't be demonstrated. I never tried to prove His existence. The idea of God is different in every man, and one can never give another his own religion."

He brought the third writing on the setting for *The Prophet*. How, as he walked on, he saw from afar the men and women leaving their fields and vineyards and hastening towards the gates of the city. And he heard many voices calling his name, and men shouting one to another from field to field telling of the return of his ship. And he said to himself, "Shall the day of parting be the day of gathering and shall it be said that my eve was in truth my dawn? And what shall I give unto him who has left his plough in midfurrow, and to him who has stopped the wheel of his winepress. Shall my heart be as a fruitladen tree, that I may be—and shall my desires become as a fountain, that I may fill their cups? Am I a harp that the hand of the mighty may touch me, and a flute that His breath may blow through me? A seeker of silences am I. And what treasures have I found in silences that I may dispense with confidence? If this is the day of my harvest, in what unknown fields have I sowed the seed, and in what unremembered seasons? If this be indeed the hour in which I shall lift up my lantern, it is not my own flame that shall burn therein. Empty and cold shall I raise my lantern, and the guardian of the night shall fill it with oil, and he shall light it also." This he said in words. But more remained in his heart unsaid. For he himself could not speak his inmost silence.

And when he entered into the city, all the people came together to meet him and they cried unto him as with one voice. Then the elders of the city stood forth and said unto him, "Go not yet away from us. A noontide have you been in our twilight, and your youth has given us dreams to dream. No stranger have you been among us, and not a guest, but our son and our beloved. Suffer not yet our hearts to hunger for your face." And the priests and the priestesses said unto him, "Let not the waves of the sea separate us now. You have walked among us, a spirit, and your shadow has been a light upon our faces. Let not the days you have passed in our midst become a memory that feeds upon the heart. Much have we loved you. But speechless was our love, and with veils has it been veiled. Now does it cry aloud unto you, and would be revealed before you. And ever has it been that love knows not its own depth until the day of separation.

"And many others came also and entreated him; and he answered not, but bent his head. And those who stood near him beheld his tears falling upon his breast.

"It was written down in a hurry," said Kahlil. As we got into the text, we began at once to condense the connecting phrases. We always have a fine time over a manuscript, because one can talk to Kahlil as to one's self. There is no pride to guard, and no treasuring of phrases. He likes to work on and on and over and over until the thing is SAID. Sometimes we have to leave a thing to ripen in Kahlil. Never before has he written so systematically on an English book. So we are doing more than usual. Usually, he keeps things to show me, until he has completed them. But this *Prophet* prologue he brings in its first or second writing down. He says the final form comes quicker than when he prunes it alone. Our method is, first, Kahlil reads it through aloud to me. Then we look together at the text, and if we come to a bit that I question, we stop until the question is settled.

He *knows* more English than any of us, for he is conscious of the bony structure of the language, its solar system. And he *creates* English.

"I have been teaching myself to prune and to try for consciousness of structure. And this consciousness of structure is fundamental." When I said I loved "working" at his manuscript better than anything else in the world, he said, "I'll bring you every line I ever write."

Early in the summer of 1920, Florance Minis invited Mary to accompany him on a trip to Egypt. Minis had traveled extensively in Europe, and was to cross the Atlantic more than one hundred times during his life. Mary looked forward to the adventure of visiting the pyramids. Unfortunately, the trip was postponed.

Beloved Mary,
[New York]
September 20, 1920

I am so sorry that your trip to Egypt has been postponed. But Egypt was *there* six thousand years ago, and will stay *there* another six thousand years, and you will visit it, and you will see the strangeness and hear its silence. Why hurry? That which time has left about the dust of Egypt is almost changeless.

I had a good summer. The days which I spent in the country were very beautiful and cool and large. And we talked much, you and I.

The Prophet will come out early in October. It is a good month for books. I always feel that October is the beginning of something.

Love from
Kahlil

CAMBRIDGE SCHOOL

36 AND 40 CONCORD AVENUE

CAMBRIDGE, MASSACHUSETTS

Beloved Kahlil,   10/10/20

I've been writing to you every few days and never sending the letter. I dearly love the pictures. Late at night, I've opened the packet and spread them about. And it has been wonderful to have them here beside the pictures on the walls. It has taught me to see in more ways than before. O, K.G., it was dear of you to trouble in the midst of the crowdedness of your return to send the drawings to me. *Thanks!*

I never sent my letter to you, because of a cloud within myself, and because I both wanted to talk to you about it, and did not want to tell you about it at all. For I was hurt, and telling would hurt you too. But I'm going to tell you.—A lady told me she would not send a daughter here to School because I had *The Crucified* hanging on the wall. And two or three of the teachers said they thought the *Mother of Heaven* might be unwise to hang—and even *The Lamb Prayed in His Heart.* Even yet I can hardly believe it, and it makes things look black before my eyes, to write it. Worst of all, to write it to you. If I could hide the face that people can feel thus, I would hide it. They say the pictures might make *girls* feel uncomfortable and that girls cannot feel "the spiritual" quality of the drawings.

What I feel about nude figures in the pictures here is that the girls are exceedingly fortunate to have them about among the people they love and respect. Their presence teaches that there is nothing shameful in nakedness or in the body—and that it is not taboo among desirable people—and that it need not make a girl uncomfortable. The pictures are a silent reassurance. And if a girl wants to see naked bodies, why, let her see them openly here and be saved from shame at her desire. If she wants to see nakedness, is the desire deplorable? I don't see that it is. Why not satisfy it?—To have here every picture I love, would be the finest single thing this school could do for young people—and not one word need be said about a single picture, to make them effective. Their very being in this place says to the girls, "What you see in us is well, and it is well that you see it."

Anxiety about the effect of these drawings on girls seems to me just a part of the very complicated and fear-beset and harassed mind toward life that people are always giving me glimpses of. I say to myself, "It is necessary"—and remind myself how much of it I too had and still have. But what I do not quite know, is how fully to meet it, or when to disregard it, if school is concerned. And, not knowing what to do, I've done nothing. I put *The Crucified* into my own room, and *The Beholder* looks very lovely in *Crucified*'s place in my office.

Love from
Mary

—◆{ KG }◆—

[New York]
Monday—October 11, 1920

Beloved Mary,

The wisest and the kindest thing to do is to take down from the walls all the pictures that offend the girls and their mothers. The thought that a drawing of mine is making someone uncomfortable, in body or in spirit, is a source of pain and unhappiness to me. We cannot teach the chastity of the nude. People must find it for themselves. We cannot lead people to the hearts of life. They must go by themselves, and each one must go alone.

I beg of you, dear Mary, to take down every drawing of which you have heard the slightest *uncomfortable* remark.

And after all, why should this thing trouble you or me?

There is nothing in it that should make things seem black before your eyes or before mine. What people feel or think is
part of Life, and you and I have always accepted all of Life.
The root of a tree is not lower than its highest branch.

Love from
Kahlil

-⊷❴ *MH* ❵⊶-

[JOURNAL]

[Cambridge]
December 18, 1920

I asked Kahlil about his reading tour. "That is off; I can't
help being glad. It was like a heavy weight on my soul. Somehow the idea of reading that *Prophet* from city to city, under
advertisement was sacrilege to me. It is my religion, my most
sacred life. I love to read it here in this studio to little groups,
or to certain gatherings. I should love to read it in a church.
In fact the first reading of it is to be in a church in New York.
Two or three are open to me for it. I don't care what I do
with anything else I've written.

"—My life has a great deal of seeing people in it, just individuals, one by one, and groups as well. And I want it to be
so more and more. I want to *live* reality. Better than to write
ever so truly about fire, is to *be* one little live coal. I want
some day simply to live what I would say, and talk to people.
I want to be a teacher. Because I have been so lonely, I want
to talk to those who are lonely.

"I spoke at a dinner to Tagore and gave Tagore the dickens.
You know Tagore has talked about America as a money-
grabbing land without a vision. I tried to say that spirit may
be manifest in machinery, that material and spiritual are not
opposed, but that spirit is in all of life and in everything.

"I told you about the thing I wrote for *El Hilal*—'You have your Lebanon and I have my Lebanon.' Well, the censorship in Syria cut it out of the magazines and out of the Syrian papers that reprinted it, and out of the papers coming into Syria from New York and Cairo and South America that printed it. But they didn't cut my name and the title out of the Table of Contents. So now everybody knows the piece was there, and they are determined to get it, and will do more than if the government had let it alone."

✣ *1921* ✣

[JOURNAL]

Cambridge—Tuesday—January 3, 1921

Kahlil for the afternoon. I showed him the white ink I had got, neither of us had seen any before, and we got out the brown piece of paper to try it on. But Kahlil got started with an ordinary pencil and he found that his eraser made a whitish mark, so he was soon well along with a Christ profile—very beautiful. Three hours later he took up the same profile, and after a few strokes on it said, "See what changed it!—Just a few lines now have made it a good drawing."

"Mary," he said, "I wonder if you have any idea how much you have enlarged my consciousness. You are always tap, tapping at me, and making me find new things." "I am always hungry for you to do it," said I, "for I feed on your consciousness."

"The thing in *The Madman* and *The Forerunner* which is nearest to people is the Last Watch. Everyone has experienced that truth: that love, like a running brook, is disregarded, taken for granted; but when the brook freezes over, then people begin to remember how it was when it ran, and they want it to run again."

358

"We ought to come to our work as we come to a beautiful child, with reverence and love."

We had the kerosene heater going and as darkness fell, its light, through the circles in the top, made a shadowy, moving light-flower over all the ceiling—most deep and wonderful.

I told Kahlil about Betelgeuse (Alpha Orionis), just measured by Michelson's* method using interference of its light rays. How it is 27,000,000 times the size of the sun, 7,000,000,000 the size of the earth and would almost fill the orbit of Mars. When Kahlil hears a stupendous reality like this, his soul almost leaves his body. He says nothing, but if he were alone, I'm always sure that rapture, what he describes as "floating," would begin then and there, and he would be gone out to meet God, for I know not how long. His consciousness expands, as with a breath, into the firmaments, and in the firmaments it dwells, even while he talks on and thinks on with me also. It is always in me then to cut the string and say, "talk no more. Fly away. Seek the sun!"

"It takes two to talk. There must be an ear to hear; there must be that which *lets* one talk."

[JOURNAL]

Cambridge—Thursday—January 6, 1921

Kahlil completed the beautiful profile of Christ on the brown paper and put it into its frame. "It is less strong than the other full face of Christ. But it has a majesty and a sensitive consciousness of its own." Louise Daly† came in and he

---

* In the early 1920's, Albert E. Michelson and Francis G. Pease measured the diameters of seven stars, among them Alpha Orionis (Betelgeuse).

† Mary's sister.

showed it to her. She spoke of its "peace," and her eyes filled up with tears.

He feels very deeply in her all she has suffered, in losing her children, "especially the unborn children. It is perhaps about the hardest suffering women are called on to bear."

"Loneliness is the great suffering upon the earth, the desire to be loved, to be understood, to have some other heart to be near to."

[JOURNAL]

Cambridge—Saturday—Jan. 8, 1921

Often people say that at the heart of life and reality is conflict. This is not so. At the heart of things is Movement. Trust and love are important. The most important thing is to love—to love everything.

-⁘{ KG }⁘-

[New York]
Beloved Mary,   Wednesday—Jan. 12, 1921

You *do* need a good long rest. Miss Fifer suggested over the telephone a week in the country. I think it is a fine idea, and I hope you will have the desire to go. I know the willingness of your spirit, Mary, but the body has its own will and its own needs. I feel quite certain that a week or ten days in the country will satisfy both the will and the needs of the body.

Please do not write. I shall telephone Miss Fifer again with the hope of hearing better news.

Love from Kahlil

[New York]
Friday—Jan. 21, 1921

I am so very very glad that you are well again. I would love
to come on Sunday afternoon and see you. I could come
Monday, or later in the week, or some evening. *Do* let me
telephone you on Sunday morning and be sure that you feel
strong enough to see me.

Love from
Kahlil

[JOURNAL]

Feb. 5, 1921—Saturday evening
New York

I've never seen Kahlil so depleted. The flesh seemed to have
dropped away from his body, and his legs, instead of being
erect and firm and solid, seemed limp. His clothes hung upon
him. "I've had about the worst time in my life," he said.
"There seems nothing left in me, and I've no creative life.
I've lost even my dreams when I sleep. Certainly nothing is
easier to me usually than to write Arabic letters. Now it seems
a burden to write even them. But under all this stillness is a
volcano. That's why I can't rest.

"I think perhaps it's my heart. My heart always beats 110
times to other people's 100 times. The doctor told me that
such a rapid heart beat occurs not oftener than in one among
500,000 persons. I'm just conscious of wanting to sleep. I'm
tired, played out. I need six months rest. Yet I've had none of
the three or four things that usually make a man physically
tired. I've no love affair, I'm not hungry or cold or doing hard
physical labor. I'm fighting all the time. Life in this city isn't
easy. I have to fight women, because I don't want women in

my life. I have to fight men, because the men are all critics. And there's the life I must lead as a Syrian, of which you can know nothing. Going to Cohasset is not different from going to Boston. In Boston the Syrians come whether I'm sick or well. Every little Syrian town represented there wants to send its own delegation, to be kind to me, or to ask something.

"Sometimes, when souls are small, and all things are small to begin with, we have to let them alone in their dark moments, to come through in their own season. But the letting alone must be loving.

"Mary, you are the only person in the world with whom I feel wholly at home. You are the most wonderful person in the world to me.

"The bond between you and me is greater than either of us knows. Between us the bond can't be broken."

--⋇{ MH }⋇--

[JOURNAL]

Feb. 8, 1921—Tuesday—New York

Kahlil looked much better. "The doctor says that my heart's all right. 'Your heart is just your own heart,' he said. 'There's something in you always struggling to express itself and find a vent. You are like a pot boiling, and if what's inside can't get out, you'll burst.' What drives me is not only the something in me that seeks expression, but also the sense of responsibility, that I must be always producing. With you I feel less responsibility than with anyone else; yet even with you I want to have something to show, or to read, every time you come to New York or I come to Boston. What I ought to do is to wait until the things in me give me their own expression. I can never do anything well by driving myself.

"Jesus had two leading conceptions: the Kingdom of Heaven, and a piercingly constructive critical consciousness. In this day he would be called Bolshevik and Socialist. The priests killed him because he criticized them. He first perceived the Kingdom of Heaven in man's own heart, a world of beauty, of goodness, of reality, of truth, and he was willing to die for that consciousness, because he believed that his death would bring it home to the people as nothing else could. He never said he was the King of the Jews. But when they saw his tremendous personal power, those foolish Jews applied to him all their old prophecies about a conqueror who should spring up from among them and rule the world. The priests used the people's praise of him as an excuse. Jesus could probably have saved himself, simply by showing that he had made no claims. But if he had refused thus to die, and had not later fulfilled the Jews' hope of a conquering King, he would have lost many of his disciples. Whereas if he died then, they would not forsake his memory and his teachings. His courage in not seeking to escape death, would attach them to him more than anything else could. I believe he had complete consciousness of this and that the decision to die must have been reached after great struggle within himself. He died, that the Kingdom of Heaven might be preached, that man might attain that consciousness of beauty and goodness and reality within himself. Jesus was the most powerful personality in history."

He opened a little jewel-box and showed me the meteorite. "You've given me many things, but this is beyond all the rest. Often at night I go to sleep with it and when I wake up my hand is tight clenched, holding it. It is to me the most wonderful reality. It takes me into all space."

---&{ *KG* }&---

[New York]

Beloved blessed Mary,   3/23/21

I am so glad you are coming soon to New York. Let us dine together Tuesday evening. I shall be here waiting for you. And if you can see me at any time during the following Wednesday or Thursday, you know in your heart that I shall not want to see anybody else or do anything else. We will talk about that on Tuesday evening.

Love from
Kahlil

[JOURNAL]

July 19, 1921—Cambridge

Kahlil was already in the office when I came, coat off, in his white shirt, and his beautiful gay smile.

He looked at the wee little book of views of the Palatine Hill and mended it with Grippit. "One of the first great steps in architectural consciousness," he said of the Arch.

"There are so many beautiful things in Constantinople. And not one of all these beautiful things was made by the Turks. Some sultans may not have been pure Turk; some of them may have had Christian mothers.

"The English have always loved the Turks. If it hadn't been for the English, the Turk would have been driven out of Europe by the Russians, and the people of the Near East would have been free, or have been swallowed up by Russia. Better Russia than Turkey, for Russia is young and full of creative power.

"The Ensemble of life is sweet and good. And everlasting."

[JOURNAL]

August 12, 1921—Cambridge

"Unless life consists in bodily things, elderly people are more alive than young ones. They have more wisdom, understanding, consciousness. Eighteen- to twenty-year-olds are not fully alive. They are imitative, in fashions, tho't, and manners. They have no opinions of their own. If one cares for a smooth skin, a bright color, and swift movements, that society feeds one; if one cares not for these, one can starve among the 18- to 20-year-olds.

"Most people have no inner life. But there is more inner life among old people than young. The fulfillment of one stage makes the next stage possible. Nature seldom makes a sudden break. She does not crush the young branches: she lets the tree die when it is old. At least there is a strong sense in us that that is the natural way. We call it the natural way.—I sometimes imagine myself, my bodily part, after death, lying in the earth and returning to the elements of earth: the great loosening, the change everywhere, the opening into simpler things, the widening out into those things from which anything may be built up again, the great Return, such deep quietness and a passing into the substance of things. Age will have been preparing my body for this blessedness. The autumn of the body leads to winter, and this winter is necessary to another spring. The spirit too must move from one season into another. Each season has its faults; each has its virtues. But our virtues can ripen only with living."

[JOURNAL]

August 30, 1921—Tuesday—Cambridge

Kahlil was looking lovely in every one of his thousand aspects. The day was hot. His skin was soft and transparent, his eyes shining, and he was full of that radiant smile of his, the freshest, gentlest, brightest play of light in any human face.

He has written the Farewell of the Prophet, and read it to me. His same message, of the Greater Self, and the Oneness of Life, and the lovingness of the Greater Self. And his English, of course, singularly pure and new and beautiful.

How absolutely the Prophet is Kahlil, although Kahlil has several times said, "This is not I, but the Prophet."

Immediately after the reading we went over the whole in detail. It was the longest piece of writing that we have ever taken at a sitting.

[JOURNAL]

September 6, 1921—Tuesday—Cambridge

Kahlil copied the whole Farewell of the Prophet. I dictating from his ms. That took us all afternoon, and more. It was 7:10 when he left. His ms. is exceedingly careful and accurate and clear.

[JOURNAL]

September 9, 1921—Friday—Cambridge

Kahlil goes on Monday.

He copied the closing paragraphs of *The Prophet* and then reread aloud the beginning of the book.

"I may have said this or that badly, but the *amount* in this opening must be kept. If certain parts are poor, they must be replaced with something else of equal length. The beginning, the middle, and the end has each its proper weight, and if we misjudge any one of them, a certain harmony is lost to the whole book. The Prophet is going to talk for several hours to these people and say a hundred things. The reader must be told how and where and why he is going to do it, and the same way about the ending of the long talk.—The music of the telling must be suitable to all that the Prophet says. It must last long enough to be really taken in by the reader. That which is not said must get over to the reader.

"The purple sails on the Prophet's ship are the mark that the ship is known by. All the people know the ship when they see it coming."

On November 16, 1921, Mrs. Florance Minis died. Receiving the news, Mary immediately traveled south.

—⊸⊱ *KG* ⊰⊶—

Beloved Mary,   Thursday—Dec. 8, 1921—N.Y.

I would like to see a modern city without street lights. The lower part of New York would be as beautiful and as terrible as the Pyramids if one can see it in the light of the stars and the moon and no other light. What a vast difference there is between a light from above and a light from below.

Love from Kahlil

❧ 1922 ·❧

[JOURNAL]

January 5, 1922—Cambridge

Kahlil has been ten days in Boston, but I've been south with my uncle Florance Minis, and am just back. Kahlil looks *well*, has gained a little flesh.

I told him I had been debating going to live with my uncle but couldn't decide to leave this school. "Wait," he said, "you will know presently. The collective mind is interested to concern itself with you and me and each of us. That collective mind will decide what is best, and you will know then. Perhaps you won't have to sacrifice school to uncle or uncle to school. Just don't hurry your decision.

"I brought another picture that I think ought to go in the Exhibition." * He unwrapped *Thirst*, the beautiful pale head. Then he made a second *Thirst* two thirds as large again, and even far more beautiful, a truly gloriously radiant worn face, full of history, of feeling, of experience, of consciousness.

We chose the wash drawings for the Exhibition, and wrote the list of their numbers and titles—forty-two in all. Patrick

* At the Women's City Club of Boston.

will clean them, put in screw eyes, and take them in on Saturday and Monday p.m.

When I said, of the new Face, "That's one of the finest heads you've ever done," Kahlil flushed with pleasure.

[JOURNAL]

Monday—January 9, 1922—Cambridge

Met Kahlil at the Women's City Club, 50 Beacon St., where Mrs. Peabody and I had hung the exhibition of his wash drawings. The rooms were very disappointing, reading rooms in the first place, where one has to be quiet, and full of furniture and ornaments, no quality of exhibit in them. Had Kahlil known, he would not have sent the pictures; but he was philosophical about it, kind and unirritated. We went for a walk, the length of the Esplanade and back to Park Street for my car, our first walk for a long time, and the first in Boston since he left in 1911.

We talked again of my inner debate, whether to go to live with Florance or keep on with School. And again he said, "One gets a desire, and it grows, and after a few days it is greater. Perhaps then it ripens and falls, and is gone, and we've lived through it, or else we may come to feel that it is a lasting thing, and act upon it.

"If you like your uncle there's no question about my liking him too. We've always liked the same people. As for congeniality, you'll never find congenial people to live with, never the one in a million to whom you can always say everything. But does that really matter after all? The relation with people can still be sweet. What is ordinarily called being understood enslaves something in us. The great thing is increase of realization."

I did most of the talking for I wanted to open my heart to Kahlil about the possibility of going to live with Florance. Kahlil said, "If I went to live with a person like that—one thing I'd never do. I'd never criticize. The man who faces his age so squarely and who writes to you as he does, who loved his wife so genuinely, who did so good by his parents, and adds to servants' wages secretly because he thinks them too low, must be fundamentally kindly. What other people say or think of a man is unimportant, if you yourself know his real being—!"

[Cambridge]
January 12, 1922

"In marriage the main thing is to give, give, give. And never to forget that human beings are eternally separate.....The period before marriage is a wonderful time in which to approach each other, to talk many things over, learn each other's attitude, and understand more of each other; when the greater nearness of marriage comes, it is not all new or unforeseen. What breaks marriage, most often is the too constant contact —morning, noon, afternoon, evening, night—and again and again and forever. The two need relief from each other."

January 14, 1922—Saturday—Cambridge

"I can get people to please me most by letting them alone— letting them do what they want to do. If I try to make them do a certain thing just to keep their balance they have to lean a little in the opposite direction. And no one of us is wise enough to make a decision for another. I cannot have an opinion about you going to live with your uncle. I can only say don't hurry. You have outgrown the school work.

"There is only one law to observe—and that is honesty. Always be honest—and always praise the comparatively best. A person's best deserves recognition as the best of his achievement.

"Find out the best in a person and tell him about it. We all need that. I have grown up on praise—and it has made me humble. It will always make a person long to deserve the praise. And any real consciousness is aware of something much greater than itself. Praise means understanding. We all *are* fine and great, fundamentally; overestimation of one another is impossible. Learn to see the greatness and the loveliness in one another—and to tell one another of it when we see it.

"The first great moment that I remember was when I was three years old—a storm. I tore my clothes and ran out in it. Do you remember when you first saw the sea? I was eight. My mother was on a horse, and my father and I were on a beautiful large Cyprian donkey, white. We rode up the mountain pass, and as we came over the ridge, the sea was before us. The sea and the sky were of one color. There was no horizon and the water was full of the large Eastern sailing vessels with sails all set. As we passed across the mountains, suddenly I saw what looked like an unmeasurable heaven and the ships sailing in it.

"I remember when I was taken to the ruins of Baalbek— the most wonderful ruins in the world. I was about nine then —my father was on a horse, and my mother was on another. I was on a pony, and our two men on mules. We stayed about four days at Baalbek—and when we left I wept. I have a notebook of the sketches I made there."

[JOURNAL]

January 19, 1922—Thursday—Cambridge

Kahlil read his "Counsel" of Pleasure to me. We changed a phrase or two for rhythm and closeness of fit—and then copied it. Kahlil in his notebook while I dictated from his paper.

It was 7 when Kahlil left. He missed a car—didn't run hard for it. He does not run hard for things now—he is determined to be fit—and to get his heart in good shape again.

------ ~⊰ *KG* ⊱~ ------

[New York]
February 7, 1922

Beloved Mary,

May God bless you, Mary, for all the sweet and dear things you say to me. But do you know that whenever you talk to me about myself I feel a delicious pain in my heart. You are always pointing at the summit of a mountain and saying to me, "When will you be there?" And it seems, Mary, that when you speak of what I am today a voice within your voice is saying, "This is what I want you to be tomorrow." But it is so good to be shown the summit of the mountain. And it is so good to know what you want me to be tomorrow.

May Life sing in your heart. And may Life keep you in her most sacred heart.

Love from
Kahlil

------ ~⊰ *MH* ⊱~ ------

[Boston]
February 22–24, 1922

Precious Kahlil, when I see you this time, let's look at a good many of your pictures. Wear your rags, so that we shan't mind dust, and keep a sheet or a towel out of the laundry to cover me with, too, so that we shall be really all right. It's been so wonderful to me to sweep with my eye over all of your things that I have here, from *The Dance of the Thoughts* to this last new beloved head. They are drenched with many kinds of tears, some of dew and some of iron, as the earth is drenched with many kinds of water—the nebulae of consciousness are there, and the crystals—that which alights on wings from the sky, and that which labors up bleeding through the earth—and always the fragile, mighty, little human hand doing them, and the human heart beating in them —and God's hand holding the Circle of them all as in a cup, that nothing shall be wasted.

Love from
Mary

--◦❦{ *MH* }❦◦--

[JOURNAL]

March 12, 1922—Sunday—New York

Our third evening, from 5:30 to 3:45 a.m.—and Kahlil said, "This has been the most wonderful of all our evenings. We have made many things clear to each other.

"Mary, when you are deciding whether to go to Savannah, follow your heart. Your heart is the right guide in everything big. Mine is so limited. What you *want* to do is determined by that divine element that is in each of us. Be guided by that in your school as well."

Kahlil told me the whole story of our relation from his side. Something led me to confess I had thought that he must have cared for me and that love for me had been killed in him by me, and that he had had such patience with me always because he felt—as he said to me once years ago—"I want to die your friend, Mary" and that he had sometimes seen me just for my sake when he had found it a task. "Well!" said Kahlil—"I am going to TELL you things.

"I was drawn to you in a special way the first time I saw you. It was at the exhibition of my drawings in Mr. Day's studio. You were wearing a silver something around your waist. I loved talking with you that day, and when you asked to have the pictures in your school I was glad to have them there. You were a child then.

"I saw more of you while they were there, and I liked you better and better. I liked your sister too, who was then with you. And I liked the atmosphere of the place, and your books and the way you had things fixed. And I liked the way you talked about everything. Even the way you talked about me and made me talk about myself. You used to ask me questions, and sometimes they embarrassed me; but I loved even the embarrassment, because of your spirit and the sweet understanding way you met everything. I knew many people in Boston at that time, but I liked you best of all. And when you asked me to your house, I never refused.

"The others found me interesting. They liked to get me to talking, because I was unusual for them. They liked to watch the monkey. But you really wanted to hear what was in me. You kept making me dig for more. That was delicious—and it is delicious to this day.

"You did not ask me often at that period—not until I began to draw at 314. The first thing was that little profile of myself. Then you had me to meet Charlotte and I drew her, and then to meet Micheline and I drew her! Then you asked me about Paris—about going there. I was glad to have you do it, and glad to take help from you. I was offered money to go, by others, and I never considered for one moment accepting it from them. I never could take anything like that from anybody except from you. But you said something about money then that I have remembered ever since. You said money was impersonal, that it belongs to none of us, but simply passes through our hands; a responsibility, not a possession and that our right relation to it is to put it to right uses. All the while I was in Paris, I felt your faith and warmth. When I came back to Boston you were the same, sweet, kind wonderful spirit. Then the very day after I spoke to you of marriage you began to hurt me.

"Paris was a time of self-discovery to me—as was the period that preceded it—and the first few years after my return. I was studying myself—hungry and thirsty for myself. —I saw everything as it affected me—if it did affect me. And so I tell the story of things—not as they were, but as they seemed to me.

"You kept hurting me. But when you had hurt me, the next time we met—I was seeing you once or twice a week —you would say, 'Kahlil, I realized afterwards that I had hurt you last Wednesday'—or Friday, as it might have been—and 'I am sorry. I did not mean to.' And you would be so sweet and lovely that I would say to myself, 'Yes, this is Mary again.' And sometimes before that very visit was out you would say something brutal to me again. Nothing that I could do or say seemed able to avert it. It would just come and half kill me. I kept saying to myself, 'If I accept the sunshine and warmth I must also accept the thunder and the lightning.' And I tried to—but something in me was dying all the time.

"In my work that was a dead year. And so I left Boston and came on to New York.

"At last two things hapened. One day—shortly after you had had Charlotte's flat for a week or ten days, and we had been so much together and were right in the midst of so much sensitiveness and nearness and difficulty—Charlotte said to me, 'Mary was here last Monday. Did you see her? She told me not to tell you she was coming. She stayed two or three days at my flat with me.' Well, I felt simply shipwrecked.—

"Then, when you were in New York another time, and we were walking home from Gonfarone's one night, you said it was the fact that you have given me money that kept the bond between us. That night I made up my mind to raise the full sum of money that I had received from you and send it to you. And I set about it the next day. You had meanwhile gone back to Boston—when I had a letter from you. It was the loveliest letter—so dear, so near, so full of everything that meant everything to me—that I felt again 'How can you receive such kindness from a soul, and then make such a return as you are promising to make her!' and so I waited and kept on hoping—and hoping. I could not make out how you could be two such different people. And then came the crash.

"One night in Boston, while we were spending the evening at Marlboro Street—the bell rang. It was your brother and his wife—you hesitated about letting them in—but decided to do so. There was a peculiar feeling about their finding me there and you felt uncomfortable. When we met two days after, you were still a good deal upset. And you said something to me about your brother's attitude toward me—that he would consider me much in the light of such foreigners as you call dagos. That finished me. And the very next time we met, you were your sweetest self—just as if nothing had happened. But with me something had happened. The man in me towards you had to change, for self protection. But until I learned that I could not work. I could not see friends normally—I could not be sane, and keep going through what you were continually putting me through. I said to myself, 'On any personal, intimate, daily plane, relations with this woman are impossible. They must be restricted to the spirit and the soul.' And I told you openly that you had hurt me so much that love had to seek another form. And then, you stopped utterly any hurting me. You were never brutal again. And then Charlotte married and went away—and all our meetings were blessed.

"But it was only the lesser thing in me that changed toward you. The deepest thing of all, never was moved. That deepest thing, that recognition, that knowledge, that sense of kinship began the first time I saw you, and it is the same now—only a thousand times deeper and tenderer. I shall love you to eternity. I loved you long before we met in this flesh. I knew that when I first saw you. It was destiny. We are together like this"—(He clasped his two hands together)—"and nothing can shake us apart. You cannot change our relation; I can't and God himself can't. If I had been able to love other women, I have had plenty of chances. In Boston I knew them. In Paris I met many. But you and I have kinship; fundamentally we are alike. I want you to remember this always. You are the dearest person in the whole world to me. That kinship, that togetherness in our spiritual being, would not be changed if you should marry seven times over, to seven other men. .... If we had had a so-called sex relation, it would have parted us by this time. And marriage would have parted us, too. Either would have been destructive. The course of our life together has been guided and we were saved from a sex relation. You have helped me in my work and in myself. And I have helped you in your work and in your self. And I am grateful to heaven for this you-and-me.

"I cannot ever visualize it when you tell me, as you sometimes have, that nobody loved you as a child. You are different from everybody else—and surely you know that you are. You speak of yourself as if you were homely. You have a remarkable face; there is a beauty in it all your own. You know that I find beauty in you. You know I use your face again and again in my drawings—not an exact likeness but you!"

"If we had married you would not have put up with my wanting solitude for ten days at a time."

"I cannot start painting until *The Prophet* is off my hands. He dominates me now. I must just yield myself to possession by that spirit until I have finished it."

He showed me a new picture—*Silence*—with her finger

upon her lips. She looked to me like myself and in Boston I asked Kahlil whether he had meant her to. He said, "Of course! If you could not see that it would be because you did not wish to see it."

[JOURNAL]

April 14, 1922—Friday—Cambridge

Kahlil for the afternoon. As he approached from the car, I was walking from House to School and so saw him. He walked slowly—and when we met at the door, he was dark and thin, and his face full of shadows. He is not well.

"I must get away from New York. New York is a hard place to live in. Here I can rest, and do what I please. Presently, Mary and I will find a little place in the country." He is going to consult a specialist for heart and nerves, and I am to look one up. I started then and there to call up Elizabeth Day for inquiries but he said, "Couldn't you do that sometime when I am not here, Mary? I would rather talk with you." And as we talked that wonderful smoothing out came in his face, that I have seen so often—the whiteness and the width—with the faint flushing.

He had brought me a little head he had found in a notebook. He had done it he knew not when but it is very beautiful..... I confessed to him that Mayer had looked from *Silence* to mine and from mine to the *New Face* again and again as if he were seeing likeness there—and that I had been ashamed to say so to Kahlil. Kahlil cried out, "Of course, of course, and in half a dozen other faces you know you see it. You have the face I want to paint and draw—the eyes with their ins and outs all around them. It is the face that I can say things with."

I showed him the beautiful things of my aunt's that my

Mary Haskell

uncle had given me in Savannah. "She must have had much taste. And you ought to have beautiful clothes too."

"Whenever two people talk there are always four talking. The two who are visible have a relation quite different from that of the invisible two. They may quarrel violently—yet the invisible be at peace and undisturbed, or they may be at one in the flesh, and yet the invisible be absolutely apart."

"One notices more a man's eyes and a woman's mouth. In men the eyes tell most, in women the mouth."

On Saturday I sent Kahlil some thyroid with directions for taking—and on Sunday he phoned me. "The thyroid seemed to do just what I needed, Mary. Last night I slept better than I have slept for two months—and I waked feeling quiet and rested. And today I feel better—fresher—and stronger. It is just opposite to the effect of the other (Adrenalin)." Adrenalin was disagreeable, deadening. He says he will go to see Dr. William H. Smith—anyhow, however well the thyroid suits—but not before Tuesday.

---⊰ *MH* ⊱---

CAMBRIDGE-HASKELL
36–40 CONCORD AVENUE
CAMBRIDGE 38, MASSACHUSETTS

Beloved Kahlil,   Saturday, April 15, 1922

Dr. Hilbert Day has telephoned to the doctor, who says he will be glad to look you over most carefully. He is Dr. William H. Smith, 8 Marlboro St., Tel. B.B. 1502. He says, call him up, and he'll make an appointment with you.

Dr. Smith is called "inhuman" in his manner at times, but you won't mind that. His inhumanity seems to consist actually in silence!

The new-drawn face is near me. I brought it over to my

room. It speaks to me as if it were speaking of this very moment—of the ceaseless uncertainty, incertainty—of the Question that is always being asked, though sometimes we hear it more forcefully than at other times. I love the uncertainty and the Question.

Suppose, when you are going to Dr. Smith's, that you take no thyroid that day, but carry the vial in your pocket, so that if he wants to see the effect you can take some on the spot for him. Just in case!

Mary

--------------------------------- ⊰ *MH* ⊱ ---------------------------------

[J O U R N A L]

April 18, 1922—Cambridge

Kahlil this afternoon. He looks better—though he had taken only three grains of thyroid in the past two days. I gave him one of my two-grain tablets and a piece of candy—and it made him feel better.

I did most of the talking, for I told him all about my visit with Florance. He sees Florance's point of view as clearly as mine. And to me he says as he has said before, "Mary, don't do anything out of pity or kindness—nor from a sense of duty. Do things because they are really your desire. What you have to find out is, What is your desire. Trust your heart. Don't decide from your head."

--------------------------------- ⊰ *MH* ⊱ ---------------------------------

[J O U R N A L]

April 19, 1922—N.Y.

Kahlil looks not quite so well, but not badly, and he has persevered in not working just to be working. And as yet *The Prophet* is not finishing itself within him.

[JOURNAL]

[Cambridge]
April 21, 1922

"Do you know that you have a book in a binding which I designed when I was fourteen years old? The Maeterlinck books all have that binding—I did several then—but I have never been able to trace any of the others.

"You know, Mary, how you can stand at night and look up at the starry sky."

And here Kahlil lost himself in what he was saying. He stood in the middle of the rug—his face lifted, every feature soft, his eyes wide open, upraised, swimming in light. It was a rapt and wonderful look....."and you see not only the beauty and the majesty of it. You see the terror of it too. It is not points of light that look terrible. It is the great realities they are expressions of."

[JOURNAL]

April 25, 1922—Tuesday—Cambridge

Kahlil came more than an hour late—about 3:20—having been to see Dr. William H. Smith at 12:30. Dr. Smith had found nothing organically wrong. Had called it a nervous heart, and had asked Kahlil to go to the Mass. General for some further examination. "He was almost the most talkative person I have ever seen!"—(because I had told him how Dr. Smith has examined a woman for ¾ hour without a word, and had thus upset her nerves)—"a solid, well informed, intelligent man. He gave me a little dissertation on the artistic temperament—how with our minds fixed on other things we are apt to forget regularity—and about the body as a machine and the care of a machine—and said I might be paying now for ir-

regular eating and sleeping during all my long working life—
he did not tell me why I am so nervous. I don't know myself
why I am. What I do know is that I've got to stop working
and learn how to live."

I told him I had written Florance more plainly about the
fools' paradise than ever before—and we had a wonderful
talk about Florance's point of view. At the end Kahlil said,
blushing with that impulse from his overwhelming reserve that
is always with him, "I have talked too much this afternoon—
more than I ought to have." When he does push outside of
his skin, at rare intervals as he does it, it is always wonderful.
It is so far from the thoroughgoing expression and unreserve
that others use. "His [Minis's] blindness is the most natural
and normal thing for him. Not only have you given him more
evident affection than he has probably ever received but he
has been able to express his own heart as he was never allowed
to do. It has all been not just a joy and a liberation—but also
a miracle and he is lost in it. He can see only that. To you,
what you have given is a crumb; to him it is a feast. The
meanest gift within a higher Kingdom may surpass the most
royal gift within a lesser Kingdom. He can only interpret
you by his own Kingdom. And so he is puzzled to understand
how it is that you won't marry him. Pain, yes, pain is all right.
It is the nearest thing to joy. We are the richer for it. But
misunderstanding?—No. Uncertainty? No. You and I know
personally the horror of misunderstanding. It is darkness and
confusion and lostness. That is what you want not to create in
his heart. People's faults can be cured only by loving them.
We can love a greenness into ripeness—or love the owner or
sufferer from the greenness into such ripeness as is in him to
develop. We cannot scold or frighten him into it." When I
said, "I am rough sometimes," Kahlil looked me straight in
the eye for just a second's pause, and then said "Yes" and
laughed. It was a triumph of that beloved candor that he has
deliberately espoused toward me for my sake and for the sake
of that cloudless openness that has unfolded between us. In

the saying we mounted another one of those broad shining steps that we are ascending together.

[Cambridge]
April 28, 1922

"Demonstrations of love are small, compared with the great thing that is back of them."

Florance cannot see that demonstration is unimportant. "Perhaps he can't learn to see it. It belongs to another order of being. He is behind you in development. But don't think of one who is behind as unworthy. Some people are like the seed of the tree of human life. But bark too is necessary. All the tree is for the seed. And the seed is for a tree too. They depend on each other. And if we are as seed to some other people, we are also as bark to those others who have gone beyond ourselves.

"People who are further on are simply the best servants for the race—the most useful to all. The eye that sees more sees for the others. The mind thinks for them—the ear hears for them. Every picture is a portrait.....a self-picture.—Every poem is an autobiography—every discovery a self-discovery.

"We are not radiators of light—but radiations—from the great light. We are light from the Source."

May 5, 1922—Friday—Cambridge

Kahlil came in with his brown manuscript-holder—in it thirty-two typed sheets from *The Prophet*. He went to the

Mass. General Hospital this morning. "I had to breathe into something, and evidently a record was mechanically made somewhere, for a little pointer was moving. They will send a report to Dr. Smith and he will let me know if he wants to see me again."

We set right to work on *The Prophet*. It has been simply paragraphed. Now we are to begin on its final rhythmic forms.

In the opening of *The Prophet*, at the passage "Only one more breath," Kahlil said, "Why does this move people to tears? It often does."

"It is better to have people puzzle a little than to have them pass a thing over because it seems so easy"—(apropos to my saying they might find it clearer in the Marriage "Counsel" if he said, "Think not that you drink from one cup—and eat the same loaf").

"Let us make the divisions by ideas—so that each division whether it is one line or several shall be in itself a complete thought and can be taken alone. I want the division to be a natural one—not according to rule—but just the actual pauses of the thing itself—the freedom of free verse without its eccentricities.

On work. "If there is one thing I am glad to have written, it is that expression 'proud submission.' We are expressions of earth and of life—not separate individuals only. We cannot get enough away from the earth to see the earth and ourselves as separates. We move with its great movements and our growth is part of its great growth."

"I am full of new things for the book. Even now I am thinking of the Prophet saying something to himself as he sits on the deck of the boat between the two lands—just himself and the mists."

May 9, 1922—Tuesday—Cambridge

Kahlil looks steadily better—"I saw Dr. Smith again today. He says there's absolutely nothing organic the matter with me. Heart, lungs, kidneys—are sound.—But I've a nervous heart, and I've lived under a strain for twenty years. I have to live differently—and get more rest.—He says, work when you really want to, and if ideas come, write them down; but don't feel you have to finish a certain thing at a certain time. Don't work more than three or four hours a day.....Neither he nor any other doctor seems to notice the pain in my heart— the dull sort of pain.....My greatest pain is not physical..... There's something big in me and I can't get it out. It's a silent greater self, sitting and watching a smaller me do all sorts of things. All the things I do seem false to me; they are not what I want to say. I am always conscious of a birth that is to be. It's just as if for years a child wanted to be born and couldn't be born. You are always waiting, and you are always in birth pain. Yet there is no birth. But if I die before this thing is born I'm going to keep coming back until it is born .....People say such wonderful things to me—and it hits me like a blow—because I am so conscious I am not doing what in me is waiting to be done.—You say wonderful things to me, Mary, and I love to have you say them. Yet they hurt—because I feel how far away what I do is, from what I would do."

Kahlil was walking up and down. His face was dark—he had never spoken before so avowedly of the pain of his long waiting and his inmost silence—"All that I can say and do is foreign to the real thing that I would say and cannot.—Only the Prophet has shadow of that thing—a bit every now and then."

We spaced the rest of *The Prophet*—and I read Kahlil from Florance's letter. "If he felt your letter hard and harsh, then it really was hard, I suppose. Yet you are sound and right in your position.

"Apparently he can't see things through your eyes and you can't persuade him to. Well, keep your own eyes steadily fixed on what you would have him see—and perhaps at last his eyes will follow yours, even though he can't listen to what you say."

[JOURNAL]

[Cambridge]
May 12, 1922

The beauty of Kahlil's personal presence in these last two visits has been, even for him, whose silence is like a world of tongues and music, like the beauty of whole zones of gardens. Nearness with him is different from nearness with anyone else. It is not an emotion—not a forgetting or a mood—not a regard one for the other nor a turning of thought or eye one upon the other. It is a living one's own life as one does when one is alone—but leaving the door open, or opening it, to the other. There is no bidding you in; rather, you are shown about in there only incidentally, if it so comes about—and nothing is changed or arranged for your benefit. In silence he says, "Be at home," though he may be busily talking at the moment. Never was there so utter a genuineness, such absence of plan for effect, such willingness for your eye to see just what is.

When he is at ease and happy and free and busy, something exquisite happens in his face—I see it as I sit by him while he writes a letter, as he did the other day, or copies a bit in his writing, or draws. He flushes a little, his skin softens and glows, his eyes shine and deepen, his lips lie softly and almost smiling together, his nose seems straight, and the whole contour of face and head is regular, vivid, serene. He is all electricity and velvet. There seems a bloom upon him. And though he is sitting right there, a most perfect companion, he is also very far away—like music in the distance—or a bird flying past in the air—or a falling star.

--·❦ *MH* ❧·--

[JOURNAL]

May 19, 1922—Cambridge

An exquisite afternoon—working most leisurely on the spacing of *The Prophet*, and stopping to talk at will.

About the style of *The Prophet*,

"Poets ought to listen to the rhythm of the sea. That's the rhythm in Job—and in all the magnificent parts of the Old Testament. You hear it in that double way of saying a thing, that the Hebrews used.—It is said—then said right off again—a little differently. And that's like the waves of the sea. You know how a big wave rolls in—whish!—and carries the big pebbles with it in a crashing noise. Then some of the pebbles roll back again, with a smaller noise, a sort of undercurrent of sound—and then a second wave will roll up, smaller than the first—whish!—And then there's a pause.—And soon another big wave will come—and the same thing happens all over again.

"—That's the music to learn from—and the music of the wind—and the rustle of leaves."

--·❦ *MH* ❧·--

[JOURNAL]

May 26, 1922—Friday—Cambridge

Kahlil looked so ill—so fagged—and he freshened only at intervals during the afternoon. Near the end of our visit he was speaking of what he is seeking in a house for the summer

—of his need for solitude and of the doctor's command that he go to the seashore—and he suddenly looked burned out.

"I *ache* for solitude. The only place in the world where I'm alone after a fashion is in my studio. But even then there's that telephone. I don't mind seeing people sometimes—but I want to be able to get away. I want walks alone, and hours alone—I want the bulk of time alone for a while.

"In a house I prefer not to have a great deal. But I need a few little things around of beauty. But if anyone knew enough to steal them for their value, he also would be worth while. Those little things are necessary to me; they are like colors in my palette."

He brought the larger wooden head again—more perfect—and with a most beautiful hand added across the breast. "I ought to have begun it lower down—and turned it downward instead of up, but these fingers I carved first, and they were so nice I hated to cut them off." And a wee full-length statuette, lovely—"This is wonderful wood. It's pine.—No, I couldn't find any chisel small enough.

"You know a sculptor works from within outward—he builds up his statue.—He doesn't cut it out. He builds arms and legs and trunk on wires, that are to keep the clay from falling to pieces by its own weight. And when he has built the statue the stonecutters copy it in stone. And their work too is an art—they are artisans. Rodin didn't make his statues in the marble. He often put further touches on the stone when the workmen had finished."

[JOURNAL]

May 30, 1922—Tuesday—Cambridge

Kahlil looks better. He says the Boston milieu is much easier than that in N.Y.—simpler in every way. Will go to Rose Cliff tomorrow and look up the Robbins House.

We worked on the line-spacing of the "Counsels."

Once when we were laughing I said, "I think of it at night and in the day—how perfectly delightful you are—and I wonder how you ever happened to be." Kahlil blushed like fire, and said, "Now you spoil it all by telling me—you 'spirit my charm.' How can I be delightful when you call me delightful?

"I think I'm going to write a 'Counsel' on receiving— everybody has something he wants to give—and so often no one will take. I may have a house and invite people to it. They will come and accept my house, my food, and my thoughts even, but not my love. And yet love is what most of us want most to give. People often say women want to be loved. But they really want much more. Many women want to bear children; and their very being wants to give the children life. She often desires man just as a key to the child that it is in her to give life to.

"A tree am I heavy laden with fruit. Overburdened am I with my fullness"—is the poem I mean.

"Yes, I've done a little on the talking to the mist. It's personal, his personal experiences and feelings—more lyrical with less of wisdom. He talks to his sister Mist: 'We two shall not part again until you are dew in a garden and I a babe on the breast of a woman'—and of the Mist he says, 'All my smiles were on her face and all her tears were in my eyes.'—I could say, 'All her tears were in my heart,' but I think 'eyes' is better.

"Yes, there's a sort of promise of the time when he's on the island, in *The Prophet*—just as there is a sort of promise of the Prophet in the farewell of *The Forerunner*. The farewell is the best thing in *The Forerunner*—and the farewell of *The Prophet* is the best so far in that. Each 'Counsel' is a sort of development leading to one thing that the 'Counsel' says; but the farewell is all of gold. And the Mist must be a step beyond the farewell. *The Madman* ends with the bitterest thing in it; *The Forerunner* with the sweetest."

June 6, 1922—Tuesday—Cambridge

Kahlil looks badly still. Maybe he won't get well until he has left both N.Y. and New England.

I showed him Michelson's "Map of the Sky." * We saw there a "Vaporous bird" of the sky in a cloud, or a something, of the Milky Way.

"You are kindly—Mary—and there are two things for you to remember: patience—to let things work themselves out— and to act according to your own realest desires.

"People like each other either because they are alike, or because they are opposites. Sometimes they are a mixture of like and unlike. You and your uncle are alike and unlike. He feels in you a world he would like to belong to, though he doesn't understand it, and though you don't talk to him about it, he knows."

He put the beautiful colored strip of silk around the waist of my dress as a girdle, and liked it very much. "Keep it, Mary—and I'll be a partner in ownership while you use it."

June 16, 1922—Friday—Cambridge

The last time I shall see Kahlil before I sail. He looked badly, still. When he boarded his car at leaving, his shoulders looked forty years old, for the first time. An unutterable pain and sadness filled my heart all through our visit.

He was speaking to me of the "little sermon" Dr. Smith had given him about always working. "He said, 'My friend, it's pretty nearly chronic, and you won't last. When you find

* See footnote, page 359.

yourself tempted to feel that way, just remember you are burning the wrong end of the candle.'

"Death is nothing to primitive peoples. Primitive people worship their ancestors and carry food to their graves. They see in a simple, direct way, that everything changes into something else. A body rots—and it becomes a tree. And all early people worship trees. Neither primitive man nor superman believes in death.

"The other day I found about twenty cows and a bull in a pasture about a mile from us. I stopped and said, 'Hello!' There was nobody anywhere around. A white cow raised her head and looked at me. I took a little grass in my hand, and said, 'Come on,' and she came, and ate it. Then some others looked —and I waved to them and said again, 'Come on,' and they came—and then they all came. And all stood and looked at me, in a line—and I looked at them. If a photographer had been there it would have been the funniest picture in the world. I stayed about twenty minutes and I was sorry to go."

Liked my steamer hat—and would like one like it himself if I can find one—and a coat like it too. Hat size 6 ⅞.

"You can remember it by 6, 7, 8."

--- ⟪ *KG* ⟫ ---

[New York]
Beloved Mary,   Saturday, June 17, 1922

God has given me much through you. How blessed it is to be one of God's hands. And how fortunate, how more than fortunate, I am to know that hand, and to touch it, and to take from it. It is so good to be a little willow on the bank of a great river.

May God bless you, beloved Mary. And may His sweet angels be with you on sea and land.

Love from
Kahlil

393

CAMBRIDGE-HASKELL

36–40 CONCORD AVENUE

CAMBRIDGE 38, MASSACHUSETTS

Tuesday Night (Sept. 5, 1922)

—just come—since noon

Beloved Kahlil,

How are you? I'm back again. Won't you come to see me? If you'll set a time I'll keep it, whenever it is. It is beautiful to come back from great galleries, and to bow down my heart in reverence to the pictures on these walls, as I do.

Love to Mary. And love, love, love to you from

Mary

--❧{ *MH* }❧--

[JOURNAL]

September 11, 1922—Monday—Cambridge, Mass.

Kahlil came at 1, for the afternoon.—He looks well again —skin clear, bright—eye serene.

"Do you want to see something?" And he began to show me the pictures he has been doing in the past six weeks— as far beyond all his previous work as that most recently previous is beyond the work of his boyhood. These pictures can stand by the finest hitherto painted in the world, and be honored with them. They are of the rarest beauty—and their technique seems inspired.

I told him of the afternoon I spent in the National Gallery seeing just *the* form of every picture—and how some pictures by a certain single change made in their form could have been made glorious—and how all the great ones had one of those great forms. And how I'd come to care more for that great structural form than for anything else—and how Rubens, for instance, seemed glorious to me now, instead of a painter of fat flesh—because his pictures are like great rivers and storms of Form. "Yes yes yes yes"—he kept smiling and saying.

Even in the pictures of this summer there has been steady progress. "I discovered this color for flesh"—he said, indicating the pale color of *It Is Life Giving to Life*. See how little it differs from white. "In the earlier pictures the flesh was much less clear and simple and sure in color." And see this outline, how sure it is—there's no pencil mark at all. It came just as easily as if I were cutting it with scissors. My hand felt perfectly sure. It was like recovering a skill that has been lost—the waking up of an absolute knowledge of anatomy that had slept in me for years.—And see the color in these. I've been working at color schemes all summer. About a dozen of them I'd like to put in *The Prophet*. When you come to New York in November we'll decide which ones to use. And remember, Mary—when this series is complete, all are yours—to do what you wish with....."

I told him about my decision to go to live with my uncle. He is glad, because I am glad to do it.

Then I showed him the overcoats he had commissioned me to get in England—and he liked them. And the ties—and those too he liked.

Last, I showed him our jewel—the opal chain and pendant.

"Why, Mary. Glorious—glorious. It belongs to that world of jewels and crown jewels that the war has scattered, everywhere. They all came to Paris—from Russia especially—and now they are even in New York—ever so many of them. This thing is in itself a glorious piece of jewelry—just for the stones in it. And for its beauty it is absolutely priceless. But you must wear it—wear it for me. You must wear it for me."

When I said Florance was always asking whether I loved him better than anyone else in the world—best of all—Kahlil said, "Every love is the best in the world, and the dearest. Love isn't like a pie that we can cut pieces of, large or small. It's all one: It's all love. Of course you can say he's the dearest thing in the world to you.—Anyone we love and everyone we love, is the dearest person in the world to us." And we laughed—so serenely! All is well, when he looks upon it—for he understands Each thing.

"The relation between you and me is the most beautiful thing in my life. It is the most wonderful thing that I have known in any life. It is eternal.

"Yes, the people at the beach must have known I wanted solitude—for the adults hardly come at all. But there are ninety-seven children on that hill. And I must have made sixty or seventy kites for them. All kinds of kites—big kites, little kites, colored kites and white. And Syrian kites. Have you ever seen the Syrian kite—six-sided, the sides all equal—and the strings from the centre and two of the angles only? They had never seen one there—but after a while they all got to making Syrian kites—even the grown men.—And the other day they came to me and said, 'We've left you alone all summer. But won't you come now and be a judge at the Children's Parade?'; so I was a judge—and the children paraded—and they gave me quite a little ovation.—The children have been nice. When they saw I was working they would go away quietly. But when a kite flew, that was the signal—and then they all came. There was one very big kite—the biggest, the signal kite. And the great question was, Who was it going to at the end? Yes, it went to a big fat boy, one of twelve children—in a family that lives there all the year round. I loved having them around and I loved making the kites. The children are all gone now, back to the city and the suburbs for school. And we shall have to come too before very long. It's getting cold down there."

[JOURNAL]

September 30, 1922—Saturday—Cambridge

"My connections were too good today!" said Kahlil, with a laugh and a blush too, when I came in from buying things for the kitchen and found him there before one o'clock.—I had found two more Keyes cloth ties—*very* beautiful and he liked them both.

[JOURNAL]

[Cambridge]
September 30–October 7, 1922

"The difference between a prophet and a poet is that the prophet lives what he teaches—and the poet does not. He may write wonderfully of love, and yet not be loving.

"Michelangelo was not the best painter, nor the greatest artist—but he was the greatest being of the Renaissance painters. Leonardo was the greatest painter but Leonardo is on the earth—and on its remotest horizons. Michelangelo is one with the earth, and the horizons, and the sky. The greatest artist was Titian. Art is always trying to express what men love—and in all ages men have loved goodness. Not all that is beautiful is good but all goodness is beautiful.

"Velázquez is a great painter—rather than a great artist. Raphael was just a painter. Someone says of him, he has nothing to say, and says it extremely well. His best period was when he was young, still in Perugino's studio and under the influence of Perugino. After that time, his people are just *fat*."

"If one will accept himself he hinders himself no longer. As soon as a person accepts being unlovable, he becomes very lovable indeed. Let me rejoice in Kahlil Gibran just as he is, and then I'll be something for people to love who can love what I am. Nobody can love me if I'm *not* myself."

[JOURNAL]

October 7, 1922—Cambridge

"You and I are each a mother to the other. I feel a little mother in me toward you—and certainly I feel a father toward you—and you feel like a mother to me, I am sure. We have become one, Mary. You have entered my being—and you can't cut off either of us without destroying the other. But we couldn't shake loose from each other. This relation belongs to our greater selves. I can no more think and imagine and create and work without you than without myself. And a relation must be strong to endure as ours has—and to stand such a shock as that period of pain we went through. But without that period of pain I think it wouldn't have become so beautiful."

[New York]

Beloved Mary,   Tuesday, December 12, 1922

The fine warm coat and the two boxes of books are here. Thank you, beloved Mary.

I know, Mary, how much you had to do, and how much you have to do before going South. I shall surely understand if you do not pass through New York. But if you can, without disappointing anyone, and without leaving anything undone, you know how much I would love to see you.

Love from Kahlil

[New York]
Beloved Mary,   Sunday (December 17, 1922)

If you reach New York on Friday let us then dine and spend the evening together. We can do the same on Sunday, then on the following Tuesday, and then again and again until you go South.

I have promised to spend Christmas day with some very kind friends. It is the only engagement, I fear, I cannot break. And I would not have made it had I known that you were coming before the end of the month.

If you reach New York on Saturday, and want us to be together that evening, I can easily make myself free—I would love to make myself free. Just a little word from you a day or two ahead.

I have received so far three boxes of books. The blue jars, which I love, were in one of the boxes. And I have received also two parcels, two books in each. The last box arrived four days ago—perhaps you have sent others since. It would seem so from the date of your letter, and also from your mentioning the Russian spoons, which were not in any of the three boxes.

I love all the books, Mary, each and every one of them. And I would love to have others also. I know I am greedy, but books are books, and what are you going to do with a hungry soul? I shall have a great feast this winter, and I shall bless your board and your cup-bearer.

But I have always been feasting at your board, Mary, and you have always filled my plate and my cup.

May God bless you, may God fill your hands with light.

Love from Kahlil

December 26 and December 28, 1922—
Tues. and Thurs.
New York

Kahlil is well—looks vigorous—full of work—Arabic poems—and Arabic prose.—And he has been working on two of the wash drawings of the summer, with a model.

"In all my life I've known only one woman with whom I am free intellectually and spiritually—with whom I am absolutely myself. That woman is you."

"I find in you all I ask of a woman—a spirit with whom my spirit takes wing—with whom I find my best self, with whom things receive a new light and new doors open—a place where my head may rest. You are the dearest person in the world to me—and you are nearer now than you have ever been. God is everything and everywhere. The most godlike thing in man is his wonder at life—at the wholeness of life, its oneness, its simplicity. In moments of deep love or of passion, many men get this vision. To see the vision is but to open our eyes."

We went to the Natural History Museum—through the marvelous models of microscopic water forms—through rooms of mammal scenes—upstairs to see the new collections of minerals. "Everything in this museum is so thoroughly done—so perfectly. The men are artists and scientists in one.

"This is a fair room—lined with offerings to the Gods— what arrangement! What color! What stirring in the rocks! What infinite variety and difference! What strength, and yet what unsubstantial beauty." The sphere of beryl, the great small slabs of translucence rainbow colored—and at last the caves with the stalactites and the stalagmites illuminated. "The Garment of God," said Kahlil before the one of white-blue-green.

In the room of mammoth fossils, we saw a great fossil duck-bill—with arched neck bent back beneath it—wings open and legs apart—just as it has fallen dead—the one creature preserved to tell how all the rest also had died. "I come to this place often," said Kahlil, "and always there's something here I haven't seen before.

"This is such a wonderful city. It is always changing.— New buildings are always replacing ones already here and they are always finer and more beautiful. It is like a flower always opening wider."

"I wish I had known more, when we were buying this building. I could so easily have borrowed $15,000 and then I'd have had the controlling note. Now, no one can own more than $10,000 worth of stock—and two own that much already. But they are stingy, the lot of them. They wouldn't even have put toilets in, if I hadn't said, 'If you don't put them in, I'll leave.' They don't want me to leave because strange as it may seem, I'm an asset to the building. But the help downstairs are underpaid—way underpaid. They get, I believe, eighty a month, and rooms in the basement. That's for man and wife. No couple stays more than six months. They come in the first place because they can be together —in most places they can't both work—but presently they go where they can get three times as much, even if they do have to work apart through the daytime. They can still be together at night. The House Committee hasn't any imagination to see that a generous policy is good business. The other day one of them said to me, 'Mr. Gibran, this isn't any Christ-like matter—this is just plain business.' And when one man couldn't pay his rent for one month—one month, mind you— they put a sign on his door. I was so angry, Mary, I went to the head of the Committee and I said 'Either that sign goes or I go—right now.' He said, 'O yes, Mr. Gibran, certainly.' The artist came and thanked me afterwards with tears in his eyes. And another man—a married man—couldn't pay for a while—and they were going to put a sign on his door—and his wife came to me in tears and cried all over the place—and I stopped them.....Do you know what they call me? 'The Doormat,' because they all come and wipe it off on me."

We read all of *The Prophet* over.

And while we were doing it, suddenly a bell rang. Then a whistle blew and Kahlil said, "The New Year is in.....We've never seen it come in together before, have we?" And as the clanging and blowing grew to a din, he stood up and said, "Jesus lives still—through 2000 years and from 8000 miles away." Then he told me Jesus was really born on January 6. That is Kahlil's own birthday.

"Mary, if there's anything in this studio that you'd like to take with you—small or large—anything whatever—to have with you—and to keep—I want you to take it. It is yours."

He loved the old Russian lacquer bowl that I had at Marlboro Street and said he'd love to keep it—to my joy. And the lacquer spoon, too, that we used to use there for soup.

·ぷ· 1923 ·ぷ·

[Cambridge]
January 2, 1923

"I've read *The Tidings Brought to Mary* in French and in English. Paul Claudel is probably the most devout Catholic among the literary men in France. He had made himself a Catholic. It's not spontaneous—it's natural, however, that there should be something unreal in the play. There's almost always something unreal when a man has to go back to express his inner life. And Claudel doesn't live today. He lives more or less perfectly, some period in the past. To me he is like a footprint that gathers water in its hollow. The water may be sweet and clear, it may have mingled with it a heavenly elixir—but I would rather have a living spring, even if the spring were of dirty water than any kind of footprint."

Kahlil was in his pongee robes. He has worn them or the brown one on each of our evenings together. When it was nearing the time for me to go, I looked long at that wonderful face of his—and the mouth—the mouth of patience, and of all feeling—that changes almost as the pupil of the eye changes—so different is it at one time and another. The one light on the table was soft yet clear. I think all the tides of human life and planetary life flow through the mind that informs that face—that to some large unit of The Universal he serves as heart—to receive its every current and to send out again a stream made new.

"If you want to give a picture to a museum, Mary—give it one of the best things only. That is the only kind of gift that should be given. And if you want to give, and not to give pictures for which you have a special feeling because you have lived with them, write to me, and I will send them one of my best.

"Yes, we shall miss working with *The Prophet* when it is out. But I have the next book already in mind. He is on his island with his seven disciples—and he talks of the largest aspect of things. And it is of the simplest things he speaks—a drop of dew, the light from a star.

"In an eternal relation letters make no difference. I love your letters in themselves—but they don't make me nearer to you."

-----------------------------⋅⋅❧ *KG* ❧⋅⋅-----------------------------

[New York]

Beloved Mary,   January 24, 1923

I am so happy in your happiness. To you happiness is a form of freedom, and of all the people I know you should be the freest. Surely you have earned this happiness and this freedom. Life cannot be but kind and sweet to you. You have been so sweet and kind to life.

I love your description of your room, and the sea of sunshine flooding it, and the blue shadows of the park outside. It sounds cheerful and full of peace. A room, or a house, always becomes like the one who dwells in it. Even the size of a room changes with the size of one's heart. How often the size of this studio has changed during the past few years.

Love from
Kahlil

--------------- ···❦ KG ❧··· ---------------

Beloved Mary,

I am sending you the galley proofs of *The Prophet*. I have gone through them and made a few corrections, but with the feeling that they need your keener eye for punctuations and other *niceties*. And besides, I do not want to send them back to the publishers without the blessings of your hands upon them.

I must return these proofs within two weeks together with the drawings. We have plenty of time—so please do not put other things aside for them. The publishers can wait a little longer than two weeks.

The drawings are much better now than they were when you last saw them. I have worked hard on them, and if they should not come out right it will be the fault of the engravers and not mine. The frontispiece—the face of Almustafa—is also finished. I have a feeling, Mary, that you will like it more than any other face I have drawn.

Love from
Kahlil

[New York]

Beloved Mary,   April 17, 1923

I have been talking to you all the time in the past two weeks. But I had the grip, like everybody else in New York —so the silence was only in my hand.

Your going over the galley proof of *The Prophet*, and with such love, was so sweet. Your blessed touch makes every page dear to me. The punctuations, the added spaces, the change of expressions in some places, the changing of "Buts" to "Ands" and the dropping of several "Ands"—all these things are just right. The one thing which I thought a great deal about, and could not see, was the rearrangement of paragraphs in Love, Marriage, Children, Giving and Clothes. I tried to read them in the new way, and somehow they seemed rather strange to my ear. Perhaps it was *habit*. I know, Mary, that ears and tongues form habits, good and bad ones. There may be something else, more strange than habit, in my ears. I want very much to talk to you about it when we meet.

I shall be so glad to see you and listen to you and be with you. Will you not let me know just when you will arrive?

Love from
Kahlil

[New York]

Beloved Mary,   Monday, April 30, 1923

I am sending you with this the page proofs of *The Prophet* because I want the light of your eyes to be upon it again before it goes to press. I wanted to go over it myself before sending it to you, but I could not. I have one of those blinding headaches that visit me once every three or four years and stay with me five or six days.

Mary, I am always asking much of you, and like life itself you always give much. May God bless you for all that you do for me. And may God love you and keep you near His heart.

Love from
Kahlil

[New York]
May 3, 1923

Beloved Mary,

We shall surely dine and spend the evening together on May 19. You will find me here any time after 6:30 o'clock.

O Mary, how much and how many are the things I take from you. If I could only give you something which in some way I did not take from you. It is the story of the river and the ocean.

May God bless you always,

Love from
Kahlil

[JOURNAL]

May 26, 1923, Saturday—New York

Spent the evening with Kahlil. He was thin—and rather pale. We went early, for us, to Athena for supper and had excellent pilaf—and then for a bus ride—the evening being almost hot, and then back to the studio.

This time I did most of the talking. Kahlil is apt to draw

407

me out before he tells of himself—and at this dose of my first five months of life away from school and a job, and in the South, I was full of "telling."

But I put down a few jottings from him:

"Among intelligent people the surest basis for marriage is friendship—the sharing of real interests—the ability to fight out ideas together and understand each other's thoughts and dreams. Without these dreams together—the marriage would finally become like the kitchen of one's life.

"To receive all that one longs to give, is perhaps the most gracious thing that is ever done."

He has drawn the husband and father of a girl I saw once at the studio door. While we were talking his "godchild" rang him up about her mother, whom he is to paint. "She is the *sweetest* thing," he says of his godchild. But he probably has no glimmering of how lovely he was to her over the phone.

❧ *MH* ❧

[J O U R N A L]

May 27, 1923, Sunday—New York

Kahlil had a Chilean guest in the early afternoon so I went to the studio at 7:30. The Chileans are writing a book on Kahlil. One is doing the text, and the other is illustrating it with photographs of Kahlil and Kahlil's carvings and studio— and a caricature of him—for the man's profession is caricature.

And his wash drawing of the *Tree of Life* is to be enlarged into a mosaic on the wall inside of a lovely old little church —as a memorial by a father and mother to their sons.

"Marriage doesn't give one any rights in another person except such rights as that person gives—nor any freedom except the freedom which that person gives.

"The best way to take anyone is in the largest, impersonal way. Nothing is so personal as the unpersonal.

"What difference does it make, whether you live in a big city or in a community of homes? The real life is within.

"I'm so glad you are happy, Mary. That means a great great deal to me.—I care about your happiness just as you care about mine. I could not be at peace if you were not. But I am at peace within now—about myself.

"I had a strange dream a few nights ago, I dreamt I was falling. This time I was falling over a precipice—and about half way down the precipice a tree stuck out. I lighted on the tree, on my feet, and stood there for about two seconds. Then I just spread out my two arms and flew—easily and quietly. And all of a sudden there was below me a sea of people, all looking up at me. And then I performed for them —showing off soaring straight up, by a great effort—and then sliding along—again and again—enjoying myself hugely while I was doing it.

"And I dreamt of Jesus this winter. It was in Lebanon, as it always is that I see him, in a beautiful village. A stream runs down, and weeping willows border the stream at one spot where we boys often used to play.—And up the stream from the willows in my dream was a glorious rosebush; I was by the stream, gathering watercress. And He came—just the same face—with the wonderful dark eyes and the clear, out-door skin, and the abundant chestnut hair, and the strong frame, and sandals worn though not worn out—and sandals and feet both dusty.—He came from the west—and the light was behind him and made his outline glow—for the sun was declining. And I took some cress in my two hands and held them out to him and said, 'Master, will you not have some of this watercress?' He took a bunch of it, all wet, and put it into his mouth. His whole face smiled. It seemed to broaden and lift—with all the eyes and the brow—as if a thousand wings were lifting in it.—And he ate it with relish, as if the crispness were delicious to him. And he said, 'Nothing is more beautiful than green,' and then he knelt at the stream and drank. Such a good deep drink! He made no noise—and yet I seemed to hear his inside having such a good time with that fresh cold water.

"And when he rose, the water was sparkling on his moustache and his beard at the lips and he did not wipe it off. He just walked on. As he walked he turned his head and looked back at me—with such a smile—such a look of understanding and of having shared a pleasure.

"And I waked."

May 29, 1923, Tuesday—New York

Our last evening together until June 13, for which we made an appointment.

"Am I too thin? I feel well. I usually eat one meal a day —my imagination and food don't go together. I'm always keener mentally and imaginatively before a meal than after. —One day a month, or two days together in a month, I go entirely without food—regularly. If anything is wrong with me, I just starve a while—and I get well.

"I have a young friend who was ill. He went to a fast cure, and was twenty-one days without eating. The theory is, that the poor and infected tissue is the weakest in the body and that when the body has no other food, some of the body itself is consumed, or fails to be sustained, or perishes—and the weakest part goes first.

"With you I always eat well. I feel at ease—and I'm hungry and I'm not going to work after dinner. When you are not here I dine out oftener than alone."

On the door I saw a beautiful painting—small—dark unfinished—new to me. It was a great mounding wave in the sea—and flung upon it, face down, a human body—heaved with the lift of the heavy water. The sea is dark, the sky gathered full of clouds. Kahlil calls it *The Wave.* "I like the freedom of this"—pointing to the left sky—"and the cold color up here—changing to warm below and back again to cold beside the body." And he showed me what still remains to do. "And when it is done, if you like it I'll give it to you."

"Have other people seen it yet?" said I. "Very few," said Kahlil. "Don't they all want it?" said I. "Don't you know that if you like a picture I'd rather have you have it?" said Kahlil and laughed. I laughed too and kissed him and was about to say more when he said, "O Kahlil! How sweet you are! You are just the sweetest thing to give me that picture!" —and then he said, "You got ahead of me. I thought you wouldn't see it—and that when we went out, at the door I'd say, 'Did you ever see this?'"

We had another killingly gay time when I took his head and kissed the top and said, "You remind me of a rice bird," and then told him what a rice bird is. Whereupon he said— in a series—"Is it because I have a ring of feathers on my head?—and a nice round little skull?—and yellow streaks? —and am eaten by the dozen?—and sing such a sweet song? —and devour a rice crop in a day?—and have so many different names?—and they fry me in my own fat?—and am I male or female?"

And when I could speak again I said, "Will you make me laugh when I meet you in Paradise? I hope you will." For I think never a time have we met—even when we were sad —that he has not made me laugh and laugh, at something that the moment suggested to his flashing mind.

June 16, 1923, Saturday—New York

We looked at each original of the pictures for *The Prophet* —and compared it with the reproduction. "I don't see how I could ask better, for a book that is not to cost more than two dollars twenty-five," said Kahlil. "And I have insisted with Knopf that it shall not cost more than that. Two dollars for *The Forerunner* is much too high—and one seventy-five for *The Madman* is only that much less because *The Madman* sells a little less than *The Forerunner*. *The Prophet* is twice as long as *The Madman* or *The Forerunner*, with twelve pictures instead of five.

"The work of these pictures, finishing them, has been very difficult for me. Every stroke had to be with a double consciousness—of the reproduction and of the picture as a picture. And I have been unwilling to spoil the picture for the sake of the reproduction."

"I'm full of the next book now—it never leaves me."

"He returns to his island and to his garden. There he is sought out by his disciples. He talks to them of simple things. And he shows the identity of each simple thing with the whole of life. This book and *The Prophet* are like a face and the expression on the face. *The Prophet* is the face—and the second part is what the face expresses—what it tells."

"I told you, did I not, how I saw the face of the Prophet? I was reading one night in bed late and I stopped, weary, and closed my eyes for a moment. When I closed my eyes, I saw quite plainly That Face. I saw it for one or two minutes, perfectly clearly—and then it disappeared. The Prophet was my attempt to reproduce the Jesus face.—And how I have worked on *The Prophet*! Sometimes I have been sitting at a dinner table in a company—and all of a sudden this drawing would be before me and I would see just the shade, just the line, to put here or there—and I would think, I wish to God I could go back right now to the studio and put that in. And sometimes in the night I would wake up, knowing a new thing to do—and I would rise and do it."

"Do you see the face of the Prophet for the Second Part?" I said. He smiled and nodded and winked his eyes together in a way all his own that says Yes.—It will be more expanded or shining or projected in look—as this one is more brooding.

"I went to see the little Church where my *Tree of Life* is to be used as a memorial. It is very lovely. But I haven't found the person to do it yet."

"Women tend to eat men up. With a man, sex is sectional, in his life—with woman it is not—because she is the mother of the race. She wants to eat and drink what man does and thinks, rather than to do and think herself. Man has more intellect—but woman has deeper mind that is hers only. We call it intuition. And man uses woman's intuition.

"Things happen in my life in groups of six years—and a tremendous number of names significant in my life begin with M. It was the root letter of a root name in my mother's family; my nurse's name began with M; the steamer line we sailed on; and the steamer; my two best teachers; my sister Mary's name; your name; Marthe M.," the young widow whose spirit was with him so much in his youth.

"I like that black dress immensely just as it is, Mary. It is just right. .... You ought not to wish for smaller hips. Yours are just right. You are beautifully proportioned all round.—And don't wear girdles low on the hips, never mind what the fashion is. The figure ought not to be divided in half by the girdle. That makes the composition wrong. Nature lets the girdle rest about the hips—and that is where it makes a beautiful whole of the costume."

413

[JOURNAL]

June 23, 1923, Wednesday—New York

When I came to the studio, Kahlil had a radiant air, and looked *well*. I said, "Last time I did not see a single picture." He laughed, seated me—and at once brought out a large packet, the prints of his twelve pictures for *The Prophet*.

"Five need to be made a little richer. I'm going to see them again about those. I determined not to spoil my picture in order to make a good reproduction. The reproduction is a passing thing. The picture is a reality—and my work. I'd rather have a good picture and a poor reproduction than a spoiled picture and a better reproduction. I've done the best I could, though, for the printer, and yet keep my picture. .....I think the best of these reproductions really leaves nothing to be desired. About *Marriage*, it has occurred to me that the varnish has helped the photograph. It makes me want to try varnish on some more wash drawings.—But I can't hurry about it. I'll give the varnished one a year first—to see what happens with it." He showed me the varnished original of *Marriage*. "The varnish preserves it, you see—makes the paper much tougher, like a parchment. I use water color varnish —it's quite different from oil color varnish.

"I like this dress ever so much"—(the one I bought in Venice last summer with long fringe)—"But I like all your dresses. I never saw you in an unbecoming one. You choose carefully.....Let me help you knot the fringe." I was knotting each strand twice to keep it from ravelling. He knotted some and said almost immediately, "I've a little technique that does it fast." He just rolled the strand—and knotted it in a flash.

About Florance's distress at my absence and in my absence,

"We can always do a thing in such a way that the other

person is happy about it. What everybody wants from us is our understanding and our sympathy. They want to know that we know what they are going through—and that we care—that we understand." And later about Florance. "Do you use his language, Mary? He can't use yours. Do you translate?.....In two or three years very deep things in him will have developed—he will be different. Not through your teaching in words—but by example. Trying to change a person is a presumption. But we all change our own selves, when we come near to others in whom we feel what we should like ourselves to be."

He had asked when I first went to Savannah whether he'd better write me as "Dear Mary" instead of "Beloved Mary" —just in case Florance saw his letter and might feel ever so little hurt. And now, when I told him Florance had opened my bank statement, he suggested the change again. "If one thing has been opened, another may be—and our relation is so solid and as rich in reality beyond words—that I could call you "Dear Miss Haskell" and it wouldn't make a bit of difference.

"Perhaps especially because you've told your uncle that I am near to you and because you have my picture on your desk—and because he feels such a longing himself to be the nearest to you—if he *should* see a letter from me with "Beloved Mary"—he might feel a pang."

"I'm glad you think the Prophet head finer than the Jesus head. I think so too."

"Pain can be creative. To be personal but very clear, take our own case, yours and mine. I suffered a great deal through you and you suffered a great deal through me. But that pain brought us to the big thing in life. We lived more because of it than because of anything else.....Some people reach the big thing in life through joy—and some through neither pain nor joy. They just live into it. And a great number never reach it at all."

Beloved Mary,   August 7, 1923—Boston

I am so happy in your happiness. You should have more of the beauty of earth and sky than anyone else.

Boston is different, something has gone out of it—and I do not visit Cambridge twice a week.

I go to the country once in a while and stay all day, thinking thoughts other than city thoughts, and dreaming other than the dreams of houses and streets. And it is good to be alone—there is so much of co-existence in aloneness.

Love from Kahlil

ROCKWOOD

CLARKESVILLE, GA.

Clarkesville, Georgia
Beloved Kahlil,   October 2, 1923

The Prophet came today, and it did more than realize my hopes. For it seemed in its compacted form to open further new doors of desire and imagination in me, and to create about itself the universe in nimbus, so that I read it as at the centre of all things. The format is excellent, and lets the ideas and the verse flow quite unhampered. The pictures make my heart jump when I see them. They are beautifully done. I like the book altogether in style.

And the text is more beautiful, nearer, more revealing, more marvellous in conveying Reality and in sweetening consciousness—than ever. The English, the style, the wording, the music—is exquisite, Kahlil—just sheerly beautiful. Bless you, bless you, bless you, for saying it all, and for being such a worker that you bring that inner life into form and expression—for having the energy and the patience of fire and air and water and rock.

This book will be held as one of the treasures of English literature. And in our darkness we will open it to find ourselves again and the heaven and earth within ourselves. Generations will not exhaust it, but instead, generation after generation will find in the book what they would fain be—and it will be better loved as men grow riper and riper.

It is the most loving book ever written. And it is because you are the greatest lover, who ever wrote. But you know, Kahlil, that the same thing happens finally, whether a tree is burned up in flame, or falls silently in the woods. That flame of life in you is met by the multiplied lesser warmth of the many many who care for you. And you are starting a conflagration! More will love you as years go by, long long after your body is dust. They will find you in your work. For you are in it as visibly as God is.

Goodbye, and God bless you most dearly, beloved Kahlil, and sing through your mouth more and more of his songs and yours.

Love from
Mary

---------------●❦ *MH* ❦●---------------

[J O U R N A L]

November 26, 1923—Monday—New York

Kahlil and I spent the afternoon in the studio.

"Yes—*The Prophet* has been *more* than well received. I have been overwhelmed with letters."

And he showed me a beautiful appreciation in the Chicago *Post*—in which all of "Work" was quoted.

"Knopf wants to get out a sort of little pamphlet, with extracts from letters about the book. I should like to use a few lines from your letter, too. And when the letters are all chosen from, I'll send you a typed copy of the series—to see —before it is printed."

had talked a bit—he took a little red leather
in his hand.

going to tell you the plan of the Second Book—and
hird Book—of the Prophet. The Second Book is in the
den of the Prophet—and the Third is The Death of the
rophet. He has gone to his island—and there he spends a
great deal of his time in his mother's garden.—He has nine
disciples, who talk with him in the garden. And he talks to
them about how the small things and the great things are connected—of man's kinship with the universe. He talks of the
dewdrop and the ocean, the Sun and Fireflies, of the air and
ways in space, of the Seasons, of Day and Night—of Light
and Darkness." "It deals with man's relation to the universe
—just as the Prophet dealt with his relation to his fellow men.
In the Third Book he returns from his island—and talks with
various groups as they come to him—about the air above
the earth and beneath the clouds—of yesterday and tomorrow
—the Four Seasons—Growth—Birth—Light and Darkness
again—the falling of snow—of fire and smoke. The Prophet
is put into prison. When he is freed again he goes into the
marketplace—and they stone him."

Later, when I was going, he said, "The Second Book is
being written with your spirit with me.—Nobody could write
the Prophet without you."

"Three things in my life have done most for me: my
mother who let me alone; you, who had faith in me and in my
work; and my father, who called out the fighter in me."

"I want to make a ring for you of lemon gold."—This
apropos to a ring Louise Daly had just given me that Kahlil
liked.

We walked after supper up to 40th St.—looking for a suit
I had seen and one he has seen—both pretty for him. But we
found neither.

The glass mosaic memorial is still undecided about.

"Tiffany asked $15,000—and then $12,000—for this piece

—and they promise nothing but hit-or-miss work—even though I offered to pick out all the glass. In their workshops, among one hundred pieces you see only two or three that are beautiful. The rest are merely ordinary.—The Church they were considering has only two ceremonial spaces left—and both of those are cut into by the choir stairs. So now they are considering another Church—where the old lady lived, instead of the one where she is buried. I've not seen that yet.

"Look at this. It is only a child's toy—but see!" And he showed me an optical sighter—above a little disk that turned —and on the disk he put some leaf-scraps—and I looked through the sighter and turned the disk—and saw marvellous designs in form and color made of the leaf-scraps.

"No doubt it is just like that all through ourselves."

I asked whether he couldn't send *The Prophet* to Duse*— and so find out whether she wouldn't be glad to be drawn.

"Of course I've wanted to draw her—ever since it was announced that she was coming to America. But when I saw how fragile she is—and when I learned how she lives here —that for twenty-four hours before each time she plays she must be absolutely alone—seeing no one, talking to no one— and that she is carried to the stage in a chair and from the stage at the end in a chair to the automobile that brings her home—it seemed cruel to try to see her."

"Since you don't like diamonds, nor platinum—nor white gold and do like lemon gold and since there is such beautiful jewelry in the Museum and you don't like the commercial designs—why don't you look at the museum jewelry and find something there that you'd like to have copied?"

At last he accepted the opal chain "for keeps" and I left it with him.

He does not look very well.

* Eleonora Duse (1859–1924), the Italian actress, was making her last tour of the United States. Her acting powers were undiminished but her health was failing and she died a few months later.

❦ *1924* ❧

——— ❦ *MH* ❧ ———

24 GASTON STREET, WEST

SAVANNAH, GA.

Beloved Kahlil,   4/18/24

I had hoped to see you this month—but Florance was not well.

We went recently to Florida, to try what change would do in breaking up a bronchial cold and cough that Florance had had since November—and there, four of us Haskell sisters met—in old St. Augustine—and later I saw a brother too. It was a very beautiful experience.

But I am always longing to have you see this world of beauty, Kahlil. It grows and grows upon me all the time. It is so strange, so deep, and so carelessly and painfully ravaged, and so pathetically exquisite despite all outrage.

And I want to talk with you.—It will be good to see you again. I do not know whether you are painting or writing, or waiting—ill or well. Yet I do not feel cut off from anyone nor anything. When I wake at night I often feel the universal ether about all things, like the shell about an egg. And then none of us seem separate one from another—elements—people—all.

God bless you, beloved Kahlil, and God love you and live through you, and bless us both.

Love from
Mary

[New York]
Dear Mary,   April 22, 1924

I hope with all my heart that all is well with you.

As for me, I am quite all right. I do some work every day; a little drawing or a little writing—most of it in Arabic. But I walk a great deal up and down this studio, or in the park, and I think and dream of distant places, and of things without form like the mist. Sometimes I myself feel shapeless. It is a strange consciousness. I feel as if it were the consciousness of a cloud before it becomes rain or snow.

You see, Mary, I am just beginning to live above the ground. I have been nothing but a root in the past, and now I do not know what to do with so much air and light and space. I have heard of men who, after leaving prison, find themselves so lost in the world that they go back and ask to be imprisoned again. I shall not *go back*, Mary. I shall try to find my way above the ground.

May God bless you, dear Mary, and God *is* blessing, and God is filling your generous heart with his sacred light.

Kahlil

Please let me know when you are coming north a week or ten days ahead, because I want to be here, and because there is something very important I want to talk over with you.

[JOURNAL]

May 21, 1924—New York

Kahlil and I spent the evening in the studio.

A glorious old linen of the Crucifixion filled all the lower wall—with his cerise velvet curtains at each side of it.

"About the twelfth Century—Armenian Byzantine," said Kahlil. Some friend had a beautiful collection of Art things. "When he died, he did not leave his wealth to her outright—but only certain income during her life—and if she should marry again, only a small part of that income. Well, she went to my country last year—and there she met the British consul to Syria—and she became engaged. The art treasures were sold here in New York. The trustees marked prices on them —and kindly gave the M's special friends opportunity to buy privately before the public sale. The M's had paid $2500 and $2700 for this ten or fifteen years ago—and now it was marked $100! And this little chair at its side—Spanish—$7.50! I could get $50 for it any day—and $3000 for the Altar piece. You can't imagine how wonderful it is to live with. It makes everything else look small. It is the only crucifixion I have ever seen in which Jesus is blessing with his right hand—and there is no blood from either hand, nor from the feet or the side."

"To be alone in old age! I am looking forward with untold pleasure to being alone in old age."

"Just to sit here like this, alone, in the corner of the sofa for hours at a time—is my exquisite pleasure."

"I am the most social human being in the world—but social life is a real problem, when one has lived so long in a place. The invitations are more than I can handle, and yet how to avoid them puzzles me. I write a book, and when it is brought out, a dinner is given in my honor. Two or three weeks later, the hostess asks me again—and then again—and other guests ask me, and often I come away tired and drained.

"Or a lady writes me a kind letter about my book. I am grateful, and reply. When she comes to New York she comes to see me—and presently she writes that she is bringing a group of friends to the studio—because they are so interested in the drawings—and they come. But two afternoons are simply lost to me. I can't work from two to four—and then from six to seven. Yet I see no way out of it all. I can't meet kindness unkindly.

"And there is one side of it all that is really part of my work. A woman, or a man, whom I have known for six or eight years, say, will call me up and say, 'Can I come round to the studio and talk with you?' And the voice shows something is the matter. And he or she comes and tells me the story of unhappiness. Some strange thing in me makes them use me as a confessor. Sometimes they ask just to *come* here—to *sit*—or to talk—because as soon as they get in this room they seem to find peace. It makes me feel so sad for them—and so hopelessly grateful, *so* grateful—because it means such trust they give."

--- ❦ *MH* ❦ ---

[J O U R N A L]

May 23, 1924—Friday—New York

We had dinner and a long long bus ride together.

We talked of many things.

"All my life, I have tried to see the whole of things—their ensemble—to get their structure—whether it was a building, or a person, or a book, or music—to get the motif, the key—the elements that make them.

"I was recently in the country visiting friends—and in the

morning about 6 o'clock I looked out of my window. The trees were budding, the birds were singing—the grass was wet —the whole earth was shining. And suddenly I *was* the trees and the flowers and the birds and the grass—and there was no I at all."

[J O U R N A L]

May 26, 1924—Monday—New York

A most wonderful evening together in the studio.

"We are *very late*," said Kahlil as I came in—with a little laugh and rising inflection characteristic of him when we are gay.

Silence was before the fireplace.

"Yes, I've worked on it since you saw it. It is a little more silent. I put it out because tomorrow I am going to work on it with a model—do more here"—indicating the body.

He picked up a small paper book—"Here is the third translation of *The Madman* into Spanish. It has already been done into Portuguese in Brazil. This Spanish comes to me from Argentina."

"A work of art must be done with the heart. A sort of love affair between artist and reader—it is more than an expression of consciousness. It is dawn expressed—and expressed with such sweetness and understanding, that it finds the other's heart—and makes a dawn in it too."

"At night before I fall asleep I sometimes take the meteorite you gave me—and hold it—and all its life for thousands of years is in my consciousness—from even how it came into being. That is ecstasy."

[JOURNAL]

June 1, 1924—Sunday—New York

Kahlil and I had a wonderful afternoon and bit of evening together. We went to the Museum and walked through the Park to the Orchestra Stand.

"Overpraise is painful. To be praised beyond what is warranted hurts infinitely. If you offer silver, it is pain to have it called brass or gold—what you want, is to have people say, 'Yes, this is silver'—for that is just what it is. That praise is solid. But to call it gold, just makes you feel how hopelessly far you are from making gold. It sets you down hopelessly before the heights you will never scale."

[JOURNAL]

June 5, 1924—Thursday—New York

We had a magical evening together. There is only one more together now before I go—and the coming to an end of this sweet period is so present with me that it is hard to remember much that we said.

First, Kahlil sat down and sketched at a design for my diamond earrings. "I like large earrings—and in the Orient I have seen them with drops—in somewhat this style that were very beautiful." We chose the best—and decided against anything but just the diamonds and pale lemon gold.

"The main thing in a design for jewelry, is that it shall be true to the nature of the stone used, and the metal—and the personality of the wearer. If the designer obeys the nature of his stones and his metal, he will be successful.....I like diamonds just by themselves—with diamonds only. In our earring, they will be like rain drops on the edge of the flower and falling from it."

"I have just finished a poem about a dead man—in Arabic. It is laid in a graveyard by the stone of one whose name has been obliterated by the rain and sun—by the seasons." And after supper he told it to me in detail—not translating, but literally telling, as he does in the case of his Arabic things. The speaker is picturing the release that is the dead's, from being known, from being named, from being linked to the Race—picturing his imminence in the whole. As Kahlil told it, slowly, often hesitating for words—he conveyed strangely to me, beyond the things actually said, the far horizons of the vision. He sat by his table, I on his sofa facing the fireplace. At his left, in the glass covering the green-bodied lady was reflected the purple rosy light of the colored lamp—like a moon rising far away. Past his right shone the golden tapestry and the golden things upon it, the bits of carving, the stained head of the Paris days. It was all like the great earth glowing in the twilight sky—with Kahlil bathed in the glow of it, reading from the vault of the inner sky.

Suddenly he said, "I could not do this, Mary, with anybody else in the world. You listen to so much more than I can say. You hear consciousness. You go with me where the words I say can't carry you.

"You look so well. I've seen you come from Boston tired and pale and thin, and now, I've never seen you looking so well. You look so dear and so sweet—you are so good to see. You are not stouter, yet you are round, and not thin.....I love to see you now.

"You seem to me to be having a more personal life now than you ever had before. You seem to be living more your own life."

June 8, 1924—Tuesday—New York

With Kahlil all afternoon and evening.

The wash drawings used in *The Prophet* are all mounted— they look more beautiful than ever.—

"I'm not willing to sell them. I would sell the twenty for $10,000, perhaps, asking that they be kept together. I would sell them if I had to, but I would prefer to give them to a museum.

"The Second Book of *The Prophet* is growing in silence— and the longer I wait, the larger the canvas grows. The Third Book will be called *The Death of the Prophet* and will deal with man and God. People are more aware of God than of the realities of Nature about them. The Third Book will be the simplest—the second the most difficult.

About reincarnation,

"No—I am sure Jesus has not been a man again here. If he had been we couldn't have helped knowing it.—I feel sure we have lived before. In myself I have experiences that indicate previous lives to me. I am perfectly certain I have known you for thousands of years."

"No human relation gives one possession in another—every two souls are absolutely different. In friendship or in love, the two side by side raise hands together to find what one cannot reach alone."

"The old phrase of the woman to the man, 'I have given myself to you'—how absurd! How *can* one give one's self to another? She says it as a reminder to him of his duty. And he says, 'I have taken you into myself'—to remind her of her duty. But how can one take another unto himself."

We walked after dinner in the damp and mist after the rain.

427

"New York grows in beauty actually every hour. Whenever I come back to New York after being away, I feel that here is a life always opening and lifting, up and out, with a freedom and a willingness, and eternal newness, that makes it the most joyous city on the earth.

"I have in mind a play. A man lost his wife whom he loved most tenderly—she left him a daughter, a young girl, to whom he was also deeply devoted. As time went on, a great desire grew up in the man to enter the monastery, which was across the mountains in the next valley, in a district strange to him. But if he went into the monastery, he would have to leave his daughter and the two felt they could not be separated. Still they could not help going into the monastery. The daughter cut her hair and put on the clothes of a boy—and together, as father and son, they applied to the monastery and were received. It was a custom of the monastery to send out the inmates, two by two, to ask gifts from the villages and the father and 'son' were often sent out in this way. One day they were at the Inn. The innkeeper had a daughter, a handsome, wild, impetuous creature, hot blooded and sensual. She saw the 'boy'—and she desired 'him.' What could the *seeming* 'boy' do, except in the gentlest way repel her advances. 'He' and his father returned as usual to the monastery—and within a week after their going, the girl did take to herself another man—and she conceived by him. When her condition became apparent, she told her father that the 'boy' had seduced her. They waited until the child was born—and then the innkeeper and his daughter took the baby and appeared with it at the monastery gate, and charged the 'boy' with being the father. What was the 'boy' to do or say? 'He' did not deny —'he' accepted the sin as his own. As punishment 'he' was commanded to take the child, and in a little hut at some distance from the monastery to live with it alone, and there to bring it up—and from the monastery daily, the plainest food would be brought them—enough to sustain life.—The sentence was carried out, and there the girl lived with the baby.

428

But the isolation, and the shame cast upon her, the loneliness —did their work. And one snowy night, the monks in the monastery were troubled by the crying of a child. In the morning they went early to the hut—and there the 'boy' lay dead—and the open dress showed the woman. The child was sitting beside her. And thus the girl's real story is seen."

We were discussing the earrings to be made out of my diamonds.

"Casting was my greatest delight when I was about eight years old—in the easiest of metals, lead. I would use sardine cans—and use a little oil to keep them from drying. I would make my little image first that was to be cast—usually of scrap. I would put the lead on the fire to melt, and then fill the two halves of my sardine can with the fine moist sand—press the image in between the two, and scrape away the sand that squeezed out and put the halves together. Open the can gently, take out the image, close the two halves together again, and pour the lead into the mould thus made—and tie the two halves together again—until the image had cooled. I wasn't always successful. But I loved it."

Talking of segregation, Kahlil said, "The Jews here are segregated—and they feel it as oppression. Yes, I go to a few Jewish houses—and I meet gentiles who have had a standing for several generations in New York. At the Lewisohns', for instance, I met Galsworthy, and Dunsany and Chesterton. The Lewisohns are really very delightful—a mother and daughter. I meet a good many people there, and hardly a Jew among them all. And at the Reeses I meet gentiles—really fashionable gentiles. The Morgenthaus are pretty Jewish. Gentiles go there just because he was Ambassador to Turkey and because he and his wife have contributed largely to things. And Otto Kahn goes to dinners. But I have seen him again and again turn and twist the conversation cleverly, too, until he got it round to 'what Wilson said to me' and 'what I said to Wilson.' "

[J O U R N A L]

June 18, 1924—Wednesday—New York

Another evening with Kahlil on my way back to Savannah from Boston.

"Shall I put you up some lunch, Mary? I thought you might like some cheese and some fruit." And he made a pot of coffee.

"Life is not cruel. It is great. And we kill nothing. You only change its place, you transfer it from one vessel to another. When you use sugar, you put it from a bowl on the table into your own veins. The Hindus lay such stress on physical death that they eat no flesh, but only herbs—as if the herbs have no life and are not killed in order to be eaten!"

"There are a few souls in the world who seem as if they do not belong here, but had strayed from just round the corner while they were on the way to another planet or world."

51 West Tenth Street

My dear Mary,   August 28, 1924

I remember your telling me that you are to come to New York some time in September. I am in New York now, and am on my way to visit some friends in the country. Could you tell me, Mary, when you are coming to New York? I have many things to tell you, and many questions to ask you. You are the only one in the world who could advise me about "me."

Love
Kahlil

❀ 1925 ❀

Dear Mary,   July 8, 1925

I am so glad that your days and nights are being filled with delights. But somehow I always think of you as one to whom life owes more than life can give; simply because you have given so much—so much.

Here in New York we are all struggling with the dull, heavy heat. I have visited two or three places in the country and found them not less uncomfortable. In the country it is green heat; here it is gray.

August is the hardest month of the year, and I fear that when it comes I shall find myself so tired out that I shall have to go somewhere—anywhere—just for the change. Even if I go to Boston and spend the days in Franklin Park it will be better than staying here or visiting my formal friends. My friends are most loving and most considerate, but they do not know what I have gone through, and I do not want them to know. It is better that they should think of my work rather than my problems.

I pray God, Mary, that you will continue to find real pleasure and real joy in every place you visit and everything you see and hear.

Always yours,
Kahlil

-------{ *KG* }-----

[New York]

Dear blessed Mary,   August 25, 1925

I came back today from the mountains and found your dear letter. It is so good to hear your voice coming from a nearer place.

I shall be here in New York during the first week of September, and I want so much to see you, even for a few hours, if you cannot spare more. I want to see my better self in you, once again, before you go south and I go north.

Will you not let me know on what day you will reach New York, and when I can see you? But if you cannot tell, and if you are uncertain, I shall gladly keep the first three days of September free and open so that I may not miss you.

May God bless you. May God love you always.

Kahlil

❧ 1926 ❧

---------------------------------- ❧{ *KG* }❧ ----------------------------------

Dear Mary   January 14, 1926

I am so glad to hear from you, and to know that all is well.

I am now in Boston doing a little work and going every day
to the dentist to be roughly handled. It was a serious condition and the work had to be done. Had I waited longer the
whole system would have been poisoned. But now I am doing
well, and I am being *brave* and patient—I even feel kindly towards my torturers!

Love,
Kahlil

Mary had by now been in Savannah for almost three years, living in Florance Minis's gracious house and learning to love the quiet city and its gentle tempo, so different from the life she had known in Boston. There were parties, movies, and visits with friends, old and new. Florance and Mary took many trips together, driving throughout America and also voyaging abroad.

By being persistent and persuasive, Florance finally wore down Mary's resistance. They were married on the afternoon of May 7, 1926, in Savannah.

Gibran had understood from his earlier talks with Mary that Florance was constantly pressing his suit. And Gibran had always told Mary to act in accordance with the yearnings of her heart. If her heart told her this was the right step, it was. But one wonders how he greeted the news of Mary's marriage. Mary was a true friend, a constant believer in his greatness. Mary never faltered as far as her belief in him was concerned. Gibran knew this. He knew that she believed devoutly in him and wanted him to continue growing spiritually and artistically.

He knew also that he had often taken advantage of her, that he may have mistreated her, that occasionally he may have been insensitive to her needs. But their love could accommodate an unkind word here or there, a sometimes unawareness of one another's needs.

Gibran genuinely wanted Mary to be happy and probably recognized that her life in Savannah would be far more pleasant than the rigorous routine she had been following in Boston.

Now Mary would no longer be coming to New York for short stays, discussing his latest paintings or spending hours together working over a new poem. This did not mean, however, that there would be no communication between them. It was understood that he would continue sending her his writings and that she would keep on with the work she loved— polishing a phrase, refining a thought, commenting on other possible ways of expressing certain ideas, correcting spelling.

Around this time, Barbara Young, who later wrote This Man from Lebanon, *a book in which she recounts her years with Gibran, entered his life. Yet, they were never so close that Gibran told her of Mary. It was only after Gibran's death that Miss Young began to get a clue as to the quality of that secret relationship.*

--◦⊰{ *MH* }⊱◦--

24 Gaston Street
Savannah, Georgia

Kahlil,   April 14, 1927

Ever so many questions. How is your book of Jesus? How has the winter been? What has happened with you? Please write me a letter.

Are you in Boston or New York for the next two weeks? I want to send a clipping which I don't want to have lost, nor even delayed in reaching you—and so I must know your address.

How I wish you could see this Spring—and could have seen and felt the winter here! The world is like a green sea of a million waves—with flowers floating upon it. The sun is so white—the shadows are so black. There has been almost no rain. We have had birds all winter. And two weeks ago we took a several days' drive—to Charleston and back again. In Charleston, up the Ashley River, rather, from Charleston, are two Gardens from old Southern days—Magnolia Gardens and Middleton Gardens. Probably the world holds no such other concentration of dreams in a garden. This soft climate and the moist coastal plains give the azaleas a wild, giant gorgeousness—and the semi-tropic trees—the palm, the magnolia, the live oak and the long-leafed pine—that might perhaps be found elsewhere, here are hung as far as eye can see with veil upon veil of long-fray Spanish moss—so that you are always imagining what you do not see, and not really seeing what is ————. The depths look infinitely profound—for the farthest glimpses within it are closed by the gray moss—and you know that behind the gray moss are always more and more forests. The secret is always palpable, and never fathomed.....It is the moss that makes the mystery, the illusion, the romance, the heartache, universal in this landscape—and that makes it so different from other exquisite landscapes. The more I live here, the more this sheer beauty sinks into my heart as a great experience.

Were it not for the pests of this climate, population would swarm here. But in this glorious sunshine, and in the cool dark shadows, and filling the air under the great moss-hung trees on a still day, are innumerable millions of "sand-flies"—gnat-like things that settle softly and bite hard—and troops of mosquitoes—and underfoot in the scrub palmettos and under the thick vines, that make the earth an enchanting carpet, there may always be a rattlesnake or a copperhead.

These pests disappear before man, but only before man-in-numbers. Therefore our population grows but slowly. And therefore only breezy spots are as yet habitable in summer. Winds blow away the sand-flies and mosquitoes, and cold makes them and the snakes, too, dormant. Therefore in winter we have people here from the North. But in summer only the natives can endure it all, and in the old days before quinine and window screens and automobiles and electric fans, death took an awful toll here. Most of the tombstones cover people who died before they were thirty-five, and a tragic proportion of them died before they were twenty.

Our winter has gone as usual, but with Florance less beset with grippe—with all our household well, in fact, for the first season in my experience. We entertain as always two to four times a week—and not very informally. When we have a good cook and good butler, a formal dinner is as easy as any other—and this year, for my first time, we have a good cook. Always we have a good butler.....My job here, besides Florance, is the food and the shopping. We have a Scotch housekeeper who sees to the cleaning and the linen; to my intense relief, for this is a big, big, complicated and over-furnished house, and to keep it clean is an occupation.

Sewing has become quite a by-product with me. We get so slowly to meals and away from them, that just to keep from restlessness and impatience, I keep a bit of sewing with me. Then I do not care how long I sit waiting upon this or that. I read occasionally, instead—but often sewing is possible when reading would be rude. And I have to have so many more clothes than elsewhere, that the sewing is doubly useful.

The other day an Alabama woman, a stranger, dining here and looking at my portrait, suddenly said, "It reminds me of another painter—I wonder if you know him and of his work—named Gibran." I took her upstairs to my room and showed her my twenty-seven pictures on the walls.

This is a long letter. I could write on and on, if there were time, my lord having made the earliest start to his office which history records, and I having found my duties all done by 10:45 a.m. We have an old lady staying in the house, with whom I have pretty constantly to be, but she too is off at her dressmaker's and at a sort of scapegrace son's—so I have had an hour and a half without interruption or claim.

If you are with Mary, give her my love.

Lovingly,
M.

KAHLIL GIBRAN
51 WEST 10TH STREET, NEW YORK, N.Y.

Dear Mary,   November 7, 1928

Jesus the Son of Man came out about two weeks ago. A copy was sent to you at that time. Perhaps you left Savannah before it reached Savannah. I hope you will like it, when you see it in spite of the many little mistakes. My publishers seem to be happy over it, and my friends here say kind things about it. More than once, during the last few days, I was *made* shy by expressions of nearness and love and understanding. May God bless the world and everyone in it.

My summer was not a happy summer. I was in pain most of the time. But what of it? I wrote much in Arabic, songs and prose-poems. I did more than that. I told the people of Mount Lebanon that I have no desire to go back and govern them. They wanted me to do that. And you know, Mary, I am homesick. My heart longs for those hills and valleys. But it is better that I should stay here and work. I can do better in this strange, old room than anywhere else.

Yes, I need warmth this winter.

Kahlil

❄ 1929 ❄

—❦ KG ❦—

[Boston]
Dear Mary,   May 16, 1929

I am in Boston now. I have been here quite a while trying
to find rest and quiet in this humble place with my sister. I
do not feel well. I think it is nothing more than nervous "tired-
ness." The Autumn and Winter were hard.

The book is doing splendidly here in America and abroad.
It is loved, they say, for its poetry, but I feel in my heart
that it will be loved in the future for something better than
what *they* call poetry.

My book on Shakespeare is still a thing of the mind. Sometimes I feel as if I could write it in a month. But I am really
tired for the present. The little Arabic work I do takes so
much out of me. Perhaps I better work on *The Garden of the
Prophet* before working on Shakespeare.—Do you not think
so?

My sister sends her love to you. I shall have to leave her
soon. There are some things in New York which I must look
into, then we both go together for a short summer vacation.

K.G.

KAHLIL GIBRAN

5 1 W E S T 1 0 T H S T R E E T , N E W Y O R K , N . Y .

Dear Mary,   November 8, 1929

Yes, I was ill in Boston during last winter. It was a general breakdown that ended in my legs—rather painful—but I *walked* through it nicely. I have had a good deal of troubles with my teeth and my Boston dentist; may the heavens forgive him.

My responsibilities in the East are over. I shall not undertake anything of that sort unless I am absolutely certain of my tomorrow. It was in my heart to help a little because I was helped much.

K.G.

❧ *1930* ☙

[New York]
November 21, 1930

I will stay in New York till Christmas. Then I will go to visit my sister, who lives now at 281 Forest Hills St., Jamaica Plains, Mass. Whatever you wish me to do I will do it gladly and gratefully.

And may our God bless you and keep you always.

K.G.

1931

 KG

[New York]
March 16, 1931

I am here in New York, and I shall stay here a few more weeks.

The Earth Gods came out two days ago, and I am sending a copy together with this. I hope you will like the drawings.

I am preparing another book, *The Wanderer*, and the drawings for it. It is a book of parables. My publishers wish to bring it out next October. I thought it is going to be too soon after the publication of *The Earth Gods*; but they would have it, and here it is almost ready. I must turn over the manuscript and the drawings within a month. I wonder if you should care to see the manuscript with your seeing eyes and lay your knowing hands upon it before it is submitted?

May God love you.

K.

Western Union

1931 April 12 AM 11 28

KAHLIL PASSED AWAY FRIDAY NIGHT   WE TAKE HIM TO BOSTON ON MONDAY WRITE 281 FOREST HILLS ST JAMAICA PLAINS MASS

MARY GIBRAN

442

ON THURSDAY MORNING, Mrs. Anna Johansen, the caretaker of the Studio, the building at 51 West 10th Street in New York, walked up the four flights of stairs carrying Gibran's breakfast. For some time, she and a number of his close friends had been concerned about his health. He had not been looking well; but his illness was a mystery.

When she saw him that morning, his condition so alarmed her that she telephoned Mrs. Leonobel Jacobs. Mr. and Mrs. Jacobs had once been residents of the Studio; they had rented the apartment directly under Gibran's for many years. Although they had moved, they continued to keep in touch with him. Mrs. Jacobs had left her telephone number with Mrs. Johansen.

The doctor whom Mrs. Jacobs brought examined Gibran and insisted that they leave at once for the hospital. Gibran, however, wanted to remain in his apartment that day and night and go instead to the hospital on Friday. Both Mrs. Jacobs and the doctor felt that Gibran might be moved safely the following day.

Early that afternoon Barbara Young came to the studio. She remained with Gibran all that day as he talked of his current work, unfinished drawings, and future books. The unfinished drawings bothered him: "These hands must still do some work upon them before they can go forth." At about 8:30 that evening Mrs. Jacobs returned with the doctor and again discussed taking Gibran to the hospital. Once again, he refused, determined to remain in his studio through the night.

Barbara Young stayed with him until after midnight. That evening he talked much of Lebanon, of his dead mother whom he revered, and of his sister Marianna, who lived in Boston.

The next morning at 10:30 he was carried into St. Vincent's Hospital at Seventh Avenue and 11th Street. His sister, Marianna, received a telegram from either the hospital or the doctor shortly after he was admitted. She called her cousins Mrs. Rose Diab and Assaf George and took the first train to New York. When she arrived at the hospital she was told that Gibran had fallen into a coma at about 2:00 in the afternoon and could no longer recognize anyone.

At dusk the doctors advised Marianna that Gibran's death was merely a matter of hours. At approximately five o'clock Barbara Young had telephoned the office of *The Syrian World*, a New York monthly magazine, to advise his Syrian friends of Gibran's serious and worsening condition. Mischa Naimy answered, and hastened to the hospital.

On the third floor, in the ward to which Gibran had been taken, Naimy was greeted by Barbara Young, whom he had met occasionally at Gibran's studio. She informed Naimy that nothing could be done. Did he wish to confess and to commune? asked Naimy. Barbara Young told him that one of the sisters of the hospital had asked, "Are you a Catholic?" and that Gibran had answered a gruff "NO." When he fell into a coma, however, Chor-Bishop Francis Wakim, pastor of St. Joseph's Maronite Church in New York, arrived and began to shout at the dying man at the top of his voice, "GIBRAN! GIBRAN!" Gibran never answered. Barbara Young was so provoked by the priest's behavior that she told Naimy she wanted to have him thrown out of the hospital.

When he died, Barbara Young and Mischa Naimy were at his bedside. In an adjoining room were Marianna with her two cousins, Mrs. Jacobs who had been there all day, Mrs. William Brown Maloney, and Miss Adele Watson.

He died at ten minutes before 11:00 p.m., Friday, April 10, 1931, the first Friday after Easter. According to Naimy, an autopsy revealed that Gibran died of "cirrhosis of the liver and incipient tuberculosis in one of the lungs."

Marianna sent a telegram to Mary Haskell, now Mrs. Florance Minis, and residing in Georgia. It reached Mary at 11:00 o'clock Sunday morning. Although Florance had always known about Gibran and Mary, he was never altogether reconciled to their relationship and was not particularly enthusiastic about Mary's departure to attend Gibran's funeral. Nevertheless, Mary took the 1:35 p.m. train for New York and Boston. She wired Marianna that she would arrive on Monday at 7:00 p.m.

GIBRAN'S BODY WAS TAKEN to the Universal Funeral Parlor on Lexington Avenue, where, banked with lilies and orchids, it was on view Saturday and Sunday.

Accompanied by members of Ar-Rabitah, the Arabic literary circle he had helped to found and of which he had been president, Gibran's body was taken on Monday to Boston. At 5:00 that afternoon, the train pulled into South Station. It was met by Gibran's close friend Chor-Bishop Stephen El-Douaihy, the priest of the Church of Our Lady of the Cedars. Covered with the Lebanese flag, the casket was borne to the Syrian Ladies Aid Society at 44 West Newton Street.

Mary arrived in Boston at 8:00 p.m. She joined Marianna and took a light meal with a few of Gibran's friends. They broke bread for him and sipped coffee, calling it a last supper for Kahlil.

On the following day, funeral services, in Syriac, were held in the Church of Our Lady of the Cedars. From the church, the congregation moved to the vault on a hilltop where the casket was to be placed temporarily. Marianna Gibran had decided that her brother would be buried not in America but among his beloved Cedars of Lebanon.

On April 16, Mary, Marianna, and Marianna's cousin Rose Diab took the night train for New York. They arrived the next morning and stayed at the Hotel Holland at 351 West 42nd Street. Later that day, at Gibran's studio, they spent hours looking through his papers and packing. Mary noted that he had had a pint of ginger ale daily since January.

With Barbara Young and Marianna, Mary went to William Saxe, an attorney whose offices were at 31 Fifth Avenue. They spoke with Saxe about administering Gibran's estate. At this meeting it was decided that Barbara Young would live in the studio until Gibran's affairs were straightened out. Until this could be done, Gibran's estate would pay the rent. The estate was eventually valued at $49,459.

On April 18, Mary, Marianna, and Barbara Young met a tax consultant and a Mr. Shea, who appears to have been an officer connected with the Manhattan Bank and Trust at Union Square. Gibran's bank box was opened. In it they found only the shares to the Studio, and his wills of 1911 and of 1913. These wills, as well as Gibran's later and final one, left everything to his sister, Marianna, to Mary, and to the village Bsherri, where he was born. "Everything found in my studio after my death, pictures, books, objects of art, etc. go to Mrs. Mary Haskell Minis, now living at 24 Gaston Street West, Savannah, Georgia."

Mary arranged for the Metropolitan Museum of Art to see Gibran's private collection of paintings. The Metropolitan accepted five: (1) *Head of John Masefield*, (2) *Albert Ryder*, (3) *Toward the Infinite* (Gibran's mother in death), (4) *"I Have Come Down the Ages,"* (5) The smallest pencil drawing from the book *Jesus the Son of Man*, called *The Life Circle*.

On Monday, April 20, Mary was in the studio all day. She locked up many letters, sketches, notes, drawings, and manuscripts. Because Barbara Young was ill, Mary worked alone.

Barbara Young, however, suggested that Mary call on Mischa Naimy for help. She reached him at *The Syrian World*; he joined her at 5:00, and was with her for what hours he could be free.

They put away drawings and objects from around the studio in a closet on which they put a padlock, as they did on the studio door.

A few days earlier, Mary and Barbara Young had pulled out a large box. When it was opened, Mary recognized her letters to Gibran—the letters she had written when they first met, when he had gone to Paris to study, when he had left Boston for New York—those hundreds of letters spanning more than twenty years. When she realized what the letters represented, Barbara Young implored Mary to destroy them, and Mary agreed they should be burned. Later, however, she returned to the studio and removed all of them. After saying goodby to Naimy, she took the 10:20 train for Savannah.

Mary wrote Barbara Young that she could not agree to the destruction of the letters: she had always believed in Gibran, been certain of his greatness—her correspondence and their relationship were part of his history. She placed these letters with his letters to her, all of which she had saved. There they remained until they were given to the University of North Carolina.

AT THE TIME OF HIS DEATH, Gibran was working on *The Wanderer.* He had read the manuscript with Barbara Young, had shown her the drawings for it and where, in the text, each drawing was to be placed. He had then sent the manuscript to Mary, asking her to look it over, as she had everything he had written. Mary had the manuscript in Savannah when Gibran died and so, when she returned, she resumed her work on it.

Marianna soon wrote Mary that she and her cousins would be taking Kahlil's body to Lebanon. On July 23, during a light rain, Gibran's body was moved from Boston to Providence, where it was placed aboard the Fabre liner *Sinara*. More than two hundred Lebanese from New York, Boston, Providence, and Fall River were at the pier. A wreath from seven hundred Lebanese living in Providence was placed at the base of the casket. Wind instruments played the Funeral March from *Tannhäuser*, "Asa's Death" from the *Peer Gynt Suite*, and "Nearer, My God, to Thee."

The ship sailed at 2:00 p.m., and almost four weeks later, on the morning of Friday, August 21, arrived in Beirut, Lebanon, where the body was received, with military honors, by the High Commissioner. After a service at the Maronite Cathedral, the funeral procession started to Bsherri by way of Tripoli, winding up and through the mountains.

At every village along the road, under evergreen arches, the procession halted for addresses by village leaders. Toward sundown the procession reached Bsherri, where a large platform decorated with evergreens and white-and-black flags had been built in the square of the village.

Companies of Bedouin horsemen met the funeral procession, which, according to A. C. Harte in a letter to *The Christian Century* in 1931, "appeared more like a triumphal entry than a funeral. The ringing of the church bells and the general atmosphere of pride emphasized this. I came across a relative who took me to the place where once stood the very small house in which Gibran was born. Part of the walls are still standing. The village fathers have decided to use the site as a museum and monument."

It is fifty miles from Beirut to Bsherri. By the time the body reached Albahsas, which marks the parting of the ways between the coastal and mountain roads, there were more than two hundred cars and one hundred horsemen.

Gibran was buried in the grotto of the little monastery of Mar Sarkis, his childhood church.

AFTER GIBRAN'S DEATH, Mary's life in Savannah remained as it had been since she had married Florance Minis in 1926. It was a quiet and pleasant existence that they shared. The beautiful old house on West Gaston Street continued to be the gathering place for family and friends.

Unlike her hectic years in Boston and New York, her life in Savannah was leisurely and uncomplicated. Unlike her relationship with Gibran, her relationship with Florance was uncluttered and seems to have been rather simple. Florance sincerely wanted Mary to have lovely things, to be comfortable, and to be happy. His persistent efforts to get Mary to spend money on herself met with little success. Her frugal habits were not easily discarded. He wanted to be looked after, and this Mary could do well and with ease. Their quiet life together ended with Florance's death on September 3, 1936.

Mary was now sixty-three. After Florance's death, she took a few years to close up their large home—a home filled with lovely furniture, all of which she gave away to friends and relatives. She then moved to the DeRenne Apartments, where she lived for some years, later moving to a still smaller one-room-and-kitchenette apartment nearby. Here she lived almost as a recluse in the simplest surroundings.

For five years before her death she was a resident of Telfair Hospital in Savannah. During these years she had arthritis and was no longer aware of her surroundings. Mr. A. Minis, Jr., Florance's nephew, described this time:

Her own estate was not large but she had given practically all of this away prior to her death and lived solely on that portion of her husband's estate which she was entitled to as a life-time beneficiary. From the way she lived I am sure that she spent only a small portion of the income and turned the rest over to charities or members of her family. When the time came when she was not able to look out for herself she, her maid, and I decided that the hospital was the best place for her; and that is where she stayed until her death.

Mary's will read: "I desire that no funeral ceremony be held for me, and that my body enjoy speedy and simple oblivion. It shall be cremated and the ashes not collected. My name shall be added to my husband's on his tombstone in Laurel Grove Cemetery thus:

Mary Elizabeth Haskell
Second wife of J. Florance Minis, m. May 7, 1926
Born 12/11/1873
Columbia, South Carolina
Died ———"

And so it is, with the date of her death added: October 9, 1964.

A Note on the Type

This book was set on the Linotype in Janson, a recutting made direct from type cast from matrices long thought to have been made by the Dutchman Anton Janson, who was a practicing type founder in Leipzig during the years 1668–87. However, it has been conclusively demonstrated that these types are actually the work of Nicholas Kis (1650–1702), a Hungarian, who most probably learned his trade from the master Dutch type founder Dirk Voskens. The type is an excellent example of the influential and sturdy Dutch types that prevailed in England up to the time William Caslon developed his own incomparable designs from them.

Composed and bound by The Colonial Press Inc., Clinton, Massachusetts. Printed by Halliday Lithograph Corp., West Hannover, Massachusetts.

Typography and binding design by CLINT ANGLIN.